FIRST CLASS

THE U.S. POSTAL SERVICE,

DEMOCRACY, AND

THE CORPORATE THREAT

CHRISTOPHER W. SHAW

FOREWORD BY RALPH NADER

City Lights Books | Open Media Series
San Francisco

Published in association with the Center for Study of Responsive Law.

Open Media Series Editor: Greg Ruggiero

Cover: Mingovits Design

ISBN: 978-0-87286-877-9
eISBN: 978-0-87286-855-7

Library of Congress Cataloging-in-Publication Data

Names: Shaw, Christopher W., author. | Nader, Ralph, writer of foreword.
Title: First class : the U.S. Postal Service, democracy, and the corporate
    threat / by Christopher W. Shaw ; foreword by Ralph Nader.
Description: San Francisco : City Lights Books, [2021] | Series: Open media
    series | Includes index.
Identifiers: LCCN 2021013804 | ISBN 9780872868779 (trade paperback)
Subjects: LCSH: United States Postal Service--History. | Postal
    service--United States--History. | Postal service--Deregulation--United
    States. | Postal service--United States--Reorganization.
Classification: LCC HE6371 .S497 2021 | DDC 383/.4973--dc23
LC record available at https://lccn.loc.gov/2021013804

City Lights Books are published at the City Lights Bookstore
261 Columbus Avenue, San Francisco, CA 94133
www.citylights.com

PRAISE FOR CHRISTOPHER W. SHAW'S *FIRST CLASS: THE U.S. POSTAL
SERVICE, DEMOCRACY, AND THE CORPORATE THREAT*

"Christopher W. Shaw's *First Class: The U.S. Postal Service, Democracy, and the Corporate Threat* makes a passionate and well-argued case for a healthy USPS. Shaw organizes his methodical argument around decades of attacks on the USPS; in doing so, he effectively refutes the flawed (and often anti-democratic) cases for privatization and deregulation. The USPS is essential for a democratic American society; thank goodness we have this new book from Christopher W. Shaw explaining why."

—DANNY CAINE, author of *Save the USPS* and owner
of the Raven Book Store

"In gripping detail, Christopher W. Shaw's *First Class* tells you who's trying to sabotage the national treasure that is the U.S. Postal Service and why (hint: corporate greed). Shaw's clarion call to protect the postal service explains what's at stake for our communities, our democracy, and our economy. While he celebrates USPS history, Shaw's gaze is primarily forward-looking. In a time of community fracture and corporate predation, he argues, a first-class post office of the future can bring communities together and offer exploitation-free banking and other services."

——ROBERT WEISSMAN, president of Public Citizen

"Christopher Shaw makes the case for the importance of the Postal Service to democracy in the United States. He argues compellingly that we should be looking to rebuild it, rather than tear it down and privatize it."

—DEAN BAKER, co-founder of the Center for
Economic and Policy Research

"The 'Save the Post Office' movement has long needed a definitive manifesto, and now it has one. Christopher Shaw's *First Class* shows how special interests, along with anti-government and anti-union ideologues . . . justify cost-cutting measures like outsourcing, closing post offices and slowing down the mail. Piece by piece, an essential national infrastructure is being dismantled without our consent. Shaw makes an eloquent case for why the post office is worth saving, and why, for the sake of American democracy, it must be saved."

—STEVE HUTKINS, professor of English at New York University
(retired) and founder/editor of savethepostoffice.com

"Shaw's excellent analysis of the Postal Service and its vital role in American democracy couldn't be more timely. As the current Postmaster General is about to implement a ten-year plan that will eliminate all airmail service, greatly reduce delivery times, and cut hours and available services at post offices, it is important to be reminded that a fully functional postal service is essential for elections, for delivery of life-saving medicines, for assistance when communities are dislocated in times of disaster, and for rural community identity. *First Class* should serve as a clarion call for Americans to halt the dismantling, and to instead preserve and enhance the institution that can bind the nation together."

—RUTH Y. GOLDWAY, retired chair and commissioner, U.S. Postal
Regulatory Commission, responsible for the Forever stamp

"Christopher Shaw reveals the U.S. Postal Service's historic contributions to the welfare of all Americans, from operating an essential communication and transportation network, to pioneering public banking, to functioning as a linchpin of elections. While the Postal Service's enemies assert its inevitable demise, Shaw presents hope for a rejuvenated public service that plays an integral part of a democratic future."

—ROSEANN DEMORO, former executive director of
National Nurses United

CONTENTS

FOREWORD
by Ralph Nader

The preventable plight of our U.S. Postal Service is an important issue for all Americans. When President Donald J. Trump's donor and henchman Louis DeJoy became postmaster general in 2020 and proceeded to dismantle the agency, millions of citizens participated in demonstrations that revealed a deep civic commitment to preserving the people's post office. While DeJoy triggered a crisis that immediately threatened the presidential election process, attacks on the Postal Service have been an ongoing problem for decades. The anti-postal campaigns of corporate interests have remained a continuing source of frustration to those of us who have observed the Postal Service's decline due to unimaginative management, a deck stacked to favor profit-driven entities such as FedEx and UPS, and unfair financial obligations imposed by Congress.

The Postal Service is facing a manufactured financial crisis that is primarily the result of a congressional mandate dating back to 2006, which required the agency to pre-fund the next seventy-five years of retiree health benefits in one decade. This pre-payment requirement is something that no other federal government agency or private corporation attempts to do—not to mention that there is no actuarial justification for such an accelerated payment schedule. The pre-funding requirement effectively forces the Postal Service to fund retiree health benefits for future employees who have not even been born yet. Despite these facts, Congress has refused to correct the host of problems resulting from its requirements.

In fact, the congressional mandate delivers Trojan horses that fulfill a number of purposes. One is to deliver more profit to parasitic private corporations. Another is to deliver real estate, after closing post offices, to developers and their brokers. There are more than 30,000 post offices that are community outlets, non-profit outlets, gathering places, spaces where federal information about citizen needs and rights can be posted, where people can talk and meet as well as get postal services. Postal officials do not want to acknowledge the intangibles that post offices provide to the community. The discussions that would not otherwise occur. "Hi Joe, how are things?" one resident says to a man walking up the steps. "What's the latest?" We have all heard these neighborly exchanges before. "The Red Sox won again," says one patron to another. "Oh, there's a town meeting next week," a resident reminds her neighbor. "Are you going to go?" What kind of price do you place on conversations like these?

The need for postal reform is not just a matter of endangered post offices, disappearing blue mailboxes, slow mail delivery, or the fight to maintain delivery on Saturday, important as these issues are. The Postal Service is a fundamental institution that binds the country together. It can and should be updated and freed from the shackles of corporations. Our first postmaster general, Benjamin Franklin, was known for his can-do verve and his appreciation of efficiency and innovation. As a stand-alone structure, he never thought post offices would mutate into a counter or kiosk inside a Staples store—or some other big-box store or shopping mall—as recent postmasters general have urged and advertised.

The U.S. Post Office I knew as a child in Connecticut during the 1940s was a symbol for reliability, punctuality, and friendliness. In the 1910s, the Post Office endeavored to connect the farm with the city dweller. This program would pick up fresh eggs, butter, poultry, fruit, and vegetables from farmer Jones and then deliver them to consumers as quickly as possible. Compare this bold venture to the recent attempts of DeJoy to crumble the postal system! He would have us believe that tough decisions are being made to modernize the Postal Service, but nothing could be further from the truth.

Instead of dismantling the Postal Service, this is the moment to expand postal services. Congress must act to protect rural communities, small businesses, the elderly, and the disabled, among others, by reasserting its authority over the Postal Service and putting a stop to irresponsible cutbacks. These policies not only threaten the future of the Postal Service in the long term; in the short term they harm the ability of small businesses to carry out their operations in a timely manner and inhibit the elderly's ability to receive essential medications by mail. They also drive ever more consumers away from the Postal Service and toward private delivery corporations such as UPS and FedEx. Post offices ought to offer an honest notary service (badly needed in an era of robo-signings), sales of fishing and hunting licenses, and an option to have gifts wrapped, among other new services. The Postal Service should accept wine and beer for delivery as FedEx and UPS do, and start delivering groceries as well. In addition, there is the widespread need for postal banking, given the many millions of Americans without bank accounts. This service actually existed until 1966 when the political lobbying of bankers terminated the successful and accessible program in communities throughout our country.

Fortunately, there is a single solution that would go a long way toward defending the Postal Service from DeJoy and his ilk: the proposal for an independent nonprofit Post Office Consumer Action Group (POCAG). Several million Americans would join. All that is required is a simple law directing the Postal Service to send residential postal patrons a letter four times a year giving them the opportunity to pay a small amount of dues in order to join a POCAG staffed full time, with regional offices. If organized postal patrons united with postal workers they could forge jointly a more robust and vital Postal Service. This unstoppable coalition could ensure an expanding and vigorous U.S. postal system that would make Benjamin Franklin proud.

My favorite legal tender is the two-dollar bill because of the historic scene memorialized on the back. This reproduction of the famous John Trumbull painting shows the patriots who gathered in Philadelphia to sign the Declaration of Independence on July 4, 1776. Postmaster General Benjamin Franklin was among them. They had decided to cast off the tyranny of King George III. These individuals thought they were signing their death warrants. They were facing the most powerful military force in the world at that time. More than two centuries later, we are thankful these people showed up and rejected the British monarchy. Showing up is half of democracy, so the question for citizens today is "Are we going to show up?"

Citizens and local Postal Service employees have a lot of good ideas that need to be exchanged and discussed with others. Maybe some of them are quirky, but they can work. Some of them may even save the Postal Service. In Washington, D.C., we can focus on what citizens are doing on the local level, where it counts. But civic activism provides our strength. It is like a magnifying glass. The sun's rays shine on the sidewalk; they are not very hot, but a magnifying glass can focus them. Yet the magnifying glass on the congressional and White House politicians in Washington and the hovering corporatist lobbyists cannot focus if citizens do not give us the sun's rays. You are the sun's rays.

INTRODUCTION

In a vast, diverse nation, the United States Postal Service provides a unique common bond. The familiar footsteps of a uniformed federal employee arriving with the mail. The creak when the handle of the blue mailbox on the street corner is pulled to drop a letter inside. The Stars and Stripes fluttering in the breeze in front of the post office. The postal clerk behind the counter whom you have known for years. Unlocking your mailbox in the bank of boxes inside the lobby of your apartment building to see what arrived today. The ubiquitous eagle profile emblazoned on the side of a mail truck navigating a busy city street. The tunnel-shaped mailbox standing alongside a country road, with its red flag raised to signal the need for a collection. These are all part of the everyday experience of being an American.

The postal system is a great national resource that belongs to all citizens of the United States. For more than two centuries, the U.S. Mail has occupied a central place in American life. The reliability of our national post office is a hallmark that generations of Americans have depended on and taken for granted. Given this history, there was widespread shock and outrage when events during the summer of 2020 suddenly made the vulnerability of the Postal Service widely apparent. In the middle of a pandemic, with a fast-approaching presidential election that demanded an unprecedented reliance on vote-by-mail, Louis DeJoy—a major Republican Party donor who had no previous experience at the agency—became postmaster general and launched a program "to drive cost out" that thoroughly disrupted postal operations, slowing down mail delivery, cutting window hours at post offices, removing mail processing equipment, and uprooting blue mailboxes.[1]

Rallies to "Save the Post Office" arose in cities and towns nationwide, and DeJoy was called before Congress to account for what looked like an attempt to dismantle the agency. "After 240 years of patriotic service delivering the mail," Representative Stephen F. Lynch (D-Mass.) asked, "how can one person screw this up in just a few weeks? Now, I understand you bring private sector expertise. I guess we couldn't find a government worker who could screw it up this fast." Like many observers, Lynch concluded that "either through gross incompetence, you have ended the 240-year history of delivering the mail reliably on time, or . . . you're doing this on purpose. . . . You're deliberately dismantling this once proud tradition." The strong reaction both from the public and inside Congress forced DeJoy to halt his plans. This responsiveness to citizen action was an encouraging development, since for years the public has lacked adequate representation when postal policy is determined.[2]

While DeJoy's policies were unusually severe and startlingly abrupt, they fit a well-established pattern. For decades, corporate interests and anti-government ideologues have sought to transform the Postal Service from a government service that exists to benefit the public into a business that operates to meet financial objectives. Although its purpose is to provide universal service to all Americans—uniform service at uniform rates to all corners of the nation—this objective is under attack because it conflicts with commercial calculations and market imperatives. Anti-government ideologues want to eliminate the public service philosophy and transform the Postal Service into just another profit-maximizing corporation. This aim is one part of their broader campaign to eliminate and privatize government services generally.

There are three main categories of corporations that take an active interest in postal policy: major mailers and the Postal Service's competitors and contractors. Major mailers—corporations that send out bulk mailings—want low postage costs, which means they deem postal functions that are not directly involved with injecting their mail into mailboxes expendable. The major mailers remain wary about privatization because they want to maintain the reach offered by universal service and ensure that the mail continues to be delivered. A Postal Service that obeys the commercial logic and calculus of a business would be useful to major mailers, because it would privilege what the industry wants over what the public needs. But a postal system operated solely to make money would seek to divert the profits that mailers collect to its own bottom line.

Postal delivery and courier services are a source of concern to two of the most powerful corporations in Washington, D.C.— FedEx and UPS. While the package delivery behemoths have an ideological bent toward privatization, this prospect is troubling because the Postal Service would gain new freedom as a business competitor. Corporations in adjacent lines of business are similarly concerned with containing the agency and preventing it from offering additional services. Other corporate interests are eager to see postal functions outsourced so they can acquire these contracts. Such businesses would like to see postal operations privatized piece by piece until the Postal Service is privatized in all but name. Although various pro-corporate interests are not in complete agreement about postal policy, they all are pushing to make the public postal system more "businesslike."

The political influence that corporate interests exert over the Postal Service is extensive, but the agency's official governing authority is its Board of Governors. The president appoints, and the Senate confirms, as many as nine governors to seven-year terms. No more than five of these officials can belong to one political party. The presidentially appointed governors select a postmaster general, who becomes a member of the board as well.

This body then picks a deputy postmaster general, who also joins the board. Congress has authority over the Postal Service, but for years has exercised minimal oversight of the agency's operations. Setting postage rates is the most contentious postal policy issue, and overseeing this matter is the Postal Regulatory Commission's responsibility. (Prior to 2007 this body was called the Postal Rate Commission.) Five commissioners who review rate changes are appointed by the president and confirmed by the Senate for six-year terms. The president selects one of the commissioners to serve as chair. Like the Board of Governors, the Postal Regulatory Commission is designed to be bipartisan: no more than three members can belong to one political party.

The questions that postal officials face evolve constantly. Twenty-five years ago, email was still a novelty. Today, a vast range of electronic communications have an increasingly central role in daily life. Yet, as the one universal means of communications, the Postal Service retains its relevance both socially and economically. The agency delivers more than 140 billion pieces of mail every year, and the number of package deliveries has doubled over the past decade. Millions of Americans live in rural areas where broadband internet connections are not available, and millions more lack sufficient income to afford home internet service. A 2020 study found that approximately 42 million people in the United States do not have home broadband connections. COVID-19 demonstrated just how essential the postal system is: the U.S. Mail delivered federal stimulus checks, medications, and numerous other items that allowed people to manage during periods of shelter-in-place. During the presidential election, the Postal Service made the electoral process more robust through vote-by-mail.[3]

Despite the central role the postal system plays in the nation's economy and society, the Postal Service has been cash-strapped for its entire existence. Operating under a mandate to be self-funding through the sale of postage ever since the Post Office Department became the United States Postal Service in 1971, the agency has functioned on a hand-to-mouth basis. And the enactment of a 2006 law that instructed the Postal Service to pay $5.5 billion every year for the next decade to pre-fund its future retirees' health care created severe financial difficulties by converting long-term financial liabilities into short-term ones. No other government agency or private corporation is required to follow such an aggressive payment plan. Congress imposed this onerous requirement in an attempt to avert an increase of the federal budget deficit. The yields on the Treasury bonds that the Postal Service's retirement fund were invested in had exceeded expectations, producing a massive overpayment. Since returning this surplus to the agency would add to the deficit, the pre-funding formula was devised to avoid this financial impact. When the economic downturn following the financial crisis of 2008 reduced postal revenues, the pre-funding mandate became a millstone.[4]

The daily operations of the Postal Service have maintained a steady cash flow, but the pre-funding obligation has created a paper loss that weighs down the agency's balance sheet. This financial liability is a public policy decision that has impeded long-range planning and investment, a growing problem since the postal system is handling fewer letters and more packages, which demands adjustments to the agency's sorting and transportation infrastructures. At this time, the Postal Service also is in a unique position to make important social contributions by leveraging its existing network to offer new financial and electronic communication services. Efforts to increase internet availability and the introduction of email and search engine services would align with the postal system's traditional mission of advancing access to communication and information. Banking services were available in post offices during the twentieth century, and restoring this function would promote financial inclusion. However, an acute concern with budgetary shortfalls has inhibited a long-term outlook. Moreover, the same 2006 law that imposed the pre-funding mandate restricted the Postal Service's ability to explore new services. While the negative impact of the pre-funding requirement on service standards and postal infrastructure has been substantial, the proposed Postal Service Reform Act of 2021 may eliminate this burden.[5]

While accounting concerns have dominated recent discussions of the Postal Service's future, our public postal system has existed to serve a larger purpose since its founding. Because the people's post office serves all Americans equally, the daily performance of its mission to "bind the nation together" extends beyond communication by affirming our nation's democratic aspirations. The government institution that has the greatest direct contact with Americans makes an unequivocal statement that the national government exists to serve all citizens. The U.S. Mail is a tangible expression of democracy in our daily lives. In *First Class*, I present an account of what the people's post office means to the American social compact and explain why this historic institution should be strengthened and expanded. Maintaining a vital and vibrant postal system will require citizens to counter the corporate threat to this democratic public service.

As the nation's postal system approaches 250 years of operation, a moment of decision looms. Philadelphia's "Merchant Prince," John Wanamaker—who served as postmaster general from 1889 to 1893—recognized that the Postal Service is not just another for-profit business. Wanamaker was a business innovator who founded one of the first department stores and promoted ideas that became retail basics, such as price tags and money-back guarantees. Yet Wanamaker understood that the Post Office fulfilled a special social function precisely because it was not a business. "It is for the interest of a private company," he observed, "to extend its business only so fast and so far as it is profitable; it is the aim of the government to extend its service wherever it is actually needed." Wanamaker's tenure at the Post Office ushered in a remarkable period of creativity and expansion. A skilled administrator, he oversaw numerous service improvements, including increasing the number of cities with home mail delivery, speeding up railroad transportation of mail, and establishing post offices on ocean liners. In addition, Wanamaker promoted home delivery of mail in rural areas, a postal package delivery service, and a post office savings bank, revolutionary reforms that subsequently became features of the twentieth-century postal system.[6]

A public service philosophy placed the postal system at the center of American life historically, and can guide the Postal Service to important future endeavors as well. Decades of policies that promote corporate interests over public goods have hollowed out government institutions, marking the postal system as a striking example of democratic public service in this second Gilded Age.[7] With millions of Americans lacking internet access and bank accounts, the Postal Service could promote the common good by extending affordable internet nationwide and offering banking services at its 30,000 post offices. In a period of deep social divisions, high inequality, and a diminished public sector, the Postal Service has a vital place in contemporary American society. The central role postal workers played in the 2020 election spurred more public interest in postal policies than had been seen at any other time in living memory. Sustained citizen engagement can ensure that the Postal Service achieves its full potential as an instrument of democracy and the public interest.

ONE

PRIVATIZATION

Privatization and deregulation of government services is a leading goal of corporate interests and their political allies. In recent decades, they have spent vast resources promoting the idea that sound public policy rests on turning government services over to for-profit businesses and eliminating corporate regulations. The U.S. Postal Service delivers almost half the world's mail annually— on-time over 90 percent of the time—to 160 million addresses at affordable costs. This long-standing tradition of achievement has made the Postal Service a consistent target of anti-government, pro-corporate lobbying efforts. The argument has been made ad nauseam that the Postal Service is so defective that the only solution is deregulation and privatization. Residents of numerous foreign nations with chronically unreliable postal systems would surely be amazed at what our Postal Service achieves on a daily basis, and shocked to hear claims that the American postal system should be dismantled.[1]

THE POSTAL MONOPOLY

While the deregulation of postal markets would provide privately owned corporations new opportunities to increase their profits, large numbers of people in the United States would no longer be able to send and receive mail at affordable rates. As Senator Frank Carlson (R-Kans.), onetime chairman of the Committee on Post Office and Civil Service, decisively proclaimed: "It is not now, nor should it ever be, a business for profit." Privatization would repudiate the Postal Service's raison d'être: public service. Our

9

public postal system is an essential service that exists for the benefit of the American people, not to turn a profit. Yet through the performance of its social mission this government infrastructure has furnished a foundation for commercial activity and national economic growth.[2]

The Postal Service can provide universal service for all types of mail because of the protections that monopoly restrictions bestow. The Postal Service has two monopolies: one over delivery of certain categories of mail and one over access to mailboxes. Congress first established private express statutes in 1792, and they grant the Postal Service—with some exceptions—the sole right to deliver letters, postcards, and addressed advertising circulars. Congress created these monopoly protections to "provide for an economically sound postal system that could afford to deliver letters between any two locations, however remote." These safeguards equip the Postal Service to fulfill its universal service obligations by protecting the low-cost delivery revenues that subsidize high-cost deliveries. Without monopoly earnings, the Postal Service would have to charge higher prices, offer less frequent service, and pare down its network. The agency's exclusive right to place items in mailboxes also helps to ensure the security of the U.S. Mail. In order to prevent potential abuses in markets where the Postal Service has been entrusted with monopoly privileges, the agency is overseen by the Postal Regulatory Commission.[3]

The Postal Service's monopoly protections and governmental status are both targets of pro-corporate political activists. Corporate interests bankroll a slew of policy organizations in Washington, D.C., that promote laissez-faire and its underlying thesis that "greed is good."[4] For decades, these think tanks have used millions of dollars in funding from rich individuals, foundations, and corporations to turn out policy proposals designed to increase corporate profits. As a large enterprise that lies outside the for-profit sector, the Postal Service has remained squarely in the sights of pro-corporate think tanks. When Ronald Reagan entered office, the Heritage Foundation urged radical reforms, claiming the very concept of a public postal system was outdated: "It is unclear why there should be a publicly owned . . . national document delivery company." In 1996, *Congressional Quarterly* noted that "to many true believers [in privatization], the most tempting target of all is the U.S. Postal Service."⁵

The America Enterprise Institute (AEI), the Cato Institute, and the Heritage Foundation have churned out numerous books, reports, and columns denouncing the Postal Service, calling for its monopoly protections to be rescinded, and extolling the benefits of postal privatization.⁶ "The fundamental culture of the organization needs to change," James L. Gattuso of the Heritage Foundation insisted. "Among other things, this means privatization," he intoned. "A second perhaps even more important step would be to repeal the USPS' statutory monopoly on letter mail." Edwin J. Feulner, co-founder of the Heritage Foundation, concurred: "It's time to break the post office's monopoly and privatize the delivery of mail." Frederick W. Smith, founder and chief executive officer of FedEx Corporation, is a former board member of the Cato Institute. In 2004, he testified before the Senate on the subject of the Postal Service's future. "In my view," Smith urged, "serious and systematic attention needs to be devoted to the possibilities of transforming the Postal Service into a corporation and phasing out the postal monopoly by the end of 2008."⁷

The position that FedEx's CEO presented to the Senate is one that the Cato Institute advocates today in its legislative manifesto, which declares unequivocally that "Congress should privatize the USPS, [and] repeal its legal monopolies." In wholehearted agreement with this position, AEI's R. Richard Geddes took the initiative to assemble "a plan for . . . de-monopolization, corporatization, and eventual privatization." For good measure, Bert Ely of the Cato Institute has added that "there is no unique welfare element inherent in a postal service that precludes its privatization." On the other side, Joseph A. Califano Jr., former secretary of Health, Education, and Welfare, once cautioned that "we ought to count to 10 before junking the Private Express Statutes—which assure mail delivery to all—in the name of more efficient and less expensive mail delivery for the few." Christopher Neal is the rural letter carrier for a ninety-mile route in Tioga County, Pennsylvania. "We have a lot of people who are disabled, who can't get out and move," he noted. "I physically hand the package to that person. No private company is going to do that. That's what we call the last mile."[8]

Opposition to our public Postal Service is found not only on the right of the political spectrum. The 1980s witnessed the emergence of a well-funded faction within the Democratic Party that stressed pro-corporate policies. Elaine C. Kamarck is a Beltway veteran of the "New Democrat" movement and also a critic of the Postal Service. She was an architect of the Clinton administration's initiative to "reinvent" government so that it operated more like a business. Kamarck recently proposed splitting the Postal Service in two. One organization would shoulder the burden of maintaining universal delivery for monopoly-protected services— notably first-class mail—while the remaining services, including package delivery, would be privatized. Kamarck's proposal would endanger universal service, especially since first-class mail revenues have trended downward in recent years and package delivery revenues have increased. But she also betrays a presumption that for-profit businesses are managed well and government is managed poorly. Kamarck doubted that postal officials can "innovate" and insisted the privatized company she proposed must be "managed by people with private sector experience."[9]

Advocacy of privatization arises from the assumption that for-profit businesses, with their straightforward imperative to maximize profits, produce superior outcomes to government institutions, with their broader and less easily defined public service commitments. Advocacy of deregulation arises from the assumption that corporations, therefore, should be given a free hand to act solely in the interest of maximizing their profits. Pro-corporate ideologues invoke "the market"—or even more dreamily "the *free* market"—as a universally applicable, effortless answer to complex economic problems and thorny policy questions. But the reality of the market does not comport with the utopian picture that its enthusiasts paint. Fundamentally, their framework fails to account for the complexities of humans and the societies they create. "Institutions provide the framework within which human beings interact," explained Douglass C. North, winner of the Nobel Prize in economics. "It is the institutional framework which constrains people's choice sets." Elliott D. Sclar observed in his aptly titled book on the myriad problems with privatization, *You Don't Always Get What You Pay For*, that "unlike the standard market model the real economy is not a flat playing field on which a host of atomistic and more or less equally endowed economic agents perpetually compete with one another in pursuit of wealth."[10]

Human beings simply do not behave in the predictable manner the standard market model assumes: they lack perfect access to information, and they do not constantly seek to maximize their "utility" in a "rational" manner. The eminent economist John Kenneth Galbraith observed sagely that "the consumer is very much in the service of the business firm. . . . Consumer wants are shaped to the purposes and notably to the financial interests of the firm." This manipulation of consumers underlines the power differentials that pervade economic activity. The distinguished historian William Appleman Williams noted that "large corporations increasingly asserted their control over the American political economy during the twentieth century. The economic consequences of that process are obvious: the marketplace came to be dominated by a tiny number of economic oligarchs." Contrary to the claims of free market romanticism, there is no assurance the profit motive will produce either quantitative or qualitative competition.[11]

SERVICE FIRST

Promoters of deregulation and privatization want to turn the rationale for the Postal Service upside down. Making profit has never been the principle that motivates the Postal Service. In fact, from 1851 through 1970, the Post Office Department recorded an annual surplus only thirteen times. Under British rule, the colonial postal system was expected to show a profit. But the American Post Office established during the Revolutionary War rejected this premise. Even before the revolution was under way, the patriots had worried about the confidentiality of their letters. Three weeks after the "shot heard 'round the world" at Lexington Green, the Second Continental Congress convened in Philadelphia and laid the groundwork for a new nation. The need for reliable, secure communication was pressing, and on July 26, 1775, the delegates selected Benjamin Franklin to serve as the first postmaster general.[12]

The Post Office emphasized nationhood—not profit—during the revolutionary and confederation periods, and following adoption of the Constitution, which bestowed upon Congress the power "to establish post offices and post roads." "From its creation," historian Jeffrey L. Brodie stated, "America's leaders placed the desire to spread information to the public ahead of the need to generate profits." Economist Wesley Everett Rich also noted that throughout this period there was "a consistent policy to extend the service rather than to secure a surplus." The postal network fanned out across the continent as the nation expanded westward. By 1840, there were more than 13,000 post offices, as compared to less than 1,000 forty years earlier. Between 1810 and 1835, the length of post roads was extended from 36,406 to 142,774 miles. The great postal historian Wayne E. Fuller observed that the American post office "grew faster, became larger, hired more employees, transported more mail, and, of course, cost more than any mail service in the world."[13]

Mail volume moved sharply upward following congressional actions in 1845 and 1851 that reduced postage rates. Historian David M. Henkin related that thanks to the U.S. Mail, "ordinary Americans began participating in a regular network of long-distance communication, engaging in relationships with people they did not see." Major innovations transformed mail delivery over the following years. These improvements were introduced despite resistance from politicians and others for whom deficits were the overriding concern. In the late 1850s, small mailboxes for the deposit of outgoing letters began appearing on lampposts in cities. Before the Civil War, regular visits to the post office had been necessary to collect incoming mail, because there were no letter carriers to provide delivery. But after the enactment of Free City Delivery in 1863, the growing numbers of mail routes staffed by letter carriers made trips to the post office increasingly unnecessary for residents of urban areas. In 1871, letter carriers were providing door delivery in fifty-one cities. By 1900, the number of cities with carrier delivery had increased over fifteenfold, to 795.[14]

At the close of the nineteenth century, rural Americans—especially farmers who were members of the National Grange and the Populist movement's Farmers' Alliance—mounted a spirited campaign to extend home mail delivery into the countryside. "If one could know what it was like to be isolated by muddy roads in spring and snowbound in the winter," Fuller recounted, "to feel the need to see a new face even if it were only the mail carrier's, if all these feeling could be experienced, then one would know why the farmers became so excited." After Representative Thomas E. Watson, a Populist firebrand from Georgia, secured an appropriation for a pilot rural delivery program in 1893, selected areas began receiving this service on an experimental basis. Soon farmers across the nation were inundating Congress with petitions and letters demanding that the new service be extended. One congressman who agonized over postal deficits protested that the "country had run free-delivery mad." But due to immense public demand, on July 1, 1902, Rural Free Delivery (RFD) became a permanent nationwide service. Its contribution to the general welfare was deemed to outweigh the deficits that would result. RFD brought an end to the age-old isolation of farm life. In 1947, one woman expressed the profound sense of gratitude and affection that rural Americans felt for this revolutionary government service when she declared, "Thank God and our government for rural free delivery."[15]

In addition to criticisms of the Post Office Department for providing services such as RFD that operated at a deficit, the postal system also came under attack for offering services that for-profit businesses claimed should be their exclusive domain. Once the campaign for RFD had been won, the American people drafted the Post Office into service in their battle against the five private corporations that dominated package delivery. Starting in the 1850s, this cartel collaborated to set package delivery prices and jointly agreed on each firm's territory. The result was huge profits for the cartel members, inadequate or no service in large areas of the country, and a labyrinthine pricing system that confounded consumers with 600 million different rates. In 1912, a federal official attempting to ship a package was quoted three separate rates for the exact same box at the same office on the same day. Communications scholar Richard B. Kielbowicz notes that an Interstate Commerce Commission study found "package delivery companies double charged and over charged, refused to tell customers about free delivery areas beyond rail depots, sent shipments by circuitous routes to inflate costs, discriminated among customers, and more."[16]

The cartel's control over the package delivery industry warded off any potential private competitors, leaving only the federal government to challenge its dominion. Rural Americans began agitating for the Post Office to deliver packages in the late nineteenth century, and western and midwestern farmers in particular were at the forefront of the growing outcry to break the cartel's

stranglehold on the industry. Meanwhile, as a contemporary journalist reported, critics of the idea responded that "the Government
has no right to take over what can be done by private enterprise."
But this argument was not compelling to the millions of Americans afflicted by extortionate rates and inadequate service. Public
demands for the Post Office to deliver packages intensified following revelations of exorbitant profit taking, notably in 1910
when Wells Fargo & Co. paid its stockholders a 300 percent div-
idend, one-third in cash and the remaining two-thirds in new
stock. In 1912, Thomas Clark Atkeson of the National Grange
testified to Congress that cartel members were exacting "very considerable profit." "As a choice between . . . a private monopoly
and a Government monopoly," he announced, "I am favorable to
a Government monopoly."[17]

Although a government monopoly over package delivery was
not established, sustained public support for a postal package
delivery service secured the creation of Parcel Post, which com-
menced operations on January 1, 1913. Today's privatization
promoters claim that government is inept by definition, but the
new service was an immediate success, handling approximately
300 million parcels in its first six months. "Government service is
the most inefficient in the world," one opponent of Parcel Post had
contended. Yet historian William R. Leach pointed out that Parcel
Post "quickly outstripped all rivals in speed and efficiency." While
mail order houses Montgomery Ward & Co. and Sears, Roebuck
and Co. already were prospering—and thus had not lobbied for
government package delivery—they reaped the benefits of this
innovation. Sears's revenues tripled in the five years following the
service's introduction. Still, given the consumer's nightmare that
had reigned under the package delivery cartel, ordinary citizens
were the primary beneficiaries of the Post Office's latest venture.[18]

ELIMINATING GOVERNMENT

RFD and Parcel Post delivered significant benefits to the American people. James H. Bruns, former director of the Smithsonian Institution's National Postal Museum, said the combination of Parcel Post and RFD was "like a modern-day Prometheus stealing fire from the gods of Olympus and delivering it to the mortals below. RFD and Parcel Post were acts of empowerment for Americans who lived in rural areas." Today, the Postal Service remains the single most visible presence of the national government in the United States, with an infrastructure that extends into both the country and the city, ending at every home's mailbox. No other federal institution plays a direct role in the daily lives of Americans.[19]

The fundamental concern of pro-corporate ideologues promoting privatization and deregulation is not the services the Postal Service provides. Their focus is the symbolic value of the Postal Service as an arm of government that gets the job done day in and day out. Public institutions that are not devoted to profit maximization provide threatening alternatives to a paradigm that organizes human activity on a for-profit basis. Our public postal system concretely demonstrates that government can deliver for the American people. From the perspective of anti-government campaigners that reality is intolerable. They want to minimize the government as a presence in our national life by forcing the public sector to cede its functions to for-profit businesses.

The campaign to eliminate government services is one part of an anti-regulatory movement that seeks to extinguish the government's ability to establish and enforce social and economic regulations. Corporations object to these rules because they make it harder to externalize costs at the expense of the environment, consumers, and workers. Joan Claybrook, former president of Public Citizen, was on the front lines resisting this deregulatory push for decades. She explained that "following the impressive citizen gains of the late 1960s and early 1970s—when Congress enacted a raft of new

health, safety, environmental, consumer, and civil rights protections—corporate America launched a cynical campaign to limit the
government's power." Claybrook detailed the vast resources invested
in the anti-regulatory campaign. "This coordinated attack on citizen safeguards has been propelled by literally billions of dollars of
shareholder money," she emphasized, "for political contributions,
right-wing think tanks, lobbyists, smear campaigns, T.V. advertising and fake grassroots organizations." A relentless promoter of
this deregulatory agenda, journalist John B. Judis reported that AEI
alone "produced hundreds of studies decrying government regulation of business and attacking legislation offered by the consumer,
environmental, and labor movements."[20]

When government services and regulations disappear, citizens become less likely to view the government as an institution
that provides services and enforces regulations. The influential
pro-corporate political strategist Grover G. Norquist, founder
of Americans for Tax Reform, acknowledged: "My ideal citizen
is the self-employed, homeschooling, IRA-owning guy with
a concealed-carry permit. Because that person doesn't need the
goddamn government for anything." In addition, Norquist's
"ideal" individual never patronizes the Postal Service. Planning
far in advance, Norquist has long carried around a list of political
objectives that he hopes to accomplish, and among these is privatizing the postal system. Senator Robert C. Byrd (D-W.Va.) once
explained the Postal Service's significance as a symbol of government: "I come from a rural area where the flag means something.
And in many little communities, there's the flag at the post office.
That represents the federal government. That represents the man
in the striped pants, Uncle Sam." Eliminating the lone federal
agency that serves citizens directly on a daily basis would be a
large step toward achieving Norquist's sweeping agenda of dis-
pensing with government services altogether.[21]

Norquist is also a committed Republican partisan. Postal
workers are overwhelmingly unionized government employees—a

voting bloc that trends Democratic. Norquist promotes "right-to-work" laws that suppress union membership, maintaining that if such statutes are "enacted in a dozen more states, the modern Democratic Party will cease to be a competitive power in American politics." In an article written for the Heritage Foundation, Norquist once stressed the importance of "reducing the number of Americans dependent on the State for employment." Ever the fierce partisan, Norquist has declared that "every time the government gets smaller there are fewer Democratic precinct workers in the world." He therefore has urged "essential reforms including cutting the USPS' massive workforce."[22]

The example of George L. Priest provides another revealing illustration of the motivations behind attacks on the Postal Service. One of the leading opponents of the Postal Service's monopoly privileges, since 1983 Priest has directed the John M. Olin Center for Studies in Law, Economics, and Public Policy at Yale University, which received millions of dollars from its namesake's foundation. Olin was a wealthy manufacturer who used his foundation to funnel large amounts of money to pro-corporate causes, particularly the academic field of law and economics. The liberal judicial advocacy organization Alliance for Justice described law and economics as a means to promote the interests of corporations through "its anti-regulatory orientation and its focus on economic costs and benefits rather than 'abstract' notions of right and wrong." Before closing down in 2005, the John M. Olin Foundation spent tens of millions of dollars funding the study of law and economics at universities nationwide. Priest served on the Council of Academic Advisors at AEI, another recipient of Olin money. He also was a member of President Ronald Reagan's Commission on Privatization, which proposed, among other recommendations, "complete repeal of the postal monopoly."[23]

The "dedicated service" of postal workers, Senator Ralph W. Yarborough (D-Tex.) once noted, burnishes the federal government's public image. "The glow of the fire of service you have kindled," he told an audience of rural letter carriers, "can illuminate this government [and] cause a greater respect and love for it by all the people." Government services that garner esteem from citizens impede Priest's pro-corporate agenda. He has criticized postal clerks who serve patrons by "wrapping up boxes" and "providing advice and counsel," because such service allegedly creates an atmosphere in post offices that "more closely resembles a welfare office than it does a retail business." The fact that postal employees constitute the largest unionized workforce in America has troubled Priest as well.[24]

In the early 1990s, Priest's enmity toward the affirmative concept of government that the Postal Service represents prompted him to allege the agency "embraces almost all the aspects of socialism rejected in Eastern Europe." Following the fall of the Berlin Wall, R. Richard Geddes made the same connection between our nation's postal system and politically repressive regimes. "Hungary and Czechoslovakia, two of the countries that shook off communism last year, have been talking seriously about privatizing their post offices," he wrote. "If this is good enough for people just discovering freedom, maybe we should look into it." Geddes additionally warned that "East Bloc countries that recognize the importance of competitive markets will surpass us in productivity, and eventually in economic achievement."[25]

The assumption that privatization creates competitive markets conveniently ignores the reality that a handful of large corporations dominate much of the economy. As David Dayen, editor of the *American Prospect*, stated, there is "a grave monopoly problem in America. The structure of modern capitalism now favors monopoly." Paeans to free markets fail to account for this reality. "An economy where the typical industry is shared by a few firms," John Kenneth Galbraith observed, "is awkwardly inconsistent with a theory of capitalism which requires that power to affect prices or wages or output or investment be impersonally governed by the reactions of the many."[26]

There was no acknowledgement of the shortcomings of free market ideology when the Trump administration advocated postal privatization as part of a broader 2018 proposal to overhaul the federal government. "The federal government is bloated, opaque, bureaucratic, and inefficient," claimed J. Michael Mulvaney, director of the White House Office of Management and Budget (OMB). "Major changes are needed in how the Postal Service is financed and the level of service Americans should expect," the administration declared, setting forth a plan for "USPS privatization through an initial public offering (IPO) or sale to another entity." This radical reform would be beneficial, the administration alleged, because "the private operation would be incentivized to innovate and improve services to Americans in every community." Margaret Weichert, deputy director for management at OMB, rehashed the logic that is habitually offered for converting government functions into opportunities for private profit: "Healthy business organizations are designed to change and adapt to customer needs and the demands of the free market. The United States government should be no different."[27]

President Donald J. Trump considered himself a wildly successful businessman and presumed government needed to function more like a business. Shortly after his inauguration, Trump announced a new White House office tasked with refashioning the federal government. His remarks on that day referred to "government stagnation," "widespread congestion," and "cost overruns and delays," all ostensibly results of the public sector's ineptitude. Trump's specific animus toward the Postal Service had multiple sources. In addition to his notion that government equals incompetence, Trump's hostility toward the founder of Amazon.com Inc.—a major postal customer—was well known. Wealthy corporate executives who had the president's ear and were critical of the Postal Service likely influenced him as well. The upshot was that Secretary of the Treasury Steven T. Mnuchin conducted a campaign against the agency. In 2018, the Department of the

Treasury released a report that called for the Postal Service to operate more like a for-profit business.[28]

Mnuchin's efforts bore more concrete results in 2020, when his behind-the-scenes machinations helped place Republican donor Louis DeJoy at the helm of the Postal Service. Mnuchin constructed the Republican majority on the Board of Governors that tapped DeJoy for the position. The rich owner of a logistics firm that had committed numerous labor law violations, DeJoy was a generous GOP donor—whose funding largesse included $1.2 million for Trump—and a former Republican National Convention finance chairman. David C. Williams, former inspector general of the Postal Service, resigned as vice chairman of the Board of Governors in protest of this selection. Williams revealed DeJoy was inserted into the process late, had difficulty answering questions during his interview, and did not appear to be a "serious candidate." After assuming the position of postmaster general, DeJoy launched a cost-cutting campaign in July that degraded service to an extent that shocked the nation. In an unprecedented development, multiple federal judges intervened to reverse these changes due to concerns about vote-by-mail in the November election.[29]

In March 2021, DeJoy unveiled a plan to restructure postal operations that was laden with corporate jargon and premises. In order "to define a new high performing future" for the postal "brand," the plan claimed that henceforth the agency would "optimize," "improve," "realign," "strengthen," "modernize," "revitalize," and "innovate." In actual terms, such verbiage translated to addressing budgetary challenges by raising prices, shutting down processing plants, closing some post offices and reducing window hours at others, and lowering delivery service standards for 40 percent of first-class mail. Mark Dimondstein, president of the American Postal Workers Union, points out that "anytime you slow down service you drive away business." Political circumstances were unfavorable to the concept of privatization due to public uproar over DeJoy's previous actions and the newly elected Biden administration's support of the agency's service mission. Nevertheless, while the plan included some credible proposals for increasing revenues—notably in regard to package delivery—its discussion of "transforming our business" betrayed the underlying perspective of this document, which is not premised upon the standpoint of public service.[30]

Former Postmaster General Anthony M. Frank once used the platform of a Cato Institute conference to respond directly to anti-government critics. He did not lack an understanding of business principles. Before entering government service, Frank was chief executive officer of one of the nation's largest savings banks—San Francisco–based First Nationwide Bank. Frank raised trenchant questions at this event that spoke to the heart of the matter. "Is privatization simply a code word for union-busting?" he demanded. "Is privatization an attempt to let private companies skim off the profitable segments of the postal business while leaving the Postal Service to continue to serve those groups in areas deemed not profitable?" The chief concern of pro-corporate ideologues regarding the Postal Service is not "binding the nation together." For decades, their priority has remained eliminating the concept of government service from American life.[31]

TWO

DEREGULATION

In 1976, President Gerald R. Ford warned of the threat that proposals to abolish the postal monopoly posed. "There are some companies that want to, in major metropolitan areas, move in with their postal system, which is now precluded by law," he observed. "Frankly, that is where the Post Office . . . makes money," Ford continued, explaining that universal service required these revenues to subsidize operations in unprofitable areas. Absent the postal monopoly, private competitors could cherry-pick the most profitable services while spurning the remainder of the existing postal system. Revenue losses in these crucial areas would force the Postal Service to reduce its expenses by pruning its network, making operation of a universal system unworkable. The experience of deregulation domestically in other industries, and of postal deregulation in other nations, demonstrates that a government agency is necessary to maintain first-class universal service.[1]

NETWORK INDUSTRIES

Given the vast scale of the nation's postal network, regulatory economist John C. Panzar has concluded: "I am convinced that postal service is a natural monopoly." As a natural monopoly, one single postal system can provide services at a lower cost than multiple systems, inhibiting the development of market competition. The private express statutes, therefore, protect against the emergence of a corporate goliath with an incentive to abuse its position. After all, as the great political economist Thorstein Veblen perceived, "the all-dominating issue in business is the question of gain and loss." The Postal Service's status as a regulated government service founded upon public interest commitments, combined with the Postal Regulatory Commission's oversight, protects doubly against such a possibility.[2]

Deregulation of a natural monopoly would raise other issues as well, including the potential for wasteful duplication of services in the most profitable areas. Such an outcome would jeopardize the current value of network effects that a single universal postal system offers its users—the convenience of dealing with only one institution's procedures and rates in order to reach every address in the nation. There are additional benefits to a uniform rate structure that a for-profit corporation would reject. One can drop a letter in a blue U.S. Mail box in Nome, Alaska, for example, and know that for the price of a postage stamp it will arrive at its intended address in Key West, Florida, and vice versa. The National Academy of Public Administration's 1982 conclusion that "Balkanization of the national postal system is not in the national interest" still holds true today.[3]

A deregulated postal market would not provide service in a democratic manner. Business districts and affluent urban and suburban neighborhoods would become prime candidates for cream-skimming, while rural regions and low-income areas would be unattractive to private businesses. As former president of the National Association of Letter Carriers Vincent R. Sombrotto once pointed out to the *New York Times*:

> I have no doubt that a part-time worker on roller skates, could compete with the Postal Service in delivering copy from an advertising agency on Madison Avenue to your office on West 43rd Street. . . . Do you feel equally confident, however, that a migrant farm worker picking apples in Oregon will be able to send a money order, or a birthday card, to his family in Arkansas with equal ease if we destroy the Postal Service?

Research confirms Sombrotto's contention that deregulation would have an unequal impact. Econometricians Marshall R. Kolin and Edward J. Smith found that mail routes in rural areas were significantly less financially rewarding than those in non-rural areas, and that higher-income households receive more mail because *"mail goes where the money is."* A 2017 USPS Office of Inspector General report also found that mail volume is higher in upper-income areas.[4]

Yet it is rural and low-income Americans who consistently report lower levels of broadband internet access than the national average. This digital divide means these groups are particularly dependent on the Postal Service. In rural areas, 63 percent of residents report having broadband internet at home, making them 12 percentage points less likely to have such access than others. Among adults whose household income is under $30,000 annually, 44 percent lack broadband internet at home, with 46 percent not owning a computer and 29 percent not owning a smartphone. Unequal internet access has remained a constant pattern since the World Wide Web's debut, and appears certain to persist for years to come. "As a public policy principle," observed Ruth Y. Goldway, former chairwoman of the Postal Regulatory Commission, "having this low-tech network in place is important in a democratic society."[5]

AEI's R. Richard Geddes claimed that "the experience with deregulation of other industries similar in structure to postal services suggests that postal reform would create substantial net gains." But in the case of network industries such as transportation and communications systems, transport experts José A. Gómez-Ibáñez and John R. Meyer reported that private firms "tend to skim the cream by selecting only the most economically advantageous segments." The record of deregulation in industries that require extensive networks in order to serve large geographic areas is instructive. The experience of deregulation in the domestic passenger airline and intercity bus industries reveals the social costs to this policy approach.[6]

The airline industry was the United States' first major experiment with deregulation. Prior to 1979, the Civil Aeronautics Board maintained order in the industry by determining routes and fares for airlines. Since deregulation, the industry has experienced periods of intense turmoil when billions of dollars in losses accumulated, hundreds of thousands of workers were laid off, and numerous carriers were operating under bankruptcy protections. Proponents of deregulation argued that consumers would benefit from the increased competition that inevitably would arise. But that is not what happened. In 2017, William J. McGee, aviation consultant at Consumers Union, testified: "Key promises of deregulation, especially enhanced competition and improved customer experience, have not been realized." In 1978, the ten largest airlines controlled 88 percent of the market. In 2020, the ten largest airlines controlled 90 percent of the market. "As soon as the airline industry was deregulated," economist Walter Adams explained, "you got an intensive merger movement, so that you had a conversion from a regulated oligopoly to an unregulated oligopoly." Only one or two airlines generally dominate individual airports, even in larger cities. In 2015, the Associated Press found that one or two carriers controlled a majority of available passenger seats at ninety-three of the largest one hundred airports in the nation.[7]

Service has deteriorated. Airplanes have become more uncomfortable as airlines crammed in more seats and introduced smaller planes; formerly basic amenities such as meals are no longer provided; new and higher fees are introduced regularly for items that were once courtesies; and passengers have experienced more delays, extra connections, and longer layovers. Deregulation increased the divide that separates coach and first-class passengers, with travelers in the first-class cabin now receiving the level of service that once was standard in coach. Aggregate ticket prices maintained the downward trend that had been under way for thirty years prior to deregulation, and passengers can receive deeply discounted fares under certain circumstances, especially if their travel plans are flexible. But airlines also have imposed numerous new ticket restrictions and conditions.[8]

Many smaller airports are served by only a single carrier, if they have managed to retain service at all. Before deregulation, transportation expert Paul Stephen Dempsey explained, "carriers were expected to cross-subsidize losses or meager profits earned from serving small communities with healthier revenues earned from dense, lucrative markets, and provide just and reasonable rates to both." Aviation consultant Mark L. Gerchiak has predicted that "the trend in decreasing services in small markets is going to continue." In 2007, Senator Olympia J. Snowe (R-Maine) reported that more than three hundred airports had lost commercial airline service altogether. Although a federal program exists to subsidize commercial flights to smaller airports, since 2010 communities from Jamestown, New York, to Miles City, Montana, and from Ely, Nevada, to Athens Georgia, have lost air service. Representative Thomas W. Reed II (R-N.Y.) has been working to restore service to Jamestown's Robert H. Jackson Field. "We care about our region's access to national air travel," he stated, "because working families and businesses depend on the availability of affordable commercial flights."[9]

Passenger bus transportation was deregulated a few years after the airlines, in 1982. At the time, an executive at Greyhound Corp. claimed that thanks to deregulation "the chances are good that the public will benefit from more service and not less." But economist Frederick C. Thayer observed: "it took Greyhound very little time to decide that in a deregulated environment, it should abandon 1,313 communities in 43 states." The two national bus companies— Greyhound and Continental Trailways Inc.—also raised fares by as much as 25 percent. Rural America was hardest hit, with more than 90 percent of the towns that lost their Greyhound service having less than 10,000 residents. The U.S. Department of Agriculture estimated that by 1986 bus service to 4,500 small towns had been reduced or eliminated. In 1994, there were only seventy-seven stops left in Missouri and seventy-one in Illinois, as compared to 413 in Missouri and 555 in Illinois prior to deregulation.[10]

In 2004, Greyhound—by then the sole national passenger bus company, having acquired Trailways in 1987—announced forthcoming cutbacks that would end service to 850 communities. Fully 10 percent of its total stops—269 towns in seventeen states—were first on the chopping block. A broad band of the nation between Chicago and the Pacific Northwest was most affected, with service to the entire state of North Dakota reduced to one city. In the wake of the news, the *Bismarck Tribune* editorialized:

> The news that Greyhound lines is pulling out of North Dakota—except for Fargo—is a shocker. It spells the virtual end of intercity public transportation in the state. . . . In today's deregulated market-oriented transportation economy, there can be no question about Greyhound's right to discontinue unprofitable services. After all, the company's banker doesn't care if Greyhound is providing a socially valuable service for those riders who are left. . . . But the loss to a certain kind of traveler . . . is real and usually not remediable by jetliner or car.

In April 2005, Greyhound initiated another round of route cuts: 150 more towns were dropped from its system, many in the Southwest, with sixty-two of this batch located in California alone. Greyhound then moved to close still more ticket counters and stops in the South and the Northeast.[11]

To maintain profit margins, Greyhound now focuses on routes between larger cities that are separated by 300 miles or less. (This is the same strategy that a new set of express bus lines such as Megabus have adopted.) "There are certain segments of the population," sociologist Gary R. Lee commented, "who are going to be seriously inconvenienced—either they have no personal vehicle, or theirs is too unreliable to use for a long trip." Representative John M. McHugh (R-N.Y.) expressed similar thoughts in 2005 when Greyhound announced the elimination of stops in his rural district. "In this region of the world," he explained, "we measure our trips by hours, not miles and, for the most part, mass transit is simply not an option. These cutbacks will have a dramatic negative impact on North Country residents."[12]

The deregulated passenger bus industry does not serve large swaths of the nation. Theresa Firestine, senior economist at the Bureau of Transportation Statistics, reported that in 2018 more than one in five rural residents had no access to intercity bus transportation. There is little to no recourse for a community that a private bus company has decided to leave stranded. In 2007, concerned residents of Mercer County, Pennsylvania, found themselves helpless when Greyhound discontinued service to their only stop. "It is a private business decision and there's not much more we can do," County Commissioner Brian T. Beader acknowledged. "It's supposed to be public transportation for everybody," resident Faheem Yousef reflected when Greyhound abandoned Bowling Green, Ohio, one of eighteen towns in the state that lost service in the summer of 2005. The other stranded towns included two in Wayne County where more than half of all passengers were Amish. Sidney, Ohio, was yet another casualty. "It's corporate America, that's my answer," resident Kathryn Rees declared. "The big boys are going to do what they want to do, and they could care less about the little guy."[13]

FOREIGN POST OFFICES

While the private express statutes remain in force in the United States, deregulation of postal markets in other nations reveals the importance of the postal monopoly. Europe has been at the forefront of postal deregulation, especially since 1998, when the European Union initiated a process that required its members to end their postal monopolies, claiming deregulation would increase efficiencies and service quality. But in deregulated markets, providing universal service is a liability, and foreign postal systems operating more like businesses have reduced service to the public. The results of eliminating the postal monopoly in New Zealand, Sweden, Norway, and the United Kingdom are instructive.[14]

In 1987, the New Zealand government directed its national post office to begin operating as a commercial business and announced its intention to eliminate the postal monopoly. The majority of full-service post offices dotted throughout the nation were closed shortly thereafter: 906 post offices were operating in 1986, but despite public protests, 432 of these were shuttered in 1988 when the government stopped subsidizing them. Operating under the constraints of market logic, New Zealand Post failed to take into account "the fact that post offices were acting as government agencies in these communities," said David Russell, chief executive of New Zealand's Consumers' Institute. "They provided something like ninety different services." Commercialization impacted the postal system's social mission, as the blind lost their legal right to receive free postage for talking books and Braille materials.[15]

In 1998, New Zealand's postal market was deregulated. The price of standard letters tripled over the next twenty years. Russell stated that "ideological fervor pure and simple" had created a "wild enthusiasm to deregulate a monopoly that was working extremely well." New competitors in the postal market have focused on the most profitable segments. Service cutbacks have proceeded at New Zealand Post in recent years, with New Zealanders continuing to protest the closure of the nation's remaining post offices. There were only 103 left by 2018, although there were 780 other "points of service" located inside private businesses. In 2013, New Zealand Post reduced deliveries in rural areas from six to five days a week. Sixteen months later, New Zealand Post made three mail deliveries per week the new standard in urban areas. "N.Z. Post has been mismanaged," journalist Paul Charman stated. "As I see it, a once strong N.Z. Post has been run down by successive governments whose long game has been to sell it off."[16]

In 1993, the mail monopoly in Sweden was abolished, and the postal market was deregulated and opened up to competition. Postage prices rose, delivery service in rural areas suffered, and the number of post offices was cut in half. In 2002, the *Financial Times* reported that "only one competitor of any size has emerged—CityMail—and it has largely confined itself to corporate mail in Sweden's three biggest cities." The United Kingdom's National Audit Office revealed "the introduction of competition led to . . . a breakdown of the previous uniform [postage rate] structure." The result was "price reductions for large businesses, but for individuals and small businesses outside the principal population centers prices have increased significantly." In 2005, Bengt Ingerstam, president of the Swedish Consumer Coalition, reported: "I can get things sent all the way from South America for less than it costs to send a parcel to my neighbor in the next city."[17]

There are currently no post offices operating in Sweden. They all were closed in favor of moving postal transactions into commercial stores. This decision was a source of controversy, and one result is a decrease in the number of retail outlets offering postal services in rural areas. Competition remains concentrated in the nation's three largest cities, and there are households in remote regions that only receive mail delivery two days a week. Sweden's postal officials claim that only 5 percent of the population needs to receive mail on a daily basis, and therefore, "adjusting the frequency of delivery would not affect customers . . . to any great degree." They recently declared it will become necessary for the Swedish government to provide a subsidy in order to maintain delivery service throughout the nation. "The issue of compensation needs to be on the agenda," postal officials warned.[18]

In 2002, Norway's government converted the national post office into a public corporation and stated its intention to deregulate the postal sector. Norway Post officials advised that "when the monopoly is broken up, other players will take the lion's share in the attractive parts of the market," so in order to maintain "the principle of uniform postage . . . the only possibility is that the Norwegian state covers the additional costs through increased government procurements." In preparation for deregulation, the right of newspapers and magazines to pay reduced postage was ended, because it was "incompatible with the principle of cost related prices." Norway Post acknowledged this change would "lead to a significantly higher level of costs for the newspapers and magazines." After notching record-high profits in 2005, postal officials stated their intention "to shut down as many as 150 of the 303 post offices left in Norway."[19]

Norwegian farmers are a potent national political force, and government policies traditionally have supported rural areas. The 2005 election produced a governing coalition in parliament that heeded rural concerns about maintaining adequate service levels and rejected postal deregulation. But the deregulatory push was revived when this coalition lost ground in subsequent elections. In 2016, monopoly protections for mail were removed and Saturday delivery was discontinued. Four years later, mail delivery was reduced to every other weekday. In some isolated areas, residents were told they would have to travel to towns located hours away to pick up their mail. "Suddenly, you stand there utterly confused," one woman reflected, "and understand nothing about your society anymore." Postal officials warn that service "must be further adjusted in line with changed market conditions," and that it is "vital" for government subsidies to cover "the net costs of the commercially non-viable services."[20]

Royal Mail, the United Kingdom's postal system, was long considered a highly successful—even beloved—public service. In 1993, the head of Royal Mail could claim it was "the best in the world." Given its two deliveries every weekday, plus Saturday delivery, for one of the lowest postage rates in the world, his claim rested on solid ground. Under Prime Minister Margaret

Thatcher, the government had privatized numerous public assets, but did not touch Royal Mail. "People feel very strongly about it," Thatcher acknowledged. Nevertheless, despite high regard for Royal Mail—and its consistent profitability—Thatcher's successors in the Conservative Party began pushing privatization, leading the *Guardian* to observe: "The plain and embarrassing political fact that the Government faces with the P.O. is that it is a public sector success story." But, of course, a major impetus for privatization was the elimination of a successful public institution.[21]

It would take "New Labour" to accomplish what the Conservatives could not. In 2001, Prime Minister Tony Blair's government placed Royal Mail on a pathway to privatization, granting its executives greater discretion to pursue commercial goals. They soon used this new authority to axe the second delivery that was traditional in the afternoon. Inexplicably, Royal Mail's management also changed its name to "Consignia"—a move that cost close to £2 million—before acknowledging the "expensive rebranding was a failure and that the new name and logo had attracted derision." It cost still more money to revert back to Royal Mail. After the postal market was deregulated in 2006, Tony Benn, a former postmaster general, concluded, "The Post Office is being systematically and deliberately destroyed." Indeed, approximately 30 percent of the post offices in Greater London had closed since 2000.[22]

In 2013, despite the opposition of two-thirds of the British public, Royal Mail was privatized. A parliamentary committee later determined the national postal system had been sold for significantly less than its full value. A separate public corporation—Post Office Ltd.—that has received considerable government aid exists to operate a significantly reduced network of post offices. Between 2000 and 2016, fully 6,750 post offices—37 percent of the nation's total—were closed. Meanwhile, the price of a first-class postage stamp rose 63 percent from 2010 to 2018, and government officials have warned that intensifying competition in profitable postal markets poses a potential threat to Royal Mail's ability to maintain universal service. In 2020, Royal Mail missed delivery service standards and increased postage well beyond the rate of inflation.[23]

In Argentina, postal privatization was reversed due to its negative consequences. Although the Argentine postal market was deregulated officially in 1994, it had been effectively deregulated since the 1970s because the government had stopped enforcing the postal monopoly and started selling mail delivery licenses to private companies. James W. Sauber of the National Association of Letter Carriers stated that as the national post office lost revenues to competitors acquiring licenses, "service quality deteriorated and its stamp price rose to rank among the highest in the world." Argentines naturally responded to the post office's difficulties by using it less, which hastened the system's deterioration. The Argentine government embraced privatization as a guiding principle in the 1990s and decided to sell the post office to a private consortium in 1997. The new owners committed to investing in improving the postal system, paying the government a concession fee, and providing universal service.[24]

At this point, the World Bank arranged financial support for the newly privatized post office, because Argentina looked like a good prototype for its postal privatization agenda. Its officials believed in "the transformation of public postal authorities into market-oriented and financially viable businesses." But in spite of this aid, the private owners failed to maintain concession-fee payments and service did not improve, even as prices increased markedly. In 2003, the Argentine government reassumed control of the post office, and back under government management it showed a surplus. Still, the postal market remained deregulated, exerting financial pressure on the post office and deterring improvements in the service.[25]

In 2002, the U.K. National Audit Office spelled out the problem with deregulating postal markets: "If competition is most pronounced for the most profitable services, [the national post office] could be left with insufficient returns to cover its overhead costs, and hence to finance remaining services without across-the-board price increases that might further erode its competitive position." The impact of deregulation on universal service in the United States would be pronounced, because the nation is so vast and the disparities between urban and rural areas—and rich and poor—are especially broad. Additionally, economic development expert Susan Christopherson affirmed, "the imperatives of the U.S. investment system are associated with firm strategies to target low-risk, high-profit markets and to discriminate among clients or customers." Her conclusion further emphasizes that the negative consequences of deregulation observed in foreign postal markets likely would be even worse in the United States.[26]

NINETEENTH-CENTURY AMERICA

For-profit postal systems have operated on American soil. In the nineteenth century, private companies that hauled freight to remote western mining camps also transported letters. This practice reached its greatest extent during the California Gold Rush, when the state's population exploded by almost 1,500 percent over four years. The postal infrastructure was overwhelmed, and private businesses cropped up to deliver mail at high prices. But the Post Office's footprint in the West expanded throughout the 1850s as Congress used mail contracts to extend stagecoach routes through areas they otherwise would have avoided due to their lack of profitability. In 1859, the Post Office Department spent almost $1.2 million delivering mail via stagecoach to California, and earned only $34,497 in the process. Still, notwithstanding the financial cost, prior to completion of transcontinental telegraph lines and railroads, these subsidized stagecoaches linked the Pacific coast to the rest of the nation.[27]

By the late 1830s, advances in railroad technology were allowing opportunistic entrepreneurs on the East Coast to challenge the U.S.

Mail. Because the Post Office used high postage rates for letters to subsidize unprofitable delivery services like newspapers, most correspondence was mailed by businesses. Without the burden of providing money-losing services, and with the aid of rapid transit on the railroads, private companies began carrying mail between major cities along the Atlantic seaboard at reduced prices. These private competitors presented businessmen in the region with an opportunity to cut their postage costs, but posed a threat to the many other Americans who relied on the Post Office, although some of the latter group could make use of local mail delivery companies that had emerged to offer low-cost delivery within cities.[28]

Given the extent of cross-subsidization in the postal system, the growth of private mail carriers endangered service in much of the nation. In 1844, postal revenues in six northeastern coastal states from Massachusetts to Pennsylvania almost equaled the total revenues generated in the remainder of the country. In these six states, only 56 percent of revenues were needed to offset expenses, leaving a large surplus to subsidize service elsewhere. Meanwhile, the remaining states and territories covered just 70 percent of their expenses. The private carriers undermining the postal system, as historian Wayne E. Fuller observed, "took the cream of the business and left the rest to the Post Office." In 1845, Congress reasserted control over the nation's mail by affirming the Post Office's monopoly on letters and slashing postage rates.[29]

Economist Kelly B. Olds and business historian Richard R. John Jr. have argued that a privately owned postal system could have supplanted the public one. They both claimed it was the interest of congressmen in using the Post Office to distribute patronage that preserved the institution. Olds alleged that if "rent-seeking groups" benefiting from existing arrangements had not taken action, "private companies might possibly have made communications in the United States more efficient." "Control of the means of communications is not a necessary prerogative of the modern nation-state." John agreed. It was patronage, he wrote, which "doomed from the start—at least in the nineteenth century, though perhaps not today—any serious proposals for thorough-going reform."[30]

When Congress upheld the postal monopoly and reduced postage, its members did more than defend patronage, they responded to a growing public demand for universal, affordable mail service. The agitation for cheap postage, philatelist David L. Straight made clear, was part of a dynamic period of social ferment that included movements for abolition, women's rights, temperance, and prison and asylum reform. The innovative postal program that educator and tax reformer Rowland Hill had formulated in Britain offered an attractive model for the United States. Hill argued that low, uniform postage rates would produce increased mail volume, thereby creating greater revenues to fund an expanding postal system. The rising geographic mobility of Americans in the middle of the century, historian David M. Henkin explained, stoked public interest in more affordable communication. Lower postage rates made it possible for practically all citizens to use the Post Office to exchange letters and remain in touch with distant relatives and far-flung friends. Developments during this period, Henkin stated, constituted a "democratization of the postal system that the Founding Fathers had designed and a realization of its most radical implications for long-distance communication in everyday life."[31]

Just as affordable postage was helping turn the United States into a nation of letter writers, an antithetical postal experiment took place south of the Mason-Dixon line. Southerners in Congress had repeatedly opposed extending the postal system, because they feared large deficits might force cuts to unprofitable services in their sparsely populated region. Additionally, the southern elite's antipathy toward the federal power to tax prompted opposition to expanding public services more generally. It was unsurprising, therefore, when following secession the constitution of the Confederate States of America declared the primary objective of its newly formed postal system was to be financially self-sufficient. Widespread agreement with this principle among members of the Confederate States Congress allowed the clause to pass easily.[32]

At the outset of the Civil War, the head of the Confederate post office bemoaned "the former prodigal expenditures in this service, and almost utter neglect of economy in its supervision and management." His policies ensured that postal rates were high, and the quality of mail delivery was low. Southern newspapers struggled under the burden of expensive postage. Both soldiers and civilians experienced lower wartime morale due to poor mail service and a shortage of reliable news. Nevertheless, at high cost to the pro-slavery cause, the Confederate post office met its fiscal mandate. Communications scholar John Nathan Anderson concluded that an examination of Confederate postal history presents "a cautionary tale of what can happen when constitutive choices about systems of mass communications are made in a single-dimensional fashion without due consideration to the consequences."[33]

PROFIT AS KING

Promoters of postal deregulation and privatization appear to be quite comfortable with negative consequences for the public. They have admitted freely that their plans would result in service deterioration. R. Richard Geddes claimed "maintaining universal service does not necessarily mean the maintenance of . . . any particular aspect of delivery quality." In fact, he stated, "universal service may actually mean providing excessively frequent service to addresses on unprofitable routes." Chris R. Edwards of the Cato Institute agreed that "policymakers should be more flexible with the idea of 'universal service.'" One specific suggestion he made is reducing delivery to "every second day." Peter J. Ferrara— an early promoter of Social Security privatization—advocated the alleged silver-bullet privatization prescription for the Postal Service as well: "Would uniform national rates be retained in a private system?" he asked. "The answer is, such rates should not necessarily be retained." But as the *Christian Science Monitor* once editorialized: "The essence of the postal service—universal service at universal rates—runs counter to privatization. Such a move likely would emphasize profit as king."[34]

Privatization also poses additional threats, notably the possibility of business failure. A private corporation could bankrupt itself, or simply decide to exit the postal services sector entirely in favor of entering an industry its executives hope will prove more profitable or prestigious. In 1997, Montana Power Company pushed electricity deregulation through the state's legislature. Executives then decided to sell the company's electricity business, abandoning its commitment to serving as a public utility. The CBS News investigative program *60 Minutes* stated that after decades of providing "cheap, reliable electricity for the people of Montana, excellent benefits for thousands of employees and generous, reliable dividends for its stockholders," Montana Power exited the "stodgy" world of public utilities in favor of entering the "glamorous" telecommunications business. Thousands of employees lost their jobs, and Montanans grappled with soaring utility bills. The telecom venture went bankrupt, while executives made off with millions of dollars. The *Great Falls Tribune* editorialized that given the fallout, "Montanans will be excused if they are angry and frustrated."[35]

The national postal system is too crucial to entrust to the vicissitudes of capricious corporate decision-making. In addition, potential foreign ownership presents a threat. In one public stock offering for Dutch Post—which implemented significant service reductions following privatization—foreign investors purchased 65 percent of the shares. "Merchants have no country," Thomas Jefferson observed. "The mere spot they stand on does not constitute so strong an attachment as that from which they draw their gains." It would be against the national interest for our postal system—a core component of the nation's infrastructure—to fall under the control of foreign interests.[36]

Elected officials on the political right tend to view government services with a critical eye, yet prominent conservatives have granted the need for a public postal system. "I know that there are some of my colleagues who believe in privatization. I do not," stressed Representative Kelly M. Armstrong (R-N.Dak.). "The reason I don't is because the last mile of delivery is obviously the most expensive." The influential free-market economist Milton Friedman made the same point, allowing that "local delivery subsidizes mail for remote areas." Senator Trent Lott (R-Miss.) once acknowledged the importance of a universal postal system as well when he affirmed, "The postal service goes into rural areas and provides a lot of services that the people probably would not receive without the monopoly of sorts the postal service has." The United States Constitution enshrined the Postal Service as a branch of government for good reason.[37]

THREE

DEMOCRACY

The postal system has been integral to American democracy. "From its very beginning," Representative James C. Wright Jr. (D-Tex.) observed, "the Post Office has existed not to make money, but to serve people." Starting in the eighteenth century, the service-oriented philosophy of the postal system promoted democratic engagement and debate. The Post Office was an indispensable conduit of news and information, delivering newspapers, magazines, and pamphlets at low cost. American voters were remarkably well informed as a result. This long tradition of service to democracy was clearly apparent in 2020, when due to COVID-19 millions of voters relied on the Postal Service to participate in the presidential election. The agency's democratic mission was conspicuous on Election Day, but preferential postage rates for newspapers, magazines, books, and nonprofit organizations promote democracy and the common good every day of the year.[1]

FOUNDING PRINCIPLES

In the years immediately following the Constitution's ratification, influential figures emphasized various possibilities for the Post Office. Alexander Hamilton favored the British model of a revenue-generating postal system, and proposed using this income to fund the national debt. Thomas Jefferson worried about opportunities for patronage turning the Post Office into a seat of political corruption. George Washington had used his skill as a surveyor to help lay out some of the first post roads. He envisioned a postal system that united the widely dispersed citizens of a fledg-

43

ling nation and sustained their pioneering attempt at republican government. Biographer James Thomas Flexner stressed that Washington "believed that the government should have the most direct possible connection with each citizen as an individual."[2]

Washington was convinced that the broad dissemination of information through the Post Office would help assure the scattered population's loyalty to the national government. Indeed, the nation's postal system did function as a crucially important symbol of nationhood. During the early years of the republic, the only tangible evidence for many Americans that the national government existed at all was the U.S. Mail. "New Yorkers and Virginians, Georgians and Pennsylvanians," historian Wayne E. Fuller stated, "were constantly reminded of their common country as they saw the United States postrider break suddenly from the forest and head into their settlement with the mail. . . . He was a living symbol of national unity, a concrete evidence that the new government existed and served all the people."[3]

The Post Office helped "bind the nation together" by maintaining communication between the settled Atlantic seaboard and the frontier. In 1789, there were only seventy-five post offices and less than 2,000 miles of post roads to serve a nation of 3.5 million people encompassing 500,000 square miles. The Post Office Act of 1792 stipulated that surpluses be used to extend service and that members of Congress—not unelected postal officials— oversee the system's development. As the nation expanded, post roads stitched together its far-flung citizenry. In the 1790s alone, the length of post roads increased over tenfold, to 21,000 miles. In 1801, the number of post offices reached 1,000, and then surpassed 2,000 in 1809. Historian David M. Henkin emphasized that "during the early national period the Post Office functioned for most Americans as the principal embodiment of the federal government and a powerful symbol of national connectedness."[4]

Washington repeatedly urged low postage rates for political information and news. He believed these sources of knowledge had a central role in the new nation's revolutionary experiment with democracy. Upon becoming the first president in 1789, Washington favored "the conveyance of News Papers and periodical Publications in the public vehicles without expence." In his first address to Congress, Washington emphasized the importance of "facilitating the intercourse between the distant parts of our Country by a due attention to the Post-Office and Post Roads." Washington persistently stressed "the importance of the Post Office and Post Roads," even envisioning this communications network as a guardian of democracy, "diffusing a knowledge of the laws and proceedings of the Government; which, while it contributes to the security of the people, serves also to guard them against the effects of mis-representation and misconception."[5]

When Washington signed the Post Office Act of 1792, he approved a law that charged the postal system with transporting newspapers at low postage rates. This act also affirmed the practice of publishers exchanging newspapers with one another postage free, which helped disseminate national and foreign news more widely. The principle of low postage for news had been established, but Washington believed postage rates for newspapers should be still lower. In his next address to Congress, Washington affirmed the "importance of facilitating the circulation of political intelligence and information," and decried setting postage rates at levels that "operate[d] . . . against the transmission of News-papers to distant parts of the Country." In response, the House of Representatives pledged that the Post Office would "merit our particular inquiry and attention." In 1794, Washington approved a new postal law that created a rate classification for newspapers that was particularly low within their state of publication and also extended lesser privileges of reduced postage to magazines and pamphlets.[6]

One of the common policy objectives of price regulations is to shift financial burdens onto those who can better afford them. This principle guided early American postal policies that promoted the circulation of civic knowledge. Letter writers at this time tended to be affluent, and Congress used higher postage rates on letters to reduce postage on newspapers. In his first annual message to Congress, President Thomas Jefferson proposed eliminating postage on newspapers "to facilitate the progress of information." This sweeping recommendation was not acted on, but the low postage rate for newspapers established in 1794 was left unchanged for decades. By the mid-nineteenth century, newspapers composed 90 percent of the U.S. Mail while supplying only one-ninth of postal revenues. Low newspaper postage was essential to ensuring that citizens in all corners of the nation remained abreast of current events. Wayne E. Fuller observed that appointing the Post Office to carry newspapers at less than their actual cost to the postal system "contributed immeasurably to the democratic process and made Americans as a whole perhaps the best informed people in the world in the nineteenth century."[7]

NEWSPAPERS AND MAGAZINES

Congress's policy of operating the Post Office as a low-cost communications network underwrote an enormous growth in newspaper circulation. Fuller noted that postage policies established in the 1790s "made possible the greatest proliferation of newspapers the world had ever seen." A mere 200 newspapers in 1801 had multiplied to 2,526 in 1850. More newspapers circulated in the United States than in any other nation in the world. Given the extent of present-day media consolidation, it is illuminating to note Alexis de Tocqueville's 1835 observation that "in America there is scarcely a hamlet that has not its newspaper." He thought this arrangement allowed for "division of the influence of the press," which prevented the concentration of political influence in a select handful of newspapers.[8]

In 1832, Congress devoted significant attention to the idea of abolishing newspaper postage outright. Jacksonians opposed such a move, however, because they worried this reform would foster the circulation of a small number of major newspapers, which in turn would "annihilate at least one-half of our village newspapers." The central role of the local newspaper in American society was further bolstered in 1851 when Congress allowed weekly newspapers to travel postage-free within their county of publication. But this was not the main feature of the Post Office Act of 1851, which was a legislative milestone because it committed the postal system to a clear-cut service-first policy. Congress decreed that neither existing deficits nor the potential for future deficits should induce officials to curtail the postal system's expansion.[9]

Newspapers continued to benefit from low postage rates in the second half of the nineteenth century, yet it was magazines that truly flourished thanks to favorable postal policy. In 1852, Congress placed magazines on an equal footing with newspapers, granting these publishers postage reductions of 33 to 50 percent. In 1885, Congress slashed postage rates for both newspapers and magazines, halving the price that publishers paid to use the postal system. Over the following thirty years, the total weight of newspapers and magazines in the U.S. Mail increased twelvefold. By 1905 the number of magazines in circulation had almost doubled, reaching 6,000. Magazines were the central medium of the "muckrakers" whose journalistic exposés raised the public's consciousness about numerous social problems, helping to create a mass constituency that favored reform. During the Progressive Era, the investigative reporting that appeared in such muckraking magazines as *McClure's*, *Collier's*, *Everybody's*, and *Leslie's* stimulated public demands for reforms that ranged from food safety standards to antitrust laws.[10]

The U.S. Mail also was crucial to the Progressives' predecessors, the Populists of the late nineteenth century—ordinary farmers and workers who advocated using government programs to promote the public interest. Falling on the wrong end of the extreme inequality that defined the Gilded Age, the Populists challenged banks, railroad corporations, and the two-party system. Because contesting such powerful interests required an alternative media apparatus, the Populists published more than 1,000 journals that sustained the movement and constituted its intellectual center. Even in the face of advertiser boycotts and hounding creditors, these reform-minded editors and publishers could depend on the Post Office to help them reach an audience. Free in-county postage for newspapers was essential to the Populist movement. Without the assurance of free distribution, few Populist journals would have been printed in the first place, and the movement would have lacked its primary source of information and education. The Populist movement spearheaded such important reforms as a progressive income tax, financial regulations, expanded public education, and the direct election of U.S. senators.[11]

In the twenty-first century, printed periodicals remain central to American democracy, and a special rate class for mailing these publications continues to promote civic engagement in public affairs. The Association of Magazine Media recognizes "the Postal Service's importance to our industry as our trusted distribution partner." The National Newspaper Association notes that reliance on printed newspapers is highest "in rural areas [and] among minorities, senior citizens, low-income earners, and those who have not attended college." With a mere handful of corporations dominating the contemporary media landscape, lower rates for newspapers and magazines—particularly small independent ones that contribute a disproportionately large share of ideas—are all the more important for promoting the diversity of voices and opinions that democracy requires.[12]

Since 2004, around one in five newspapers—almost 1,800 in total—have disappeared. When local political news coverage declines, so does citizen engagement with public affairs. As a result, voters elect politicians who are less competent and less responsive to constituent interests. At the federal level, this outcome means members of Congress provide worse constituent service and secure less funding for their districts. At the same time, political competition on the local level declines and the cost of government rises because the press fails to hold elected officials accountable. Fortunately, in the interest of promoting localism and civic engagement, small periodicals still benefit from reduced postage rates within their county of publication. The Postal Service delivers the majority of newspapers that serve small towns, rural areas, and local neighborhoods. "Community newspapers need for USPS to be stable and effective," affirms Matthew Adelman, president of the National Newspaper Association.[13]

BOOKS AND NONPROFITS

In the late nineteenth century, books served alongside newspapers and pamphlets as vehicles of the Populist movement's ideas. In the 1870s, a wave of cheap paperback books packaged as periodicals began moving through the U.S. Mail. These publications techni-cally should not have qualified for the second-class postage rate reserved for newspapers and magazines, but enough members of Congress were convinced of the educational value of paperbacks that they continued to travel through the postal system at the lower rate. In 1894, one congressman dismissed concerns about the contribution of paperback books to the postal deficit. "I care not if it does cost the Government a few dollars more than it brings in," he conceded, "provided it spreads good literature throughout the country." But this unsanctioned arrangement raised ques-tions about low-cost second-class mail generally, so newspaper and magazine publishers backed members of Congress and postal officials who condemned deficits, resulting in unwanted attention that brought an end to the practice in 1901.[14]

Books subsequently would be admitted to the U.S. Mail under a special rate class as part of the longstanding policy of employing the Post Office to support objectives such as education that serve the public interest. The American Library Association argued for decades that library materials deserved the same government support accorded newspapers and magazines. In 1886, the organization made an unsuccessful bid to include library books in the second-class rate category. A breakthrough occurred in 1924 when civic groups representing a wide range of Americans who stood to benefit from greater access to library books testified before Congress in support of the idea. The American Federation of Labor, National Grange, and General Federation of Women's Clubs were among the organizations that urged a low library postage rate. The Post Office Department backed the idea in 1928, which smoothed legislative action. This reform granted public libraries the ability to send and receive books at a reduced rate within their state or a range of 300 miles.[15]

While public libraries were waging their postal campaign, book publishers pursued a separate rate category for books in general. Their efforts received an unexpected boost due to an overlooked provision in a 1933 revenue law that authorized the president to modify postage rates temporarily. Although the reason for this provision is unclear, in 1938 book publishers recognized its potential for aiding their cause and assembled a coalition of supporters that included such organizations as the American Library Association, American Association for Adult Education, American Association of University Professors, Association of American Colleges, Carnegie Corporation, National Association for the Advancement of Colored People (NAACP), and National Catholic Education Association. In addition, a personal friend of President Franklin D. Roosevelt made the case for a special book rate to him directly. Roosevelt was easily convinced that such a rate would serve "the interests of the public, in the promotion of the cultural growth, education, and development of the American people." He created a new rate class for books through presidential proclamation that very year. But Roosevelt's order was temporary, so the coalition lobbied Congress for a law. With book rate already in operation, legislation creating a permanent book rate was enacted in 1942 with little opposition.[16]

Libraries and books remain entitled to favorable postage rates today. In 1953, films were added to the items that could be sent using book rate and library mail. In addition to books and films, at the present time the articles that qualify for book rate—which is currently called media mail—include sheet music, sound and video recordings, manuscripts, educational charts, and binders containing medical information. In 1958, the distance limitation that originally applied to library mail was removed. The institutions permitted to use library mail were expanded to include museums and herbariums nine years later. Articles that can be sent via library mail include not only items that qualify for book rate, but also academic theses, periodicals, scientific kits, specimens, and additional materials that further education.[17]

Postal developments generally follow the broader trends of American society, both progressive and reactionary. During World War I, a spasm of fear gripped the nation, prompting passage of the Espionage Act of 1917, which empowered the postmaster general to censor mail deemed detrimental to the war effort. Senator Robert M. La Follette, Sr., (R-Wisc.) protested that the law would "suppress publication through arbitrary denial of mailing rights." With the support of President Woodrow Wilson and much of the American public, Postmaster General Albert S. Burleson followed exactly the course that La Follette opposed. But this new task was not one the unprepared Post Office Department was equipped to carry out in the thoroughgoing manner that supporters of the idea demanded. Still, a southern magazine that attacked conscription, socialist newspapers, journals critical of British rule in Ireland, foreign language periodicals, and additional publications ceased operations. In 1919, congressional hysteria produced bills prohibiting the postal system from transmitting German language items, and—in an attempt to prevent labor strikes—another bill proposed making it unlawful to interfere with the mining of coal used to fuel railroads that transported mail. None of these or other similar bills were acted upon, but they reflected the fearful response to the war and the Russian Revolution that would produce the First Red Scare following the armistice.[18]

Yet World War I was also the moment when the Post Office Department implemented a policy that promoted democracy and civic life. In 1917, Congress established a special postage classification for the publications of "religious, educational, scientific, philanthropic, agricultural, labor, or fraternal organizations." Congress previously had granted nonprofit organizations the right to send their publications as second-class mail. Proponents of this reform argued that these publications were of "public character," and were "issued and disseminated not for the purpose of making a pecuniary profit but for the dissemination of information." In 1949, the question received further congressional consideration when nonprofit organizations protested that a rate increase would require them to budget additional funds for postage, leaving less for their public service work. "We are financed almost exclusively through the annual Easter Seal appeal," a spokesman for the National Society for Crippled Children and Adults explained. In 1950, the March of Dimes asked Congress to "exempt the philanthropic organizations" from a proposed rate hike. In recognition of the social contributions of nonprofits, Congress created a special postage rate for their mass mailings the following year.[19]

The social movements of the post-World War II era made extensive use of nonprofit postage rates to recruit members and raise funds. The leading organizations of the southern civil rights movement depended on the postal system for financial support. The Southern Christian Leadership Conference, Committee of Racial Equality (CORE), and Student Non-violent Coordinating Committee all relied on donations sent in response to direct mail appeals. "Direct mail was CORE's lifeline," movement leader James L. Farmer Jr. affirmed. In the late 1930s, the National Wildlife Federation (NWF) successfully used the postal system to raise funds for its conservation work, a harbinger of events during the 1960s and 1970s, when ever-increasing numbers of Americans

mailed in the checks that fueled the rapid growth of the environmental movement. The U.S. Mail helped the Wilderness Society
maintain contact with its growing membership, who sent donations and in return received a steady stream of newsletters, alerts,
and additional fundraising requests. Membership in the Audubon
Society, NWF, and Wilderness Society doubled over the course
of the 1960s. Meanwhile, the Sierra Club's membership increased
more than fivefold. In the 1970s, the San Francisco office of
Greenpeace established a highly successful direct mail program
that helped drive the organization's rise to prominence.[20]

Many of the nation's largest civic organizations owe their very
existence to the nonprofit postage rate. Consumer movement
leader Colston E. Warne of the Consumers Union, publisher of
Consumer Reports, stated, "In the early days, the greatest source
of our revenue was direct mail. . . . Direct mail sales were a central element in our survival." When civic leader John W. Gardner
founded Common Cause in 1970, nonprofit postage helped him
mail out millions of letters to potential members. In less than six
months, 100,000 Americans had joined the fledgling organization. Consumer advocate Ralph Nader founded Public Citizen
one year later. Nonprofit postage rates significantly aided the
new organization's growth, helping amass donations from 62,000
people in just two months. Organizations spanning the political
spectrum from the Democratic Socialists of America to—ironi-
cally enough—the Heritage Foundation made use of the postal
system in a similar manner. Peter Bahouth and Andre Carothers
of Greenpeace once called mail "a lifeline for the growth and preservation of the nation's ailing tradition of citizen involvement in
public issues."[21]

There have been a number of changes in nonprofit postage rates
over the years, but the principle of reduced postage has remained
the same due to recognition of the positive benefits these organizations and their publications provide to American democracy
and society. In 2004, Lester C. Hess Jr., past national president

of the Benevolent and Protective Order of Elks, observed, "Non-profit organizations are woven into the very fabric of American life." Americans rely on nonprofit organizations to provide social services, promote education, and support the arts. And, Hess testified, "to a large extent [nonprofits] depend upon the U.S. Mail . . . for their existence." In 2015, Richard K. Kolb of the Veterans of Foreign Wars stated that in recent years nonprofit postage had saved the organization a "tremendous" amount of money. Although online fundraising has grown in importance, Stacey Stewart, president of the March of Dimes, affirmed that direct mail remains an effective fundraising tool. Donors are more likely to read paper letters, plus they elicit a stronger emotional response and are better remembered. In addition, mailed fundraising appeals go hand in hand with online efforts. Sarah Valentine, vice president of development for Seattle's Woodland Park Zoo, reported: "What we're seeing more and more is direct mail triggers giving online."[22]

In addition to fundraising solicitations, the periodicals that non-profits publish play a key part in obtaining financial support and communicating with members. At the Nature Conservancy, "the magazine is a driver of inquiries and notifications for bequests," stated Theresa Duran, director of publishing. The NWF's magazine, executive publisher E. Hervey Evans explained, informs members about "where the money is going, where the work is in the field . . . and the specific projects that we're supporting." Nonprofit magazines play a vital role in advancing organizational missions. Since 1967, for example, the NWF's *Ranger Rick* magazine has taught environmental values to children. For decades, the scientific testing of products publicized through *Consumer Reports* has allowed Consumers Union to reduce consumer victimization in the marketplace.[23]

Notable among the numerous social benefits the postal system provides is the delivery of mail to blind Americans postage-free. In 1899, the Populist Representative Mason S. Peters Sr. (Kans.)

secured legislation that gave blind people the right to mail letters at a reduced postage rate. This reform expressed the Populist conviction that government had an important role to play in advancing social progress and the general welfare. The policy of preferential postage for the blind expanded over the following years. By the late 1960s, the Post Office Department permitted blind people to mail letters, recordings, educational materials, and even typewriters for free. As part of the Postal Service's mission today, this special rate class continues to offer disabled Americans an essential connection to the broader world. Without a public service mandate, the postal system would have no reason to provide such socially beneficial services. Lower postage rates for nonprofits, libraries, books, periodicals, and newspapers all result from the Postal Service's status as a branch of government dedicated to the common good.[24]

VOTE-BY-MAIL

The Postal Service is crucial to the primary requirement of democracy itself: the ability to vote. "The Postal Service plays a pivotal role in delivering democracy for America," observes Robert M. Levi of the National Association of Postal Supervisors. The confluence of the COVID-19 pandemic and the 2020 presidential election brought new recognition to the importance of a vote-by-mail option. The potential for future crises makes maintaining the ability to cast ballots through the U.S. Mail crucial to democracy. The first significant use of vote-by-mail was during the Civil War, when northern states changed their laws to permit Union soldiers and sailors to vote absentee in the 1864 election. The first entirely mail-in ballot election was conducted on a local basis in 1977 in Monterey County, California. Over the following decade, approximately 1,000 local elections were conducted entirely by mail in eight states. In 1993, Oregon became the first state to hold an all-mail statewide election. Six years later, Oregon stopped operating polling places altogether in favor of conducting its elections by mail instead.[25]

Research published in 2020 revealed that mail-in voting had not granted an advantage to either of the two major political parties. Fraud had not been a notable problem either: out of 250 million mailed ballots over the previous twenty years, there were only 204 cases of vote fraud, resulting in 143 criminal convictions. Despite vote-by-mail's successes, however, no one foresaw the critical role the national postal network would play in the 2020 election. The unprecedented public health challenge of COVID-19 presented an extraordinary test. It became necessary, in short order, for the Postal Service to coordinate with numerous state and local officials who had little experience with vote-by-mail.[26]

Unfortunately, at that very moment the impact of decades of short-sighted cost-cutting measures at the agency collided with the incompetent and destructive actions of a new postmaster general, Louis DeJoy, to create a host of mail delivery problems. The imposition of a plan to reduce the agency's total work hours proved particularly damaging. "Most processing plants are already extremely understaffed," stated Paul V. Hogrogian, national president of the National Postal Mail Handlers Union. "Eliminating or even reducing overtime can only result in increased delays . . . including critical items such as prescriptions and election materials." In the face of the impending election, DeJoy persisted in his service-slashing offensive, regardless of the impact on mail delivery. "We have fought too long and too hard to fully participate in our democracy," the NAACP protested, "to allow it to be subverted in this heinous and scandalous manner." Former Deputy Postmaster General Ronald A. Stroman pointed out that "internal documents" revealed DeJoy "specifically said leave mail behind. . . . That is a deliberate delay of the mail." "There has been a dangerous decline in mail delivery performance," retired postmaster Mark Jamison observed. "DeJoy is simply the wrong man for the job."[27]

Multiple lawsuits filed to ensure reliable ballot delivery resulted in federal judges blocking DeJoy's controversial operational changes. In the weeks prior to Election Day 2020, millions of citizens maintained the physical distance that public health authorities recommended to reduce transmission of COVID-19 by voting through the U.S. Mail. On average, mailed ballots were delivered from voters to election officials in 1.6 days, and virtually all ballots were delivered within seven days. Jeanette Senecal of the League of Women Voters commended the "dedicated Postal Service workers [who] ensured millions of Americans could safely cast their ballots." The 2020 election brought home the necessity of vote-by-mail and the trusted federal agency that provides this essential service. In the middle of a pandemic, voter turnout had actually increased. "Postal workers delivered on the election," Steven Hutkins of Save the Post Office stated, "and they deserve our immense gratitude."[28]

FOUR

COMMUNITY

"I grew up in a town of 300 people and the post office was the center of our social life," Senator Byron L. Dorgan (DNL-N.Dak.) once recalled. "In my home town, the post office was the center of where people came and visited and exchanged views about things." Dorgan's observation about the post office's vital role in his hometown is an experience that generations of Americans have shared. Post offices are an integral part of local communities and the most common federal government buildings in the nation. Yet closing post offices—particularly in small towns—has been a never-ending mission for postal officials consumed with cutting costs. But the agency realizes only minor savings when a post office is closed. In 1969, Postmaster General Winton M. Blount Jr. admitted: "It has become obvious to me that there are no really significant cost savings to be realized by closing small post offices." The inordinate stress on eliminating post offices emerges from a denial of the Postal Service's full role in our society.[1]

HEART OF THE COMMUNITY

Americans value the Postal Service because of the many ways the institution benefits their lives. Those who would like to eliminate the Postal Service advance a narrow and distorted definition of the agency that dismisses and diminishes its many functions. In 2003, a commission President George W. Bush formed to study the Postal Service issued a report that continually emphasized the importance of the institution "staying focused" on its "core business," which was defined as "acceptance, collection, sorting, transportation and delivery of letters, newspapers, magazines, advertising mail and parcels." The absence of operating post offices from this list was no oversight. Henry J. Pearce, co-chairman of the commission and chairman of Hughes Electronics Corporation, announced: "You don't necessarily need post offices." But Senator Harry Reid (D-Nev.), who grew up in the small town of Searchlight, Nevada, remarked that "over the history of our nation, post offices have come to symbolize and offer more than just the practical service of keeping people in touch with friends and family in distant locales. . . . [They] have become the heart of the community."[2]

The members of President Bush's 2003 postal commission were overwhelmingly corporate executives. "All of us came to this very complex challenge with no real background in postal issues," one member acknowledged. "We have a perspective which is informed by our role in the business world largely." The commission's report, in a section provocatively titled "Freeing Postal Service from the Post Office," asked, "[Do] most Americans *ever* have to set foot in a post office again?" The commission made clear that so far as its members were concerned, the answer should be a definite no. They rejected any suggestion that the Postal Service's physical presence in local communities is vital to the institution. Instead, commission members suggested that post offices be closed in favor of such inferior substitutes as automated self-serve kiosks and retail counters in convenience stores—privately owned businesses that can shut down at any time. They further claimed the website could be made "virtually interchangeable with a local post office." But web pages are not substitutes for post offices. General delivery at post offices, for example, offers homeless people a means of collecting their mail. The most recent letter one homeless man in Manhattan received was from his sister: "How are you?" she asked. "I hope everything is working out. Did you find employment? Don't give up hope."[3]

Post offices promote democratic values. Rising economic

inequality has reduced the number of spaces where Americans come into contact with people from different social backgrounds. Paul M. Weyrich, founder of the Free Congress Foundation, believed "the public space," which he defined as "anyplace where we do not control who we might meet," is essential. Weyrich explained further:

> If we are to be citizens of a republic and not mere con-
> sumers in an administered state, we need to both have
> and want contact with our fellow-citizens. When life is
> privatized, lived largely or almost wholly behind walls,
> doors and security control points, society withers. We
> come only to care about ourselves and those who share
> our private space. What happens to the rest of the society
> is not our concern, so long as we are OK.

The historian Christopher Lasch made a similar observation. "Civic life requires settings in which people meet as equals," he affirmed. Post offices help "bind the nation together" by offering a site where community members from diverse walks of life cross paths with one another.[4]

For generations, the post office and local postmaster have occupied the center of small-town life. Gathering the petition signatures to secure the federal recognition necessary to obtain a post office was one of the earliest collective actions a newly established community undertook. After a small-town post office on the late nineteenth-century Great Plains was operational, the regular arrival of the U.S. Mail commonly would be announced by raising the flag—a signal that drew forth the men and women who lived in the surrounding area. Once a crowd had assembled, historian Everett N. Dick recounted, the postmaster "picked up the mail piece by piece and read the inscription to the crowd. Each claimant cried out, 'Here!' in response." "Some postmasters used this occasion for making comments regarding the pieces of mail they were handing out," Dick reported. "Such an entertainment, while wholly beyond the expectations of the United States Government . . . was nevertheless highly entertaining and enjoyable to the community."[5]

The post office continues to serve as a center of small-town life today. "When I need to announce something to the community, I don't post it at the city offices," said Hubert Donaway, a city councilman in Putnam, Texas. "I stick it up at the post office. Everybody goes there." An article in the *Atlanta Journal-Constitution* about the post office in Rupert, Georgia, explained: "A post office is more than a place to mail letters and buy stamps, especially in rural America. It serves as a community's heart." Rupert resident Don Barnes put the importance of his town's post office in proper perspective: "If you do away with it, you'd do away with Rupert, really." The existence of many towns is inexorably tied to their post office. Judy Rose, village president of Brokaw, Wisconsin, summed it up: "It's part of their identity."[6]

The post office is a place where people rub elbows with their neighbors, presenting an opportunity to catch up on local events and reaffirm the bonds of community life. "People come to pick up their mail, talk with friends and the postmaster and exchange information," related rural sociologist L. Conner Bailey Jr. "It's kind of like sitting around the cracker barrel in the country store." "It's where everybody comes through," said Karen Pickett of Canyon, California. "It's definitely a hub." "It's here we get to greet our neighbors, our friends," commented Phyliss A. Hunter of West Stockholm, New York. "It's great to check in and see how everyone's doing." Fellow resident Norma J. Cyrus added, "It's the camaraderie of seeing different people." "It's the nerve center," Elswood A. Love agreed. "It's the only public place in Wellersburg," observed Bill Rowley of his Pennsylvania town's post office. Patrons not only value the civic space post offices offer for conversation with fellow residents, they appreciate familiar postmasters and postal clerks. "I try my best to perk up somebody's day," said clerk Priscilla Byzon as she served patrons in Coulters, Pennsylvania.[7]

The local postmaster occupies a prominent and respected place in small-town life. Daniel M. Heins, national president of the United Postmasters and Managers of America, explains that the contributions of postmasters commonly extend beyond their professional duties. Postmasters are leaders in their communities whose participation in local affairs ranges from service organizations to churches to chambers of commerce. "When there are community events," he adds, "postmasters will make sure they are part of that parade or festival." Local residents honor the service of their postmasters. Like many communities, Etna, New York—an upstate crossroads village—threw a party in honor of its postmaster when she retired. "It's definitely going to be weird without her; she knew everyone," said resident Robert Vantine. "We're going to miss her." Residents of Hansville, Washington, felt the same way about their postmaster, Barbara Neff. They had no need to write return addresses on envelopes, because Neff knew her patrons so well that she recognized their handwriting. Upon the occasion of Neff's retirement after twenty-seven years of service, the community awarded her its outstanding citizen award at a packed party. "What a jewel of a postmaster," June Forbes said. "She did so many things for us."[8]

The role of the local post office as a community center is perhaps more important than ever. In his influential book *Bowling Alone*, sociologist Robert D. Putnam concluded, "The bonds of our communities have withered," leaving most Americans feeling "vaguely and uncomfortably disconnected." For people like Ken Twergo of McCall, Idaho, such a sense is lessened by the community's post office. He summed up its importance to his town:

> For decades [it has] served as the daily meeting place, the place where public notices are tacked to the board and where you run into people you haven't seen. Where we

do see each other is in the post office. That's the gathering place. There isn't a community center of any other sort in a lot of these towns. There certainly isn't in McCall.

In a social environment of diminished community spirit and withered social bonds, such as Putnam identified, it is not surprising that people across America value their local post office as much more than simply a place to buy a book of stamps. These public spaces are central to the fabric of community life and cherished as a dependable focal point of residents' social worlds. Unlike new electronic forms of communication, which may actually be isolating individuals instead of bringing them together, the Postal Service has a well-established track record of uniting people.[9]

CLOSING THE HUB

In 1977, Reuben L. Johnson of the National Farmers Union insisted, "The role of the rural post office rises above the cost-analysis figures used by the Postal Service." The Postal Reorganization Act of 1970 affirms the significance of the local post office, declaring these federal facilities cannot "be closed solely for operating at a deficit." Americans receive many services at post offices that are no less valuable because they do not add to the agency's revenues. "There are people in rural communities who can't read or write," pointed out Steve D. LeNoir, president of the National League of Postmasters. "Postmasters help them read and answer mail, and fill out money orders. You can't put a dollar value on that. And these people are often the people who are most lacking representation." In Wayne, Illinois, Postmaster Maryellen Wegener alerted the police when older residents failed to make their regular visit to the post office. The local police chief acknowledged that "such calls are a key ingredient in his department's well-check program." In towns like Devol, Oklahoma, a postmaster can expect to receive telephone calls from elderly residents asking, "Did my medicine come in? Could you drop it by on your way home?" "Machines don't replace people," observed Robert M. Levi of the National Association of Postal Supervisors. "Ultimately the service is provided by human beings—postal employees—not machines."[10]

In order to close post offices, federal law requires the Postal Service to make a case that closures will improve efficiency without degrading service. An internal 1977 agency study concluded that 57 percent of the nation's post offices could be closed "without hurting service." All of these 17,000 supposedly disposable post offices were located in small towns. This finding was not acted upon, however, because of controversy over the issue at the time. In 1975, the General Accounting Office had instructed postal officials they could "economize postal operation in rural America" by closing 12,000 small-town post offices. "We agree," declared Postmaster General Benjamin F. Bailar. Although falling far short of the number the General Accounting Office referenced, an ensuing spate of closures left behind a void in abandoned communities, generating considerable public and congressional outrage. At the same time, a large number of additional post offices were placed under consideration for possible closure.[11]

In 1976, President Gerald R. Ford signed a law that protected the rural post office, placing a temporary moratorium on shuttering post offices and establishing a set of guidelines to govern future closures. The Postal Service is required to inform communities of its intention to close their post office, and can take no action until sixty days after the written proposal to close has been made publicly available. Furthermore, postal officials must hold a town meeting where residents have the opportunity to voice their concerns. Finally, any person a post office serves may appeal its proposed closure to the Postal Regulatory Commission within thirty days.[12]

This framework has not worked as well as its proponents had hoped. Only 11 percent of post office closures were appealed during the initial twenty years that the new process was in place.

This proportion is strikingly low, given the strong attachment of so many Americans to their post office. Veteran observers of post office closure proceedings note that all too often the decision has been made already, and the Postal Service is just going through the motions. They also emphasize that when post offices are being eyed for closure, lack of profitability is at the top of the list of reasons a particular post office is selected. And despite the ability of communities to appeal proposed closures to the Postal Regulatory Commission, postal officials are well prepared to make closures happen, because they have been planning for months prior to any public announcement. Meanwhile, local residents have to quickly organize, educate themselves about their rights in the matter, and prepare a response, all in short order after the plan to close has been made public.[13]

There also is the all too common occurrence of the Postal Service evading the standard post office closure process. Post offices sometimes need to be suspended on a temporary basis due to emergencies such as fires, flooding damage, or a postmaster's death. But there are cases of post offices being suspended to address temporary emergencies and then remaining closed indefinitely. "What begins as an emergency suspension," the Public Representative of the Postal Regulatory Commission explained, "at some point becomes a de facto closure that deprives customers of their right to have input into their future service and to appeal the decision to close the facility."[14]

At the end of 2010, after 103 years of operation, the post office in the small ranching community of Prairie City, South Dakota, closed for good. Postal officials said the facility lost $19,000 per year, but claimed the closure was due to a malfunctioning furnace that created "safety deficiencies." Residents had been ignored when they offered to repair the furnace. The town's postal clerks regularly posted birth and death notices and always kept a pot of coffee brewing. "That was the gathering place for people to come in the mornings . . . and visit," said Daniel Beckman. "It's totally depressing." Residents protested they now had to drive forty-one miles to reach a post office or a pharmacy. The closure disrupted the community's ability to receive medicine in a timely manner, because when the post office shut down so did the direct mail route from the closest town with a pharmacist. "When they cut these services, there are multiple spinoff consequences," Dr. Brian Willoughby observed. Prairie City residents appealed the closure unsuccessfully. "Life is changing," one postal spokesman remarked. "We have to make customers understand there are other ways to get the services we provide."[15]

Residents of other towns facing post office closure share the same sense of sadness and frustration that Prairie City experienced. "Just because we're a small town doesn't mean we don't deserve a service that has been here for 150 years," exclaimed Laura Hartman of Little Sioux, Iowa, when the Postal Service announced its plans to close her town's post office. "Rural people," Senator James G. Abourezk (D-S.Dak.) once stressed, "rightly expect the same convenient service city people take for granted." Little Sioux's residents offered to build a brand-new post office. When that offer was rejected, they suggested placing the post office in the city hall. But the Postal Service disregarded this alternative as well and proceeded with the closure.[16]

A 2018 study found that more than one-third of post offices do not generate sufficient revenues to cover their expenses—including over one-half of rural post offices. In 2003, David J. Frederickson, president of the National Farmers Union, observed, "If the Postal Service can decide the fate of a post office strictly on the basis of revenue and without regard for the needs of the community, then the very concept of the local post office is at risk in rural America." Americans feel strongly about post offices in large measure because of all the "incidental" benefits they provide as community centers, sources of identity, and civic spaces belonging to them, important features of these institutions that are not measured in dollars and cents.[17]

Postal management repeatedly has made clear its desire for greater discretion to close and relocate post offices. In 2003, Postmaster General John E. Potter expressed his frustration that "you can't close post offices for economic reasons." He remarked, "I think that we have communities that are underserved and communities that are overserved. . . . That's an imbalance that we have to correct, but I'm hard pressed to find the money to open new post offices in growing areas." Growing communities going without post offices has been a problem, and there are areas of the country that need more post offices. But Robert M. Levi pointed out "there is not as much commitment to serving communities by opening new post offices as there is to closing existing post offices."[18]

In January 2011, the Postal Service initiated a major wave of post office closures, citing budgetary problems. The agency announced that as many as 2,000 post offices were on the chopping block. "Allowing the Postal Service the ability to close offices that fail to cover their costs is a huge step toward our future viability," Postmaster General Patrick R. Donahoe stated. "It ain't right doing this in our community," responded Delmer Clark, a retired coal miner in Holmes Mill, Kentucky. The local school had closed years earlier, and reliable internet, cable, and cellular telephone reception were lacking. Clark felt that the community was being abandoned. "When they close the post office," he worried, "they probably won't even come up here anymore to clean the roads."[19]

In July 2011, the Postal Service revealed it was eyeing more than 3,600 post offices for closure. Approximately one-third of this batch were located in areas with limited or no broadband internet. Closing every post office on the list would have saved the agency 0.4 percent of its annual expenses. "That's a drop in the bucket," remarked former Postmaster General William J. Henderson. "That's not even a drop. . . . The bucket won't ripple." Not all the post offices at risk were located in small towns. Thirty-four post offices in New York City were in jeopardy too, including one in Co-op City—the largest housing cooperative in the nation, with a population of 40,000. Residents argued the high proportion of senior citizens living in Co-op City demanded special consideration. "We need as much help as possible," Grace Gourdine stressed. In upstate New York, Lackawanna's post office was also among those selected for closure. More than one-quarter of the city's residents had a disability—many of them veterans—and nearly one-quarter of all households lacked access to a car. "What are we? Chopped liver?" resident John Chentfant protested. "I mean, we're a city, for crying out loud."[20]

In May 2012, due to public and congressional opposition, postal officials backed away from mass post office closures. In the Ozark Mountains of Arkansas, for example, residents meeting in community centers and churches had organized to save local post offices. They circulated petitions, wrote letters, made telephone calls, and met with their elected representatives. This outcry caused Senator John N. Boozman (R-Ark.) to take a stand against closing rural post offices. "There are times when it's not profitable," he said, "but it's important to provide that service [anyway]." Due to similarly strong pushback from citizens throughout the nation, postal officials abandoned their drive to shutter post offices. "We've listened to our customers in rural America," Donahoe stated, "and we've heard them loud and clear—they want to keep their post office open."[21]

With closures off the table, the Postal Service announced that window service would be reduced at more than 13,000 post offices from eight hours to between two and six hours a day. Most of these post offices transitioned from career postmasters to a remote management model with a rotating staff of non-career and part-time employees. The residents of Chase Mills, New York, received a letter that made it clear postal officials wanted to foreclose any potential negotiations over the question of service reductions: Nadine Tremblay, post office review coordinator for the Albany District, stated that unless the community preferred to conduct a discontinuance study reduced hours would be maintained. But in Thompson, North Dakota, the town's mayor, Karyn Hippen, said that given the work schedules of many residents it was "very important" that hours not be cut. "It would feel like a step backwards," she added, "when everything else is moving forward." "It was only open three hours a day, anyway," said Nancy Martland in response to the reduction of hours at her Sugar Hill, New Hampshire, post office. "So the hours were already reduced, as far as we were concerned. Perhaps the most disturbing thing to many of us is the way this was handled and continues to be handled . . . with utter disregard for our community."[22]

Limited window hours in Sugar Hill were the legacy of an earlier push to shorten post office operating hours. In 2003, cutbacks were implemented regionally in the Northeast. David L. Greenlaw, president of the Maine chapter of the American Postal Workers Union, said, "It's bound to have a negative impact on customer service." Post offices in central Massachusetts started eliminating window hours in the morning, evening, and lunch hours. "This is a real pain in the butt," protested businessman Richard W. Thunberg Jr. as he waited outside the Oxford post office for it to reopen at 12:15 p.m., while fellow frustrated postal patron Nicole Case said, "It's another thing I have to worry about. . . . I have to be somewhere else in a few minutes, and this just slows everything down." Mark Kleinmeyer, postmaster of Riverside, Iowa, questioned whether cutting window hours was a wise business decision: "They're preaching 'sell, sell, sell,' and then they're cutting back hours." What their patrons understand, and leading postal officials too often deny, is that post offices are integral to the Postal Service, not an expendable cost to be eliminated.[23]

RELOCATION

Post office relocation has been another major source of contention, especially since older post offices located downtown are often central to community identity. In 1996, events in Livingston, Montana, brought national recognition to the Postal Service's disregard of local wishes when the community organized against the decision to close its downtown post office—a National Historic Landmark—in order to open a new one on the outskirts of town. The area's growth was straining the capacity of the downtown building. Unfortunately, instead of exploring options that would have allowed the historic post office to remain open, postal officials unilaterally decided to build a new post office outside of downtown Livingston. In just four days, Livingston residents had responded to this threat by collecting 1,500 signatures on a petition that opposed the move from the town's 7,500 inhabitants. Residents not only were concerned about the need to preserve a historic building and maintain good service, they also worried about the negative impact the relocation would have on local businesses and their downtown more generally. As one resident explained, Livingston's historic downtown "is very viable. . . . Losing the post office weakens the long-term viability. The only thing worse for downtown would be building a Wal-Mart." Due to Livingston's well-organized campaign—and resulting national publicity—its downtown post office is still open.[24]

Communities are well aware that there will be negative repercussions if they fail to stop their downtown post office's relocation. Richard P. Moe, president of the National Trust for Historic Preservation, made clear the importance of post offices in helping to maintain downtown business districts: "Downtowns are the key to communities' viability, and these post offices are the key to the downtowns." Surveys of downtown shoppers conducted by the National Trust's Iowa Main Street communities revealed that "more than 80 percent of the people who shop downtown in the towns surveyed do so because of the post office." Christopher M. Nevin, mayor of Hampstead, Maryland, said the post office "serves as an anchor for your downtown. . . . It generates shopping downtown, it generates foot traffic. People go downtown to the post office and say, 'I have to stop in Bob's Variety Store.'" Without post offices to draw people downtown, local businesses suffer and the surrounding area can head downhill. And when downtown business areas go into decline, property values decrease and sales tax revenues evaporate, harming the larger community.[25]

On Cape Cod, the village of Wellfleet's post office moved from its downtown location to a new shopping mall on the town's outskirts. "The pulse of our community emanated from the post office," said Kevin Rice. "When they moved it to Route 6 they tore the heart out of the town. What could be more symbolic of the paving over of America?" The residents and borough officials of Audubon, New Jersey, tried to prevent their post office in the town center from decamping to a shopping center. Citizens collected 1,300 petition signatures in support of maintaining the post office at its downtown location, and the local government attempted to work with the Postal Service to find a solution. But the shopping center proved to be more "financially agreeable" and the post office was relocated. "They just put the nail in the coffin for any walk-in traffic for any of the stores [downtown]," remarked petition drive organizer Charlotte Skeggs.[26]

In the 1990s, Pittsboro, North Carolina, lost its downtown post office to a replacement on the edge of town. The new post office was larger and able to offer more post office boxes, but, as Bill McAllister reported in the *Washington Post*, "if you're poor, or a downtown merchant, or elderly . . . the new post office is a calamity." McAllister stated that "unless you want to walk along the red clay shoulder of a busy two-lane highway, the only way to get there is to drive." In the early 2010s, a number of post offices were relocated to annexes—facilities that provide work space for sorting and delivery functions. Post office annexes are located near transportation routes but isolated from concentrations of offices, businesses, and other places where patrons regularly spend time and run errands. "As is often the case with post office closures, these relocations shifted the Postal Service's costs to its own customers, who had to drive further (if they could drive at all), use more gas, and take more time to get to the distant annex," Steven Hutkins of Save the Post Office observed. "Postal representatives often discharged their obligation to discuss the relocation plan at a public meeting by simply showing up at a regular session of the city council where they turned a deaf ear to the community's concerns about the social and economic impacts."[27]

As Hutkins noted, locating post offices in automobile-centric landscapes poses a particular problem to people who do not own or have access to a car, including many senior citizens and people with disabilities. In addition to an absence of pedestrian-friendly features—such as sidewalks, crosswalks, and "Walk/Don't Walk" signals—there are actual barriers in these spaces that discourage ease of movement, including a lack of ramps for wheelchairs and insufficient public transportation. Between 2009 and 2018, the number of people struck and killed by motor vehicles increased by 53 percent, and sprawl landscapes are particularly dangerous for pedestrians. Fueling sprawl by moving post offices to such landscapes has environmental and social costs. Reliance on automobiles generates air pollution, and new construction paves over natural areas and productive farms and ranches. The American Farmland Trust reported that between 2001 and 2016 developers converted 11 million acres of agricultural land to other uses. Additionally, as social critic James Howard Kunstler observed, there are questions about the aesthetic and spiritual impact of "the jive-plastic commuter tract home wastelands, the Potemkin village shopping plazas with their vast parking lagoons, the Lego-block hotel complexes . . . the Orwellian office 'parks'" that constitute these landscapes.[28]

HISTORY AND IDENTITY

As sprawl landscapes resembling every other sprawl landscape proliferate, the unique history and character of downtown areas is becoming more important to communities. Recently constructed post offices are highly uniform in appearance, and rather than conceiving a fitting representative of the national government, their designs prioritize minimizing expenses. Replacing a long established and widely recognized post office with these "cookie-cutter" buildings makes the Postal Service appear more akin to a fast-food chain than a storied government agency. In fact, contemporary "postal stores" were specifically designed to resemble convenience stores. Recent post office buildings of less than 1,500 square feet are identical factory-built, prefabricated structures. The Vermont League of Cities and Towns, Preservation Trust of Vermont, and Vermont Division for Historic Preservation pointed out that the "uniform, one story 'cookie-cutter' building plan . . . surrounded by lots of paved parking spaces" that the Postal Service favored for new post offices simply "[does] not fit into the unique character of most Vermont communities."[29]

Post offices built in the nineteenth and early twentieth centuries remain impressive representations of the federal government. Post offices in major cities were monumental structures occupying prime centrally located property, faced with exteriors of marble or granite, and featuring interiors that included decorative murals, ornamental bronze work, and grand public spaces. Post offices in smaller cities were built on a more modest scale, but were situated in the center of town and equally impressive within the context of these communities. After World War II, post office design shifted toward a more utilitarian appearance, and selection of sites emphasized automobile access.[30]

While local residents focus on the significance of post offices to their communities, their abstract financial value attracts attention as well. Back in 2003, President Bush's postal commission suggested the agency "obtain an independent appraisal of the current market value of its major real estate holdings." In 2020, David Ditch of the Heritage Foundation recommended that the Postal Service "have more ability to develop its real estate portfolio." R. Richard Geddes has expressed great enthusiasm about the financial potential of postal property, advising that the agency "sell valuable downtown properties." In order to accumulate cash and make the Postal Service more attractive to buyers in a potential stock offering that would privatize the agency, he recommended that it "divest itself of substantial buildings and land in prime downtown locations." The agency owns "prized real estate," Geddes continued, "including its headquarters in L'Enfant Plaza in Washington." Although the massive headquarters building has not been put up for sale, numerous post offices with value on the real estate market have been.[31]

In 2013, the Postal Service unveiled plans to sell the General Post Office in the Bronx—a New Deal landmark and focal point of life in the borough. A real estate specialist at the agency said it was time to "right-size our retail operation into smaller leased space." Shocked community members protested this decision. "It's not just a post office; it's part of my life," regular post office patron Ella Michael explained. "The community should have a say as to what should happen to that building," insisted Representative Jose E. Serrano (D-N.Y.). "And the community is saying don't sell it, and keep the services there." Steven Hutkins observed that selling off these stately monuments "is really to undo the work of the New Deal." "It was paid for by tax dollars and now it's being sold to private interests," added Charles "Chuck" Zlatkin of the New York Metro Area Postal Union. But despite broad opposition, in 2014 the post office was sold to a developer for $19 million, and then flipped four years later.[32]

A struggle to save a historic post office on the other side of the country produced a different outcome. In 2012, the Postal Service decided the time was right to sell the downtown post office in Berkeley, California. Citizens leaped into action, holding a rally one month later to celebrate the ninety-eighth anniversary of the building's completion. The civic organization Citizens to Save the Berkeley Post Office had been born. These dedicated activists marched, rallied, and lobbied. Their efforts received strong support from the city's local, state, and federal elected officials. "This building was constructed . . . through taxpayer dollars and was designed specifically as a post office," Representative Barbara Lee (D-Calif.) stressed. "It would not be serving its true and original purpose if it was something other than a post office." The city devised a creative zoning solution to protect the post office that restricted land use in its vicinity to government and nonprofit functions. This move reduced the market value of Berkeley's historic post office. In 2016, the Department of Justice objected to the rezoning, but when the city elected not to respond, the issue was dropped. The years-long legal struggle concluded in 2018, when a U.S. district judge upheld Berkeley's zoning ordinance.[33]

The firm that attempted to sell Berkeley's downtown post office had received an exclusive contract in 2011 to peddle postal property. C. B. Richard Ellis Group Inc. (CBRE) acted as realtor for the Postal Service while simultaneously representing buyers of postal properties, a clear conflict of interest. In 2013, investigative journalist Peter Byrne reported that 20 percent of CBRE's sales during the first two years of the contract went to clients and business partners, and many of these properties were sold at less than assessed value. CBRE also boosted its commissions by selling properties to landlords who then leased them back to the Postal Service for excessive rental prices. David C. Williams, inspector general of the Postal Service, led a 2015 investigation that uncovered poor recordkeeping, flawed appraisal methodologies, and problematic relationships between buyers and sellers. In 2017, postal officials ended the contact with CBRE and selected a new real estate broker. "Each contract . . . is evaluated as contract expiration dates approach," a postal official explained. "In 2016, the Postal Service determined that it was in its best interest to resolicit for a real estate services provider."[34]

The Advisory Council on Historic Properties has criticized the Postal Service's custodianship of the post offices that occupy such a prominent place in our national legacy. In 2014, the council concluded postal officials had failed to follow laws governing the sale of historically significant properties. Furthermore, postal officials neglected to consider alternatives before deciding to sell such properties in the first place. "Despite considerable objection in most cases from community leaders and preservation advocates," the council noted, "it has already declared that sale is the only option." The council pointed out the public benefits of using the Historic Surplus Property Program to transfer these properties to states, counties, and municipalities for preservation. Use of this program would ensure that postal facilities remain in the public domain.[35]

In 2014, Representative Serrano introduced legislation— co-sponsored by Representative Lee—that required the Postal Service to employ more deliberation and transparency when selling property, banned potential conflicts of interest, provided communities greater input during the process, and offered state and local governments first right of refusal on any sale. The bill did not advance to a vote, but the National Trust for Historic Preservation stated that it "would put into place sensible policies and allow people a greater say in the fate of their local post office buildings, which have long occupied a special place at the center of communities across the country."[36]

The investments of generations of Americans built the postal properties valued in real estate markets today. The Postal Service should be the custodian of this rich inheritance, not its auctioneer. A large proportion of the nation's post offices were constructed in the 1930s as part of the massive federal construction program the Franklin D. Roosevelt administration sponsored to combat the Great Depression. Postmaster General James A. Farley recalled that during the New Deal "the Post Office Department played a major role. . . . We launched a big public works program that provided needed jobs and pumped federal funds into the faltering economy." From 1930 through 1939, three times the number of post offices were built than had been constructed over the previous fifty years. These post offices are so highly esteemed today because their architecture, decorations, and ornamentation incorporate historical and regional references appropriate to their local communities. President Roosevelt himself took an interest in post office design, in some cases overseeing certain projects and even offering specific suggestions. During the hard times of the 1930s, these post offices affirmed the nation's past while inviting Americans to look forward to a brighter future.[37]

The more than 30,000 post offices scattered throughout the nation are the product of a staggeringly diverse range of cultural influences and historical moments. They are of central importance to community life in small towns and large cities, both economically and socially. Their full significance is invisible to market logic, but no less real. Neither a narrow cost-benefit calculus nor a real-estate appraisal provide an adequate and appropriate measure of their worth. Citizens and communities recognize this reality. The Postal Service should be organized in such a way that its decision makers can see beyond the commercial model that too often restricts their vision.

FIVE

CUTBACKS

"The Postal Service has forgotten the second part of its own name," Senator Paul M. Simon (D-Ill.) once stated. "It's a service, not a moneymaker." In 2002, John Gurley, a retired postal worker, affirmed, "From what I've seen over the years, there's definitely been a huge decrease in delivery service. In the 1960s, service was the thing." In recent years, large corporations that send substantial volumes of mail have used the Postal Service's financial difficulties to advocate further service reductions, and postal officials grappling with budgetary problems have pursued cost-cutting strategies even more aggressively. Although the challenges the postal system faces due to technological change are frequently presented as evidence of the agency's imminent extinction, the Postal Service will remain an important national institution for the foreseeable future. Service cutbacks, however, could ultimately threaten the Postal Service's relevance to the American people.[1]

MAIL VOLUME

The future of mail volume is a major source of concern to all who are connected with the Postal Service. In 2002, the General Accounting Office concluded the Postal Service's "basic business model is not sustainable" if mail volume declines, because population growth will increase the cost of maintaining the postal system at the same time that revenues are falling. A 1998 story in *Time* inaccurately forecast that email messages would replace 25 percent of "snail mail" within two years. The imminent demise of the Postal Service due to technological change has been predicted time and again. The invention of the telegraph in 1837 elicited predictions that mail would disappear. It was Western Union, however, that discontinued telegrams in 2006. The arrival of the telephone in 1876 produced the same claim that mail's demise was imminent. But the telephone long ago evolved into a complement to mail. Similar assertions were made when fax machines became standard office equipment in the 1980s. Yet the fax machine has become more of a niche medium than a communications necessity.[2]

The recent shift toward electronic communication is not simply a consequence of new technologies. Economic factors have played a major role in the decline in mail volume since 2007. Use of the postal system plummeted when the nation entered a deep recession due to the housing crash of 2007–2008. Historically, postal revenues drop when the economy suffers. But this time, mail volume did not fully rebound as economic conditions improved. In 2020, the amount of first-class mail was down 45 percent compared to 2007. After a precipitous drop from 2007 to 2009, marketing mail has remained relatively steady.[3]

During the Great Recession, businesses seeking to cut expenses embarked on an aggressive transition to electronic communications. They have continued this drive to reduce their first-class postage expenses ever since. This corporate push plays a major role in declining mail volume. Some companies have switched consumers to electronic billing without their authorization. There are banks that charge $3 or more per month for paper statements. But many consumers do not have internet access and do have legitimate concerns about online security. "We believe anyone who chooses a paper bill should not have to pay for it," the National Consumers League insists. Millions of Americans who use the internet on a regular basis prefer to receive paper bills, statements, and other business correspondence through the mail, particularly medical and financial items. They find paper bills and statements more convenient and easier to monitor. Consumers also worry about losing access to records if a business shuts down. "Paper bills and statements have value to most consumers," affirms consumer behavior expert Joanne McNeish.[4]

Over the past decade, mail volume has declined more than 16 percent. Individual categories of mail are legally prohibited from subsidizing one another, but they contribute differently to the "overhead" or "institutional" costs of the Postal Service that support the postal network itself. The mail "mix" is important, because although different postage classes are self-supporting, institutional costs are shared across classes of mail, since they all utilize the broader postal infrastructure. It is worrisome, therefore, that first-class mail revenues have dropped sharply since 2007, because this service makes a disproportionately high contribution to institutional costs. Still, at this point the low-hanging fruit already has been diverted to electronic communication. Fortunately, package delivery doubled over the past decade, creating significant revenues for the Postal Service. This bright spot notwithstanding, postal officials have faced major budgetary challenges in recent years.[5]

The onerous requirement to aggressively fund employees' future retirement health benefits has been the primary source of the Postal Service's financial troubles. The National Association of Letter Carriers (NALC) estimates this burden is responsible for 84 percent of the agency's losses since 2007. The Postal Service Reform Act of 2021 is designed to resolve this issue. The Postal Service also is saddled with retiree benefits from the former Post Office Department and required to invest its retirement funds in low-yielding Treasury bonds, which has further impaired the agency's financial situation. Moreover, the 2006 law that imposed the burdensome pre-funding requirement also impeded the Postal Service's ability to create additional revenue. The law directed the agency to refrain from offering new services, and prevented rate hikes that exceed increases of the Consumer Price Index for existing services where the Postal Service has little or no competition, such as first-class mail. A price index that measures inflation in the private delivery industry would be a more appropriate benchmark for postal rates. Since this framework made raising new revenues difficult, postal officials turned all the more readily to cutting expenses.[6]

CUTTING SERVICE

While the Postal Service's financial problems have worsened in recent years, service cutbacks have been an issue for decades. In 1972, Postmaster General Elmer T. Klassen claimed "significant cost reductions" were necessary and proceeded to cut mail deliveries, collections from U.S. Mail boxes, and window hours at post offices on Saturdays. In 1975, Klassens's successor, Benjamin F. Bailar, proclaimed his "doubts . . . that the total volume of mail will ever again reach its 1974 peak of 90 billion pieces." He further predicted that mail volume would drop to 84 billion pieces by 1980 and "never recover." Bailar said this imminent decline necessitated "examining the way the Postal Service operates. . . . Do all Americans really need six-day-a-week delivery? Do we really need 40,000 post offices, stations, and branches? Should all first-class letters cost the same?" Guided by his projection of collapsing postal revenues, Bailar initiated a major push to close small-town post offices.[7]

Bailar also was the postmaster general who ended twice-a-day mail delivery once and for all. At the time, same-day local delivery of mail still occurred. Two mail deliveries per day had been halted in 1950 for residences and was then phased out for businesses over the next few decades. In 1976, the Postal Service announced that the last eastern cities where businesses still received two daily deliveries—Philadelphia, Pittsburgh, Baltimore, Richmond, Va., Washington, D.C., and Buffalo, Rochester, Syracuse, and Utica, N.Y.—would receive mail once a day, and reduced business deliveries in New York City from three times a day to twice daily. (Areas of New York with exceptionally high mail volume received twice-a-day-delivery until the late 1990s.) Bailar's justification for service cuts proved to be off the mark. Instead of plummeting by 1980 as he predicted, mail volume rose: pieces of mail per capita increased 13 percent between 1976 and 1980.[8]

In a boon for gray metal cluster mailbox units and curbside mailboxes, door delivery was discontinued to all newly constructed housing in 1978. Delivering mail to the door is more costly than curbline or centralized delivery. A 1977 poll had revealed that 58 percent of Americans "don't want a cluster box." But the Postal Service disregarded the wishes of the public and—without consulting Congress or the Postal Rate Commission—proceeded to implement this new policy. As a result, millions of people in the United States who otherwise would have received delivery to the door now collect their mail from curbside mailboxes or cluster boxes. "The fact is that door delivery is far more satisfactory than curb delivery," acknowledged Lawrence F. O'Brien, postmaster general under President Lyndon B. Johnson. In order to promote cluster boxes, the Postal Service resorted to such ploys as sending residents of Dickinson, North Dakota, a congratulatory message: "Your Postal Service is upgrading the mail delivery in your area . . . [which] is privileged to be one of the first in the upper Midwest to receive this service.'"[9]

The pattern of service reductions established in the 1970s continued over the following decades. In 1991, Representative William S. Broomfield (R-Mich.) characterized the removal of the familiar blue mailbox on the corner—collection boxes in postal terminology—as "an especially sore point. . . . Too many of those mailboxes are vanishing." Reducing the number of collections from boxes and moving final pick-up deadlines earlier in the day is a less conspicuous way that service has been reduced. Postal watchdog Douglas F. Carlson has tracked this issue for decades, repeatedly uncovering instances when agency regulations designed to ensure adequate collection services have been disregarded. A presentation at a 2001 meeting of Postal Service area vice presidents is revealing on the question of collection box service. The subject under discussion was "strategies for altering customers' methods of depositing mail." Postal patrons did not appear to have problems dropping letters into collection boxes, so one must assume that "alteration" involved compelling them to change when and where they deposit their mail.[10]

In 2007, eighty-one-year-old Anne DeFilippis of Philadelphia lost her nearest collection box. She had six children, seventeen grandchildren, and twenty-one great-grandchildren. "I always send a card on birthdays, and there's quite a few anniversaries, as well," DeFilippis said. She did not consider placing outgoing mail by her front door secure, and arthritic knees plus a heart condition restricted her mobility. Local Republican Party committeeman Jim Finnegan objected that a dozen boxes recently had disappeared from the neighborhood. He thought it might be necessary to organize a protest. "You think they want Ma and Pa Kettle picketing in front of their office in walkers and crutches?"[11]

Local residents often try to save the neighborhood collection box by mounting petition drives and protesting to postal officials. The town of Otisfield, Maine, lacks a post office, so the prospect of losing its lone collection box was particularly troubling. When an attempt was made to remove the box, local officials blocked access with a snowplow and a backhoe. "It's the town of Otisfield's post office," explained the town's administrative assistant. "We can't buy stamps there, but we can put mail in there and know it'll be delivered." In 2004, an Allentown, Pennsylvania, mother and daughter taped a sign to their neighborhood's box when it was scheduled to be carted away. "Please don't remove this mailbox!" the note implored. "We will miss it too much." In 2002, Marv Tripp of Oakland, California, took action after two nearby collection boxes were removed, including one he had used for over forty years. "You have to plan so many things in your life," he observed. "You don't want to plan your life around mailing a letter." Tripp started a petition drive to bring back the mailboxes that successfully netted the return of one of them.[12]

The removal of collection boxes is an ongoing process. More than one in eight collection boxes nationwide—around 50,000—were eliminated between 2000 and 2004. Mass removals often occur on the local level. In 2014, postal officials decided to uproot one-quarter of the collection boxes in Rockford, Illinois. Five years earlier, one-quarter of the collection boxes in the Los Angeles area were removed in the space of a few weeks. Since the familiar box half a block from his home was gone and local post office telephone numbers are generally no longer listed, David Meltzer called the Postal Service's toll-free number to find the location of the nearest remaining one. "They told me to go look around, ten blocks one way, ten blocks the other," he reported. In a suburban Maryland neighborhood, mailing practices were altered significantly when the local box was taken away. "Now you have to get in your car to mail a letter," one resident explained. Allan Burnett of Queens was "shocked" when he discovered his closest mailbox had been removed. But this loss posed more of a problem to some of his neighbors. "There are a lot of elderly people who don't drive. Now what are they going to do?"[13]

The cumulative toll of the steady disappearance of collection boxes from their proverbial sites on street corners nationwide has been large. In 1972, the population of the United States had recently topped 200 million and it was served by 313,485 collection boxes. Even though the population had increased to over 330 million in 2020, only 140,845 collection boxes remained—an almost 9 percent decline over the previous five years. The removal of collection boxes has not made the Postal Service more valuable to the public. "We woke up one morning and the mailbox was gone," said Sue Florio of Teaneck, New Jersey. "It's made a lot of people very unhappy needlessly." William B. Cook, president of NALC Branch 358 in Schenectady, New York, called box removal "poor customer service." "Our competitors, FedEx and UPS, are putting out mailboxes," he pointed out. "They're expanding . . . and we're making ourselves less readily available to our customers."[14]

When the Postal Service stopped door delivery to housing constructed after 1978, homes receiving delivery before this cutoff remained entitled to retain this service. Around one-quarter of deliveries are still made to the door. Yet efforts to revoke door delivery from homes whose right to receive this service was grandfathered in have been ongoing. In response to pressure from district or area managers to reduce costs, local management has attempted to convert residences to cheaper delivery methods. In Seattle, two full-time employees were assigned to try to convert areas from door delivery to other methods. In St. Petersburg, Florida, despite a city ordinance in effect since 1968 banning curbside delivery, the change has been made repeatedly. Jim Biggerstaff, president of the Council of Neighborhood Associations, said the Postal Service is "bound and determined to put mailboxes curbside all over the city. . . . I think they're ugly." Additionally, curbside mailboxes are vulnerable to vandalism, which is an all-too-common problem.[15]

Certain postal managers hope to convert entire neighborhoods to curbside or cluster-box delivery. Postal regulations stipulate that residents must agree to any change in delivery method, but, as Rick Myers, vice president of NALC Local 1091 in Orlando, Florida, pointed out, "most consumers don't know [this]." In Durham, North Carolina, residents were falsely instructed that failure to install a curbside mailbox would result in their mail being returned to sender. Sometimes a house-by-house approach has been employed. A Postal Service spokesman revealed, "When an older neighborhood reaches a certain threshold of curbside boxes, those with on-house boxes will be asked to move their boxes to the curb." Myers stated that for decades postal mangers nationwide incorrectly informed Americans they must convert to curb delivery. Once a curbside mailbox or cluster-box unit is installed, door delivery will not be resumed. In 2019, Representative Susan A. Davis (D-Calif.) reintroduced a bill supporting the maintenance of door delivery. "I have heard overwhelming opposition to ending door delivery," she said. "A move to stop door delivery of mail would be bad for postal customers, businesses, and the Postal Service. Seniors and people living with disabilities would be hit particularly hard."[16]

Mail thieves prefer to target cluster-box units because they present an opportunity to steal from multiple addresses in one single location. U.S. Postal Inspection Service spokesman Daniel L. Mihalko reported that "the majority of thefts come from the cluster boxes often found in new subdivisions." The Postal Service has responded to this problem by installing more secure cluster-box models, creating an arms race as mail thieves develop new techniques and also search for easier targets. "I am researching 'night vision' remote control cameras (used for night animal photography)," said a concerned resident of American Canyon, California. "These robbers need to be caught and prosecuted." "Reporting to us makes a huge difference," Postal Inspector Jeffrey Fitch stated. "If cluster boxes are broken into on Saturday evening, people don't need to wait until they see their letter carrier, you can report it." Representative Davis said, "I've heard stories from constituents who are forced to use cluster mailboxes, and they report all kinds of problems with them, from theft to graffiti."[17]

Understaffing is an enduring service issue. In 2006, the *Washington Post* reported: "City dwellers are familiar with the maddening pace of two clerks plodding through a twenty-person line." "We don't have enough staffing to process the mail at any high level of service," acknowledged Eugene Gabaldon, president of American Postal Workers Union Local 380 in Albuquerque, New Mexico. Service problems at the South Berkeley station in Berkeley, California, arose when staffing was cut back to a single clerk. A petition signed by 700 patrons declared: "We support the postal clerk at this post office and want to see her receive the support and additional staffing she needs so she can do her job." An additional clerk was assigned to cover break periods following unfavorable press attention. "They could provide a two-minute wait max, if they wanted to," said William H. Burrus Jr., president of the American Postal Workers Union (APWU). "But they don't want to because they know the American public will accept a delay. They've become accustomed to it." In 2020, only two postal workers in San Antonio, Texas, were assigned to fix cluster boxes that thieves had damaged in the area, so it took weeks and even months for necessary repairs to be made. Late mail delivery is another longstanding issue. In 2005, a small business owner in San Diego complained, "We get today's mail tomorrow." In 2021, the *Washington Times* reported that "complaints about mail delays have been piling up nationwide since . . . Louis DeJoy took over the agency."[18]

MAJOR MAILERS

Postal expert Douglas F. Carlson points out that budgetary requirements demand the Postal Service either increase revenues or reduce costs. Because postal officials exercise direct control over costs, Carlson observes, "It's the easy route to take." The decisions that officials have made about which expenses to cut generally align with the outlook of major mailing corporations. The mailing industry generates significant revenues, and postal management attempts to meet its requirements. The Postal Service maintains the Mailers Technical Advisory Council, which provides a means for mailing industry executives to communicate directly with postal leadership. The major events that postal officials organize are designed to ensure the mailing industry's concerns are heard, notably the annual trade show the National Postal Forum. Unfortunately, too often this approach makes the hundreds of millions of people who actually receive mail second-class stakeholders of the Postal Service, because the services that primarily benefit residential patrons—"Aunt Minnie"—are seen as expendable when they conflict with the interests of major mailers.[19]

The overarching concern of major mailers is lower postage rates for themselves. Mailers, therefore, often advocate eliminating infrastructure and services that do not exist for their benefit. "We don't need six-day delivery," the representative of a mailers' organization once explained. "We don't need . . . small post offices . . . and we think it's unfair . . . and even immoral to expect us as mailers to pick [up] a service we neither want nor need." Post offices have been considered particularly expendable. In 2003, the large advertising mailer Valpak Direct Marketing Systems Inc. expressed frustration over the unwillingness of Congress to allow mass closings of postal facilities. "Such restraints send unmistakable signals that the Postal Service is still very much a government agency," Valpak complained, "and that Congress considers numerous policy/political objectives more important than improving productivity and efficiency."[20]

Major mailers also would like to minimize the role of postal infrastructure in costing methodologies used to determine postage rates. Every piece of mail has a unique cost. While the expense of collecting, sorting, transporting, and delivering each piece of mail varies, postage rates are uniform, because universal service is the principle that governs the Postal Service. Averaging the costs of all mail together—including institutional costs—makes uniform rates possible. Major mailers would prefer to pay only the costs that are directly attributable to each individual piece of mail. Although a separate rate class for big mailers already exists due to discounts for bulk mailing, under such a costing methodology these corporations could receive still lower rates at the expense of altering the premise of the Postal Service. As William H. Burrus Jr. stated, "bottom-up" pricing "would actually relieve the largest mailers of any responsibility for the costs of maintaining a universal system. It would almost certainly result in surcharges for service to rural communities and low-volume post offices. Such a structure would be tantamount to proposing that public education be funded only by those who have children in school."[21]

The mailing industry finds the Postal Service's social obligations a burdensome impediment to prioritizing major mailers.

Top postal management agreed with this assessment in 2004 by promoting "self-service" as part of a campaign dedicated to "increasing awareness of retail alternatives" in order "to move simple transactions away from the retail counter." In 2002, after consulting with major mailers, the Postal Service released a "transformation plan." Shrinking the postal system was a recurring theme in this document. "A rigorous network optimization process will be used to ensure that the Postal Service provides the right level of retail access at the least possible cost." Postal officials acknowledged that closing post offices would not be popular with the millions of Americans who use them, so it would "require the Postal Service to change customer behavior—particularly the mindset that all stamp purchases and mailing transactions must take place at the post office."[22]

The Postal Service further determined that "the standard for the number of delivery days and service levels should be flexible to accommodate changing conditions." With this agenda in mind, postal officials announced their intention to "pursue regulatory and legislative reform to provide the Postal Service the latitude to adjust service levels and delivery frequency to standards commensurate with the affordable universal service obligation." Valpak wanted to "allow the Postal Service to experiment with variations in service levels, including reducing the frequency of delivery from the current six days per week." After all, as its chief executive officer stated, "Valpak could manage with delivery only three days a week."[23]

In response to sharp revenue declines during the Great Recession, postal officials moved aggressively to reduce expenses, cutting postal infrastructure, lowering postal employment, and reducing service for residential patrons. Once again, Valpak supported "the Postal Service's managerial flexibility to cut costs." The mailers were in agreement on this point. The National Postal Policy Council and the Major Mailers Association declared: "It is essential that the Postal Service cut costs and save money through right-sizing its network." Mailing industry lobbyists always monitor their interests closely when significant postal reforms appear to be forthcoming. The Association for Postal Commerce (PostCom) acknowledged: "PostCom supports the Postal Service's efforts to reduce costs." Still, the organization keeps careful watch to ensure against "shifting . . . costs to mailers, rather than reducing the overall costs of processing the mail." Meanwhile, average Americans lack a well-organized lobby to protect their stake in the Postal Service.[24]

THE GREAT RECESSION

In the wake of the 2008 financial crisis, a Postal Service spokesman revealed that the agency was considering layoffs for the first time in its history. This announcement signaled that postal leadership was contemplating drastic measures. Service reductions such as large-scale collection-box removals followed, but it was August 2009 when the Postal Service first suggested a sweeping service change. "I think we have reached a breaking point with the recession and that is why we are seeking to go from six-day to five-day delivery," Postmaster General John E. Potter said. There were members of Congress who were open to such a radical move. "Unless we apply some tough medicine here and now . . . this dizzying downward spiral . . . could become a death spiral," Senator Joseph I. Lieberman (I-Conn.) opined. A few weeks later, the Postal Service offered buyouts to up to 30,000 clerks, mail handlers, and vehicle maintenance workers.[25]

In the face of a major budgetary crunch, leading postal officials had turned to the usual playbook: cut expenses through service, infrastructure, and staffing reductions. Yet the Postal Service also hired expensive outside consultants. In order to better make their case to Congress, the media, and the public, postal officials handed Accenture PLC, Boston Consulting Group, and McKinsey & Company $4.8 million to review the situation. The conclusions these management consultants arrived at matched the response the agency was already implementing. Five-day delivery, post office closures, and a smaller, "more flexible" workforce all figured prominently in the resulting "action plan for the future." McKinsey actually had floated more drastic "service level opportunities," including doubling the timeframe for delivering first-class mail, more curbside delivery and cluster-box units, delivery only three days per week, and a push for self-serve kiosks.[26]

In March 2010, with the backing of these high-priced consultants, Potter formally proposed ending Saturday delivery. Potter told representatives of the mailing industry attending that year's National Postal Forum that "the value of going to four days— removing a second day—is even greater." Still, he considered delivery three days per week a bridge too far. "I think that would negatively impact our business." Influential voices supported drastic action. The *Washington Post* editorialized that "privatization is probably the only long-term solution for the USPS." Yet the agency was "so saddled with legacy costs that no investor would touch it." Nevertheless, if Congress signed off on measures that allowed the Postal Service to cut costs—"get its house in order"—there was a possibility that "one day" the agency could "attract private capital." But there was little public enthusiasm for service cuts, and Congress was not prepared to grant postal management the free rein the *Post* advocated.[27]

Shortly before stepping down in December 2010, Potter warned that the Postal Service would run out of money at some point in 2011. This announcement set the stage for his successor, Patrick R. Donahoe, who would spend his term pushing for significant changes in postal operations. In January 2011, Donahoe proposed closing as many as 2,000 post offices, a number that subsequently ballooned to 3,600. "We believe it's something that absolutely has to be done," affirmed Gene A. Del Polito, president of PostCom. In March, the Postal Service announced it would use buyout offers to eliminate 7,500 administrators, supervisors, and postmasters. Over the previous two years, the agency had shed 105,000 full-time positions among clerks and mail handlers through attrition and early retirements.[28]

Despite the ongoing drive to reduce costs, in September, Donahoe said the Postal Service was so low on money that it might have to cease operations that winter. But sympathy for his predicament was lacking in Congress because of the service-cutting agenda the agency had pursued. "The postmaster general has focused on several approaches that I believe will be counterproductive," Senator Susan Collins (R-Maine) stated. "They risk producing a death spiral where the postal service reduces service and drives away more customers." There were also members of Congress who fully backed slashing service, however. Representative Darrell E. Issa (R-Calif.) had introduced legislation that eliminated Saturday delivery and granted postal officials new latitude to shutter post offices and mail processing facilities. Issa worried the Postal Service had "out-of-control labor costs and excess infrastructure," but his bill did not address the all-important pre-funding issue.[29]

Shortly after Donahoe claimed the Postal Service was running out of cash, the agency unveiled its plan to shut down hundreds of mail processing facilities. This network was designed specifically to process local first-class mail overnight, so closures would slow down delivery speeds for these letters to two days or more. James F. Killackey III, executive vice president of the National Association of Postal Supervisors, warned that delaying first-class mail would drive business customers to use United Parcel Service and FedEx instead. The National Newspaper Association worried that concentrating mail processing in large urban plants would "deprive the system of the efficiencies of the smaller plants and complicate the possibility of timely delivery to rural areas." The National Postal Mail Handlers Union pointed out that operating fewer plants would require mail to be transported greater distances—with the resulting expense—and magnify the consequences of equipment failures. Major mailers liked the prospect of cost reductions, but were concerned about potential negative impacts on delivery standards. Local officials and businesses in impacted communities called attention to the economic fallout of closures resulting from job losses and slower mail service.[30]

In December, the agency announced its intention to move forward with plant closures in the spring, which would largely put an end to next-day delivery of first-class mail. "There are certain items that are able to be shipped by first-class mail . . . that will now have to be moved toward express delivery," one Standard & Poor's analyst noted. Los Angeles travel agent David Hop reported he would have to look for alternatives. "We will probably have to send some of it electronically, but a lot of people still like hard copies," he said. "I'll just have to spend more money with FedEx or United Parcel Service to get mail across town." Many postal workers thought the axe being taken to postal infrastructure and service standards was an attempt to force congressional action, specifically on the pre-funding requirement. "We are being used as pawns so that pressure is placed on Congress," objected Janet Kosnik, president of APWU Local 649 in Helena, Montana.[31]

The plan to shutter large numbers of post offices had provoked a public outcry, leading postal officials to retreat in May 2012 and announce that hours of service would be reduced instead. This idea was unwelcome, but did not trigger the same level of opposition as the proposed closures. Now officials trained their attention on processing facilities. Within weeks, a plan to close almost half of all processing plants was made public. The Postal Service "must be streamlined, and this is a good first step," said a lobbying organization representing FedEx and United Parcel Service. The planned closure of 229 facilities was "not enough fundamentally to fix the Postal Service's financial problems," Senator Thomas R. Carper (D-Del.) claimed. Since the elimination of so many facilities would allow for still deeper cuts to the postal workforce, the Postal Service said it would offer 45,000 mail handlers buyouts.[32]

In October, the Postal Service tendered buyouts to an additional group of employees. A total of 115,155 clerks, custodians, mechanics, and drivers were declared eligible for this offer. Efforts to cut costs continued with the announcement of plans to make early retirement offers to thousands of management employees. Meanwhile, Valpak was disappointed that the proposed switch to five-day-a-week mail delivery remained pending. "Unfortunately, thus far Congress has been unwilling to allow this important change to be made." In February 2013, postal officials decided to press the issue, announcing the agency would bypass Congress and unilaterally stop collecting and delivering mail on Saturdays. "It's too big of a cost savings to ignore," Donahoe explained. Representative Issa applauded the move. Senator Carper thought it was an unwise step, but added: "It's hard to condemn the postmaster general for moving aggressively." It did not take too long for postal officials to conclude they had overreached. The Government Accountability Office determined the Postal Service lacked the legal authority to drop Saturday delivery. Nine weeks after Donahoe's announcement, postal officials reversed course before the policy went into effect.[33]

Management's next major initiative to restructure the postal system targeted post offices again. In fall 2013, eighty-two stores in the Staples office-supply chain installed sections that offered many of the services available in post offices. "This is a direct assault on our jobs and on *public* postal services," stated Mark Dimondstein, president of the APWU. "The APWU supports the expansion of postal services. But we are adamantly opposed to USPS plans to replace good-paying union jobs with non-union low-wage jobs held by workers who have no accountability for the safety and security of the mail." An internal Postal Service memorandum revealed that the purpose of this program was to ascertain the labor costs of using "retail partner labor" in comparison to postal workers.[34]

Senator Jon Tester (D-Mont.) thought the Staples experiment was a doubtful development and clearly of no use in large sections of the country, particularly rural areas. "I see this postmaster general . . . shutting down post offices, then saying, let Staples do it. Well guess what: I don't have a Staples." "I think he wants to privatize," Tester added. The APWU organized nationwide protests outside Staples stores that continued for years in some areas. "I'm concerned about those who come behind me," said Dena Briscoe, a postal clerk in Capitol Heights, Maryland. "They might not have the type of opportunity I've had to be here thirty-four years and being able to have . . . livable wages and benefits." Teacher unions issued calls for members to boycott Staples. The sale of school supplies produced around one-third of the chain's revenues. "We put Postal Service management and a profit-seeking corporation on notice that the quality of mail delivery is not for sale," said Joshua I. Pechthalt, president of the California Federation of Teachers.[35]

After eliminating 143 mail processing facilities in three years, postal officials kicked off 2015 with a plan to close an additional eighty-two plants and slow delivery standards. This would be the final initiative to cut postal infrastructure under Donahoe's tenure. In February, he handed the reins of the Postal Service over to Megan J. Brennan. The second round of processing facility closures ran into congressional resistance right from the start. Senator Claire McCaskill (D-Mo.) stated that "voluntarily giving up your competitive advantage and lowering standards isn't a recipe for success." It was becoming clear that delivery times were suffering due to earlier plant closures while the projected cost savings were inflated. Months earlier, fifty senators and 160 members of the House had signed letters requesting a moratorium on closures. Postal Regulatory Commissioner Ruth Y. Goldway warned the new round of plant closures would "result in a two-tier patchwork network in which service to smaller cities and rural areas will be degraded much more than major urban areas." PostCom was unhappy that the Postal Service had overestimated the cost savings from closing plants even as new requirements obliged major mailers to incur additional preparation expenses for mailings. In

May, postal officials "extended the timeline" for further closures of mail processing facilities. The USPS Office of Inspector General would reveal that the closures completed in 2015 had increased transportation costs, decreased mail processing productivity, and realized just 5.6 percent of projected cost savings.[36]

The suspension of mail processing facility closures marked a halt to initiatives that reduced the postal network. In 2012, Valpak observed, "the Postal Service has been stymied by Congress with respect to cost cutting, resulting in the Postal Service making the cuts that it could make, not necessarily the cuts that it wanted to make." In January 2016, postal officials formally announced they no longer would seek to eliminate Saturday delivery. The Postal Service had negotiated a special agreement to deliver packages for Amazon. com Inc., including for a seventh day on Sundays. As packages became a larger proportion of postal deliveries, more delivery days offered a competitive advantage. "Just imagine if we had given in to those who were advocating the end of Saturday delivery," testified Fredric V. Rolando, president of the National Association of Letter Carriers. "We would have missed out on the e-commerce boom . . . unnecessarily eliminated tens of thousands of good jobs, and weakened the Postal Service." In January 2017, Staples Inc. discontinued its postal offerings. The union-led boycott had exacted a financial toll on the company. "This victory goes far beyond Staples," Dimondstein observed. "We have strong reason to believe this was their plan for postal retail for most of the country. We believe they had a number of these deals in the pipeline."[37]

SERVICE MATTERS

Under Postmaster General Brennan there would be no major new initiatives to curtail service in the name of reducing operational expenses. Retired postmaster Mark Jamison observed that instead Brennan "let things degrade at their own pace, allowing expectations to diminish." The impact of previous cuts had placed significant strain on the postal system. In the San Francisco Bay Area, for example, mail delivery in the fall of 2016 was erratic. There were days when residents of Berkeley and Oakland reported receiving no mail at all. On other days, mail was delivered after midnight. Misdelivered mail even became a problem. The executive vice president of NALC Branch 1280 in Burlingame was dismayed. "We've never failed," Sandra Dieffenderfer said. "We've always been really proud to get out the mail. But this year I see failure, and it's sad." Understaffing contributed significantly to this breakdown. While new hiring has helped, overextended postal workers have remained an issue in the Bay Area and elsewhere. "Management is intentionally not staffing our offices," charged Miriam Bell, president of APWU Local 375 in Charlotte, North Carolina. "Many of our workers are being forced to work twelve-hour days, six days a week."[38]

The cumulative toll of cutbacks and understaffing in the 2010s contributed to the serious mail delays that became a major news story in 2020. "The various causes are difficult to isolate and quantify," Steven Hutkins of Save the Post Office observed. "Particularly because they interact and compound each other." Although problems with service performance arose when the pandemic began in March, the imposition of Postmaster General Louis DeJoy's operational changes over the summer produced extraordinary delays. In particular, curtailing work hours and reducing the number of trips that trucks made from processing facilities left mail waiting to be sorted and transported. In the weeks before Christmas, the postal system was deluged and delivery standards deteriorated significantly. Only 38 percent of one major category of first-class mail was delivered on time. In the aftermath of this breakdown, the Postal Service blamed a variety of developments that were beyond its control: rising quarantines reduced employee availability, air transportation options grew scarce, election mail required priority handling, and the agency also cited bad weather.[39]

In spring 2020, the Pew Research Center found that among

federal agencies "ratings of the Postal Service continue to stand out: an overwhelming 91% say they have a favorable view of the mail delivery service." However, the severe deterioration of service under DeJoy has put this positive opinion at risk. So long as the Postal Service maintains traditional levels of service, the public will continue to support the agency and resist calls for deregulation and privatization. But Charles "Chuck" Zlatkin, legislative and political director of the New York Metro Area Postal Union, notes that sustained poor service has consequences. He points out that in 2020 appreciation for the Postal Service was so great that citizens in the street applauded passing postal trucks and postal workers delivering mail, but adds that "if the mail continues to slow, then I don't know if there will be much applause in the future." Poor service could even lead some dissatisfied patrons to give the ill-advised push for privatization new consideration.[40]

As average citizens are the recipients of mail, the Postal Service's future rests on the satisfaction they derive from the institution. Poor service does not make the postal system more useful or relevant to patrons. In 2003, the Oregon Rural Letter Carriers' Association observed: "We see postal workers who care about doing a good job, who are seeing that their employer is caring less and less about them and quality service, and more and more about cutting wages and scrimping on service to make it look like they are running a successful business. We do not believe this is a formula for success." The agency's requirement to break even encourages management to treat service to average citizens as a liability. "The dilemma for us is 80 percent of revenue comes from big business," Postmaster General John E. Potter once acknowledged. "The economy is what drives us."[41]

Adjustments become necessary as use of the postal system changes. But service cutbacks call for utmost caution, since they make mail less valuable to residential patrons. Steve D. LeNoir, former president of the National League of Postmasters, states that "when service goes down you lose people and it's hard to get

them back." By degrading service, the Postal Service risks alien-
ating its fundamental customer base—the individual postal user.
People often call bulk mail "junk." In a front-page *Boston Globe*
article on the subject, for example, Kate Nugent of Somerville,
Massachusetts, called "junk mail . . . out of control. . . . I just
keep the recycling bin next to the mailbox so I don't even have to
bring it in the house anymore." In one revealing study, economist
Michael D. Bradley discovered a direct relationship between the
quality of service patrons receive and the value they place on mail.
Bradley found that mode of delivery influenced the amount of
attention that recipients grant advertising mail, with those who
receive door delivery interacting the most with mail and those
with cluster-box delivery exhibiting the least interest. Since the
satisfaction the public takes in receiving and sending mail provides the basis for the postal system, service reductions threaten to
undermine the Postal Service.[42]

Postal patrons want widely available and adequately staffed
post offices that are open during convenient hours; they want the
ability to send items securely at uniform and reasonable prices
anywhere in the country; they want reliable and timely six-day
delivery to their homes and easily accessible collection boxes with
pick-ups scheduled to meet their needs. "Service, not revenues,"
must be the main theme of what we seek to render to our Nation,"
argued J. Joseph Vacca, former president of NALC. "When we
deal with revenues, we concern ourselves with how much we can
take from Americans, rather than how much we can give them.
Let business continue to worry about how much the traffic will
bear, but let Government—and that is what we are—worry about
how much we can give Americans." As Vacca stated in 1977, postal
officials manage a public service, not a business. Still, there is no
reason why good service and greater revenues must be conceived
of as opposites. Improving service could increase revenues for the
Postal Service by enhancing the value of mail.[43]

SIX

COMPETITORS

The question of what services the Postal Service should provide is a perennial source of contention. In the latter half of the twentieth century, political and ideological objections repeatedly prevented the postal system from offering electronic communications services. As a result, the Postal Service ceded this emerging field of communications to for-profit businesses. During this same period, opposition from Federal Express and United Parcel Service made the postal system's package and express delivery services a controversial issue. These two corporations used their considerable political power to intrude on postal operations. In 2000, postal official Robert G. Krause revealed: "We expect to hear from FedEx and UPS every time we create an offer that has value in the marketplace." The efforts of business interests and their allies to diminish the Postal Service have done a disservice to the American people.[1]

UNDERMINING DELIVERY

Use of Parcel Post grew in the booming economic environment following World War II until Congress intervened on behalf of its ailing competitor, the Railway Express Agency, imposing complex regulations and weight and size rules that hampered the government's package delivery service. As volume declined, postal officials had to keep increasing Parcel Post rates to cover the service's costs at the same time that processing issues arose. Packages were no exception to the strained postal infrastructure's broader struggle to keep up with a rising population and strong economic growth. Moreover, uncoordinated handling procedures produced the further problem for Parcel Post of damaged contents. The number of packages passing through the postal network fell from 857 million in 1959 to 664 million in 1968.[2]

As the 1970s began, Parcel Post's main competitor, United Parcel Service, pulled ahead in package deliveries. Cherry-picking the easy-to-handle, profitable packages had allowed UPS to construct a smoothly operating network. Meanwhile, the Postal Service was obligated to accept nearly all shipments. At that moment, the Postal Service began constructing its National Bulk Mail System (NBMS), consisting of twenty-one major and twelve auxiliary facilities that were to become the processing centers for virtually all bulk mail, including parcels. Postal officials thought this new system would reduce delays and damage, helping to win back customers. In the meantime, Parcel Post volume continued to fall, dropping more than 25 percent from 1971 to 1975.[3]

When the NBMS began operating in the mid-1970s, it quickly became apparent that careless design and management were significant problems. Under postmasters general Winton M. Blount Jr., Elmer T. Klassen, and Benjamin F. Bailar, the 1970s were a period of poor leadership at the Postal Service. Blount was former president of the U.S. Chamber of Commerce and a multimillionaire construction company owner who filled postal headquarters with business executives. Klassen and Bailar were former American Can Company executives who came to the agency with no background in postal affairs. The assistant postmaster general placed in charge of the NMBS denied the purpose of the new infrastructure was to "regain any business." Edgar S. Brower questioned whether such an objective would be "proper." The NBMS actually slowed Parcel Post delivery, and the General Accounting Office deemed the project a $1 billion failure. In 1976, United Parcel Service handled 950 million items. By 1978, Parcel Post volume had declined to only 345 million packages.[4]

At the same time that postal officials restructured Parcel Post, they also began testing an experimental courier service designed for urgent business correspondence. In 1977, Express Mail became a permanent service, providing next-day—and in some cases same-day—delivery. Although Express Mail experienced strong initial growth—outpacing recently founded rival Federal Express—postal officials skimped on assigning designated workers to ensure timely delivery and failed to offer enhanced features that private competitors provided, such as pick-up and tracking. The Postal Service had greater success with the "deferred" category, encompassing mail that is delivered within a two- to three-day window. Postal officials created the deferred delivery concept in 1968 with the introduction of Priority Mail. In 2017, the *Washington Post* called this service "a particularly lucrative part of the Postal Service's shipping business."[5]

Unlike its competitors, the Postal Service has operated its package offerings under the handicap of lacking a dedicated fleet of aircraft. Delays on passenger airlines and their focus on travelers instead of cargo has affected timely delivery of first-class mail as well. In 2001, postal watchdog Douglas F. Carlson raised awareness about delivery delays in the West that were occurring because mail was hauled on trucks instead of flown on airplanes as it had been previously. The *Oakland Tribune* was provoked to editorialize that "Western residents are being treated as second-class citizens. The U.S. Postal Service has a responsibility to provide equal service to everyone." Postal officials claimed the change was necessary because "the mail now takes a big back seat to passengers."[6]

When postal officials explored the possibility of operating their own air fleet, passenger airlines with contracts to carry the U.S. Mail lobbied hard against the idea. In the early 1990s, Postmaster General Anthony M. Frank argued "that unless there is better service than commercial airlines can provide, the Postal Service's share of the overnight delivery market will be further eroded by highly aggressive, privately operated delivery companies, such as Federal Express and United Parcel Service." Bill McAllister of the *Washington Post* reported that the prospect of the Postal Service operating "its own fleet of 50 to 60 red-white-and-blue cargo airplanes . . . triggered fierce opposition from the nation's commercial airlines." The Air Transport Association of America told Congress: "We believe plans for alternative air transportation for mail should be rejected." A postal air fleet never got off the ground.[7]

The absence of postal aircraft contributed to delivery delays during the COVID-19 pandemic as airlines reduced the number of commercial flights in response to declining passenger demand. "Across the country a lack of air traffic means less of a transportation network for the Postal Service," said Thomas J. Dlugolenski, president of National Association of Letter Carriers Branch 134 in Syracuse, New York. "These disruptions have created a fragmented network and mail is waiting for flights." Former Postal Rate Commissioner Ruth Y. Goldway thinks it is time to reimagine the entire postal network. "The Postal Service," she contends, "needs a network more modeled on the internet—not highways and roads—that is very flexible so that transportation and equipment can adjust for volume quickly. It should be massively decentralized with more sorting facilities."[8]

CORPORATE POWER

For decades, two heavy hitters in Washington, D.C.—United Parcel Service and Federal Express (currently FedEx Corp.)—have interfered with the Postal Service's delivery of packages. In 1995, the *Wall Street Journal* called FedEx "a major lobbying force in Washington." "For years," affirmed Charles Lewis, founder of the Center for Public Integrity, "Federal Express has had a reputation for being one of the most aggressive special interests in Washington." From 2010 through 2019, FedEx spent $132 million on lobbyists. "I was stunned by the breadth and depth of their clout up here," acknowledged campaign finance reformer Senator Russell D. Feingold (D-Wisc.).[9]

FedEx founder and chief executive officer Frederick W. Smith made his influence felt early on, "single-handedly" winning enactment of an airfreight deregulation bill in 1977 that allowed his fledgling business to use larger airplanes. The corporation then pushed hard for deregulation of the airline and trucking industries. For decades, Smith has cultivated powerful political allies. President William J. Clinton called FedEx's founder his "friend of many years." In 2004, Smith raised large sums of money for President George W. Bush's reelection campaign. Bush was an old friend: he had been Smith's fraternity brother back in their college days at Yale University. Smith personally lobbied President Donald J. Trump to reduce corporate tax rates. Subsequent passage of legislation in 2017 reduced FedEx's tax bill from $1.5 billion to $0. Smith celebrated this victory alongside Trump and other business executives at one of the president's country clubs. "We at FedEx were very pleased," Smith acknowledged. He proclaimed the corporate tax cuts "a great achievement for the American people."[10]

FedEx is a product of the pro-corporate rewriting of economic and political rules imposed internationally over the past forty years—such as corporate-friendly foreign trade and anti-union measures—and wants to see this trend continue into the future. After the U.S. Navy's 1992 departure from Subic Bay Naval Base in the Philippines, FedEx started using the site as a regional transportation hub. In 1995, the Department of Transportation authorized FedEx to become the sole air cargo provider between the United States and China. FedEx would like pro-corporate trade agreements to encircle both the Atlantic and Pacific oceans. In 2014, the corporation funded a report promoting a trade deal between the United States and the European Union. An executive vice president of FedEx anticipated that it would "streamline rules, cut red tape, lower tariffs, and harmonize regulations." When the failed Trans-Pacific Partnership was floundering in 2016, a senior FedEx executive contended "it would be tragic to miss the opportunity."[11]

From its founding, FedEx has been fiercely opposed to its

workers organizing labor unions. In 1996, the Senate remained in session for two extra days—shortly before the November election—in order to pass legislation making it harder to organize FedEx workers. "What happened here was just a blatant example of the power of their political efforts," affirmed Senator Paul M. Simon (D-Ill.). "If the John Smith company came along and asked for the same thing, it wouldn't have a prayer." In 2009, FedEx waged another anti-union battle over a bill that would have eased union organizing at the corporation. FedEx's home state senator, A. Lamar Alexander Jr. (R-Tenn.), fully backed the company. "I'm going to do everything in my power," he pledged, "to make certain that the final legislation doesn't include a provision that changes labor laws." After a two-year struggle, the offending passage was stricken from the legislation. FedEx had spent $42 million lobbying against the measure.[12]

United Parcel Service Inc. is a major force on Capitol Hill as well. In 1980, a senator's aide said, "I got a call from a local UPS manager in our home state saying he liked a certain version of the truck-deregulation bill. That's all it took. We were for it, too." UPS knows how to cultivate powerful allies: in 2000, in order to "reward" corporate donors and raise money for his political action committee, House Majority Whip Thomas D. DeLay (R-Tex.) flew more than thirty lobbyists to a golf tournament in Las Vegas on board an airplane that UPS contributed for the purpose. DeLay himself made the trip separately aboard a FedEx corporate jet. From 2010 through 2019, UPS spent $68.2 million on lobbyists.[13]

Like FedEx, UPS has opposed pro-worker measures and promoted pro-corporate foreign trade. Campaign finance reformers Micah L. Sifry and Nancy Watzman cited UPS—"with its thousands of brown-uniformed employees lifting and straining all day"—as "one of the staunchest enemies" of the ergonomics standard that was repealed in 2001. UPS ranked first in money spent scuttling the regulations designed to reduce repetitive stress injuries in the workplace, handing out $2.9 million. FedEx came in a close second at $2.6 million. In 2003, UPS "applauded" the signing of a trade agreement between the United States and Chile that the company had helped spearhead as co-chair of the U.S.-Chile FTA Business Coalition. UPS's chief executive officer claimed that "removing restrictions to the free flow of goods, information and funds is critical to the world's economic health and certainly to UPS as an enabler of global commerce." More recently, UPS championed the Trans-Pacific Partnership.[14]

Although FedEx and UPS are business rivals that have butted heads, the political interests of the two shipping giants frequently align. In 2017, Smith and UPS Chief Executive Officer David P. Abney jointly proclaimed their wish for corporate tax cuts and additional pro-corporate foreign trade agreements. At the top of the list of items FedEx and UPS agree on is the need to keep the Postal Service as noncompetitive as possible. FedEx's former lead lobbyist once acknowledged the corporation wanted to "curb [the Postal Service's] intrusion into express delivery and other markets." The two companies have promoted this position aggressively and successfully.[15]

In 1996, FedEx—with the support of UPS—went ballistic when Priority Mail experienced a strong increase in volume after an advertising campaign pointed out that this two-to-three-day delivery service was similar to FedEx and UPS products costing twice as much or more. Seeking an injunction to stop the advertisements, FedEx filed a lawsuit in federal district court in its hometown of Memphis, Tennessee, that accused the Postal Service of "false advertising and unfair competition." FedEx claimed that because it offered a money-back guarantee that it would deliver within the specified time frame, and the Postal Service did not (although Priority Mail did average two to three delivery days), the two products were not comparable. FedEx then launched a retaliatory advertising campaign featuring actors portraying incompetent postal workers—a smear the corporation had pressed in previous advertisements as well. Smith denounced the Postal Service and called its publicizing of Priority Mail "false and misleading." Bill McAllister reported that Smith "vowed to take his lawsuit to the Supreme Court, if necessary, and also urged Congress to force the Postal Service to stop making the claims." This intense campaign compelled the Postal Service to pull the offending advertisements, but not before FedEx had responded to the new competition by cutting its price for two-day delivery from $11.50 to $7.45.[16]

In 1998, the chief executive officer of UPS claimed the Postal Service "wouldn't last one day in the free and open market of real competition." The political efforts of UPS aimed to ensure the agency would not have the opportunity to prove him wrong. In 1997, UPS—with the support of FedEx—successfully blocked expansion of the Postal Service's Global Postal Link program, which was designed to help shippers' parcels clear customs faster. In rate cases pending before the Postal Rate Commission in 1998, UPS attempted to make Priority Mail less attractive to customers by adding an extra $1 to the price of packages sent with electronic delivery confirmation. Later that same year, UPS unsuccessfully contested Postal Rate Commission decisions regarding Parcel Post and Priority Mail in an effort to inflate the prices of these services. In 1999, UPS continued its offensive against the Postal Service by delivering packets to every member of Congress filled with materials denouncing the agency. In 2000, UPS filed testimony before the Postal Rate Commission seeking to increase Priority Mail rates over 40 percent.[17]

UPS has pushed to end the Postal Service's delivery of packages altogether. In 1977, a UPS director opined, "Parcels are not mail at all. . . . There is good reason to believe that they perhaps, shouldn't be under the aegis of the Post Office at all." In 2003, UPS's chief executive officer insisted that "movement of goods . . . should not be part of the Postal Service's core mission, or even its broader mission." FedEx has joined UPS's efforts to remove the Postal Service as a competitor. In 2004, Smith went beyond calling for elimination of parcel delivery and proposed the Postal Service itself could "be wound down in an orderly manner as competitors are able to take over its functions." When making this argument, he has noted, "There are many institutions that long ago passed into history." "Closing down the Postal Service," Smith concluded, "like any other government agency that has outlived its usefulness, is an option that ought to be considered seriously."[18]

In recent years, FedEx and UPS have softened their opposition to the Postal Service delivering packages. Lacking its own air fleet, in 2001 the Postal Service entered into a no-bid transportation contract with FedEx. Postmaster General William J. Henderson called the agreement "a major step forward in the Postal Service's increasing collaboration with private business." After stepping down from his position at the agency, Henderson claimed the Postal Service should become a private business, contending, "What the Postal Service needs now is nothing short of privatization." In return for $6.3 billion over seven years, FedEx started using spare aircraft capacity to carry mail. An additional feature of this arrangement gave FedEx the opportunity to plant more than 10,000 drop-off boxes both in front of and inside post offices nationwide in return for between $126 million and $232 million (depending on the total number of boxes placed). The corporation expected to net $900 million in new revenues from these sites. One postal official suggested that locating FedEx boxes at post offices offered a means to recruit new customers for the Postal Service. The agency would eliminate 3,841—almost 30 percent—of its own Express Mail collection boxes from 2001 through 2004.[19]

The Postal Service subsequently renewed the FedEx agreement and inked air-transportation contracts with UPS. The private delivery companies have often used the Postal Service to complete the costly, labor-intensive final leg of their deliveries. FedEx and UPS process the packages until they start to lose profitability, at which point they are turned over to postal workers. These business arrangements have reduced tensions. Still, in 2014 FedEx and

UPS protested loudly when the Postal Regulatory Commission signed off on changes to Priority Mail rates designed to increase volume. In 2018, a federal circuit court ruled against UPS when the corporation disputed the method used to determine prices for Postal Service package delivery. UPS was attempting to raise prices for these services by around 7 percent. Instead of pricing Postal Service packages on the basis of letter carriers completing these deliveries as part of their daily rounds, UPS would like to base prices on the hypothetical expense of special trips made solely to drop off packages. The result would be higher prices to ship items via the Postal Service. Meanwhile, FedEx is building out its ground delivery infrastructure and recently started to bring packages back into its network that previously were handed off to the Postal Service. In 2020, FedEx asserted that "there is no necessary relationship between the postal monopoly law and the provision of universal postal service."[20]

POSTAL PACKAGE DELIVERY

The delivery of packages by the Postal Service has become more vital than ever due to the rise in electronic commerce. Regardless of what future position FedEx and UPS take toward the Postal Service, there are at least three very good reasons for packages to move through the U.S. Mail: these services generate revenue that helps maintain the postal infrastructure; only the Postal Service delivers to all addresses; and additional competition is in the interest of consumers, especially given high market concentration in the package delivery sector. The Federal Trade Commission stated that the Postal Service's "unique legal status appears to cause it to suffer a net competitive disadvantage relative to its private competitors." Nevertheless, in recent years packages have replaced revenue from declining mail volume and have made increasing contributions to institutional costs. "If you look at what the Postal Services does," advised former Representative John M. McHugh

(R-N.Y.), "packages are the most profitable piece of its business." In 2018, Postmaster General Megan J. Brennan underscored that "our package business plays a significant role in providing critical funding to help pay for the infrastructure, which enables us to maintain that universal service obligation."[21]

Unlike the Postal Service, FedEx and UPS assess costly fees for residential delivery. A FedEx spokeswoman once explained "it costs us more to deliver to residences. . . . It was time to have a special surcharge." In 2019, when FedEx's residential surcharge was $3.80 per package and UPS's was $3.95, logistics consultant John R. Haber noted these fees exceeded 40 percent of the total average delivery price. FedEx and UPS also impose special surcharges on deliveries to locations they deem "remote." Many places that incur these fees do not meet the definition of this word as it is normally understood. In 2003, the *Wall Street Journal* reported that "the number of ZIP Codes the carriers consider remote is swelling even as America is growing more urban." At the present time, private delivery companies levy surcharges on shipments to a majority of zip codes—more than 23,000 in total. "They don't want to send somebody there on a twenty-five-mile drive to deliver one package," said Frank Wozniak, a rural letter carrier in Washington County, Pennsylvania. Additional fees are applied to the noncontiguous United States. In 2020, the Federal Trade Commission stated: "Not only do delivery companies frequently cost more for destinations in Alaska and Hawaii . . . the companies' most expedient options may not be available."[22]

In 2003, UPS argued the Postal Service "should be subjected to the same antitrust scrutiny as the private-sector entities with which it competes." The postal system is a regulated government monopoly because it serves the public interest. UPS and FedEx pursue their own financial interests. Despite constituting a duopoly, these two corporations have faced little antitrust scrutiny. An antitrust legal theory called the Chicago School that gained ascendancy in the 1980s claimed such enforcement was largely unwarranted. "Anti-antitrusters," economist James W. Brock explained, "condemn structural antitrust policy as just one more costly, counterproductive political interference with the beneficent functioning of free markets." Agricultural economist Willard F. Mueller called attention to the fact that this theory "tends to resolve all disputes concerning the intent and consequences of particular [business] practices in favor of the businessmen making them." When confronted with UPS's substantial share of the ground parcel delivery market in 2005, Chicago School disciple James C. Miller III, chairman of the Federal Trade Commission under President Ronald Reagan, replied, "I'm not worried about UPS's share of the market; it's a pretty open marketplace."[23]

Despite theories that dismiss the dangers of market concentration, consumers of shipping services have consistently favored the Postal Service delivering packages. Former Postal Rate Commissioner A. Lee Fritschler once observed that "they want to maintain competition in parcel shipping." Small businesses in particular benefit from shipping items through the postal system. *USA Today* small business columnist Rhonda Abrams has reported that "many small businesses would go out of business if it weren't for USPS." Without the Postal Service, the package delivery market would become even more oligopolistic. In 1981, Frederick W. Smith remarked, "We are so much bigger than anybody else. . . . It would take a corporate behemoth to muscle its way into our business." FedEx has only grown over the past forty years. In 2004, Timothy J. May, general counsel of the Parcel Shippers Association, called the Postal Service "indispensable for promoting competition and giving consumers of package service a choice." In 2019, the Package Coalition testified that "the Postal Service is crucial to the success of America's thriving e-commerce economy."[24]

ADDITIONAL SERVICES

There are political reasons that post offices lack offerings available at UPS Store and FedEx Office outlets. Struggles have ensued when the Postal Service attempted to offer additional services. In 1975, Congress instructed postal officials to remove recently installed coin-operated photocopy machines from post office lobbies after a trade association that complained its members were losing business waged a lobbying campaign. "Copiers are most convenient in post offices," a National Consumers League spokeswoman replied, "because of their central location and because of the frequent need to mail whatever has been copied." "In some rural areas it is the only photocopying service available," noted a Consumer Federation of America spokeswoman. Patrons were not pleased with the decision: the Postal Service received over 12,000 letters of protest within a month—significantly more than a recent postage increase had elicited. The copy machines were returned, but a policy was established that anyone who needed to make "more than a few copies" would be "directed to nearby commercial establishments." Additional machines would not be installed in post offices unless postmasters determined no copiers were available for use at nearby businesses.[25]

In 1995, the Postal Service inaugurated a pack-and-send service at selected post offices that offered patrons the option of having postal workers prepare their parcels for shipment. "We're trying to be customer-friendly and respond to what our customers want," Postmaster General Marvin T. Runyon said. He explained that patrons "don't like to come in and have to buy a box from us . . . and then they have to wrap it. . . . So we started doing it." The new service provoked an outcry from the Mailboxes Etc. chain and other private packing stores. "It's something our customers are screaming at us to do," said Runyon's successor, William J. Henderson. "I mean it's obvious. If you take packages, you ought to provide [packing services]." Private packing store owners maintained the service was unfair government competition. "The fact is, they're competing with us," replied Runyon, pointing out that the nation's postal system had existed far longer than packing stores. By arguing that the service was priced too low, the packing stores successfully lobbied the Postal Rate Commission to permit pack-and-send services only if prices rose to noncompetitive levels.[26]

Starting in the late 1950s, the Postal Service made a number of attempts to offer electronic communications, but pro-corporate ideology among postal officials combined with private business interests lobbying from outside to undercut these efforts. In 1959, Postmaster General Arthur E. Summerfield—an enthusiast of new technologies—prepared to launch Speed Mail—a facsimile communications system that promised to transmit letters nationwide in mere hours. "Here is truly the 'wave of the future,'" he raved. "Here is speed incomparable to other means of transmitting messages set down on paper." Although the Post Office Department partnered with private companies on the venture—including lead contractor International Telephone & Telegraph Co.—Western Union perceived Speed Mail as a threat to its business. The telegraph company rallied opposition against this "socialistic scheme" among airlines and railroads worried about fewer contracts to transport mail. In 1961, the Kennedy administration's new postmaster general, J. Edward Day, decided to scrap the program. An internal department report concluded this decision "was based on more than simply economic considerations."[27]

In 1977, the Commission on Postal Service issued a stark warning about electronic communications: "*The impact will be of sufficient magnitude to constitute a major threat to the basic business of the Postal Service.*" In its multi-volume report, this message was the crucial one. The Post Office Department had started investigating electronic communications in 1968, but in the 1970s business-oriented members of the Board of Governors and the postmasters general—Blount, Klassen, and Bailar—had failed to act. Paul J. Krebs, chairman of the commission's subcommittee on electronic communications, criticized the agency's leadership for not taking action "to meet the changing communication needs of the American public." In fact, he had "detected a predilection against any involvement [in electronic communications] at all." Representative James M. Hanley (D-N.Y.) was similarly frustrated. "All three Postmasters General . . . have been reluctant," he noted. At a hearing on the subject, Hanley further observed that "present postal management does not see the need to put greater emphasis on the research and development of new electronic message systems."[28]

The future of electronic communication was a major concern of postal union leaders as well. J. Joseph Vacca, president of the National Association of Letter Carriers, advised: "We stand in danger of losing, literally, the postal service as we now know it unless we involve ourselves in this electronic revolution." Vacca said the inaction of postal officials revealed that "this newly assembled group of expert businessmen not only lack a commitment to service but they also lack the prime requisite of business, a will to compete." James L. LaPenta Jr., president of the Mail Handlers Division of the Laborers International Union, alleged that "Blount, Klassen, and Bailar have neglected this aspect so long that . . . I think they've been successful in doing what they set out to do . . . wind down the Postal Service and put it out of business." Vacca agreed that the "failure to aggressively pursue mail business must be attributed to an unexpressed desire to preside over the demise of the U.S. Postal Service." He urged the agency to incorporate the new technology under its "constitutional mandate." "Failing such decision," he warned, "the present control of the people of the national [communications] network through the people's Postal Service will be transferred from the people to corporation directors."[29]

Bailar acknowledged the connection between electronic communications and the Postal Service's future as well, even predicting this development would "mean the traditional Postal Service is going to have less volume and be less important." But he worried that providing electronic communications services would "run counter to . . . notions of free enterprise." "I don't see any reason," Bailar added, "why the government ought to be in a business which private industry is willing and able to take care of." Bailar reiterated his position after leaving the agency to become executive vice president of United States Gypsum Co. "I think [electronic communications] ought to be left to the private sector," he affirmed. In 1991, Bailar asserted, "It's time to end the U.S. Postal Service monopoly on the handling of letter mail."[30]

Upon assuming leadership of the Postal Service from Bailar in 1978, career postal employee William F. Bolger pursued an electronic communications service called Electronic-Computer Originated Mail (E-COM) that was designed for large-scale mailings. In the initial plan, major mailers would send the text of messages electronically to the Postal Service's central mainframe computer. Messages would then be transmitted to one of twenty-five select post offices to be printed out, placed in envelopes, and delivered as first-class mail. "The individual has no place in E-COM," postal expert Kathleen Conkey observed. The proposed service faced strong opposition from telephone companies developing their own electronic mail products, and mailers concerned that revenues from existing services might be used to subsidize E-COM, resulting in higher postage rates.[31]

Federal regulators sided with E-COM's corporate opponents, claiming the service would suppress competition in electronic mail. The Postal Rate Commission's ruling on the matter prevented the Postal Service from transmitting electronic messages between post offices. Communications scholar Ryan N. Ellis stated that this decision "reassured private industry that electronic communication would remain beyond the scope of the postal monopoly." When E-COM finally debuted in 1982, clients needed to contract with private companies to transmit messages to post offices—an awkward feature that complicated the process. E-COM's debut was disappointing. The service's deficiencies were further compounded by its lack of allowance for inserts or return envelopes and its use of non-color printers that could not reproduce corporate logos. The plug was pulled after only two and a half years. "We're hard-copy delivery folks," a spokesman for the Board of Governors stated.[32]

As use of the internet increased rapidly at the turn of the millennium, the Postal Service floated the idea of assigning Americans postal email addresses. In 2000, Postmaster General Henderson observed that electronic communications "is just moving mail from hard copy to electronics. . . . It's just an extension of creating universal service." Yet the electronic services the agency actually rolled out were much more restricted. Nevertheless, the Postal Service still was attacked for meddling in areas that corporate interests thought they should automatically be awarded. When a new, secure postal email service (PosteCS) was unveiled in 1998, UPS—which was introducing its own secure email product—filed a complaint with the Postal Rate Commission. "This is another example of how the Postal Service is illegally competing with the private sector," a UPS spokesman claimed. More electronic services were introduced, including eBillPay, Mailing Online, Digital Certificate, and Electronic Postmark. This push soon was abandoned, however, as political pressure to exit electronic services mounted and financial returns did not come quickly. The corporate-dominated 2003 postal commission recommended "leaving electronic products and services to [the] private marketplace." In 2004, Postmaster General John E. Potter told a Senate committee: "I have eliminated practically all of those [electronic] ventures." The 2006 postal law subsequently erected barriers to the Postal Service offering new services generally.[33]

AUCTIONING AWAY TRUST

In recent decades, postal officials have approached new services with great misgivings, but there has been less reluctance to auction off the Postal Service's image. Proposals to commercialize this public institution have emerged repeatedly. In 1981, the agency announced it "was considering the sale of commercial advertising space in post offices and on postal trucks, mailboxes and other postal property." There have been no lawsuits or lobbying against commercialization of the postal system from the corporate sector. Instead, corporate interests have encouraged the agency to hawk their products, and the criticisms the Postal Service receives are from civic groups and individual postal patrons. "What if the government is seen as tacitly endorsing a company that turns out to be a polluter or a monopolist?" asked Gary Ruskin, director of Commercial Alert, an organization that challenges rampant commercialism.[34]

In 2001, the Postal Ad Network was introduced to sell advertising space on postal property. "We're looking for every opportunity to find additional revenue streams," said John H. Ward, vice president of core business marketing. Apparently, undermining the integrity of the Postal Service as a public institution in the pursuit of slight new revenues was an option that fit the bill. The *New York Times* reported the Postal Ad Network was intended to help advertisers find opportunities "where they can put ads that ambush consumers." Our surroundings had become so cluttered with ads that advertisers worried that seizing our attention was growing more difficult, so they were scouring all available spaces and moments for opportunities to commandeer our consciousness.[35]

Ward contended patrons were "very enthusiastic" about the idea of "using Postal Service assets as an ad medium." Notwithstanding his claim, people like Merri Dewinter of Mishawaka, Indiana, objected. "They've got the T.V. and newspapers and radio and billboards (for advertisements), that's enough," she said. "These days," the *Omaha World-Herald* editorialized, "it seems as though you can't look or listen anyplace without being shilled for a product or a service, rather than having a moment's peace. Please: no further contributions from the public sector to this growing harangue." A trusted government institution selling itself to the highest bidder presented a troubling proposition. "Ben Franklin must be weeping in his grave," the *World-Herald* stated. "Some things shouldn't be for sale, and in our view this is one of them."[36]

The Postal Service also developed a particularly visible advertising arrangement with the Hollywood studios Universal and DreamWorks. As a result, billions of letters were cancelled by postmarks with movie marketing slogans like "Happy Who-li-days" and "Greetings from Rodney and Fender." Such postmarks displaced traditional cancellations that observed national holidays and offered public service announcements. These messages were deemed a waste when postmarks could be transformed into an item with commercial value. The "spirit" of postal employees was put up for sale too. While letters were being postmarked "Happy Who-lidays," a postal spokesman declared: "Postal employees embody the spirit of Whoville and the Who-lidays." Those who imagined postal workers embodied the spirit of public service and the higher value of binding the nation together were discouraged to hear this declaration that in fact they personify an advertising pitch. Jane Mackie of Evanston, Illinois, stated: "Christmastime and crass commercialism are inseparable in the United States, but I find it offensive that I cannot send my grandmother a Christmas card without making her the subject of this marketing."[37]

The studios paid for this advertising by alluding to mail in these films. *Shrek 2* included the "Far Far Away Post Office"; *How the Grinch Stole Christmas* incorporated a character who worked at the "Whoville Post Office"; and *Robots* featured a talking mailbox. It was all part of an "ongoing promotional campaign with DreamWorks that aims to mold public perception of the Postal Service as cutting-edge." The advertising campaigns were thorough: in addition to billions of postmark cancellations, movie ads were placed throughout post offices nationwide. Prior to the *Robots* release, postmasters were instructed that post office lobbies "should be displaying . . . a standee and poster featuring the colorful characters from *Robots*." Gary Ruskin observed, "It's not the purpose of the federal government to get kids to nag and whine at their parents to take them to a movie."[38]

The Postal Ad Network's vulgar and gaudy additions to recently constructed cookie-cutter post office buildings offered a stark contrast with the grand post offices of an earlier era that remain architectural landmarks in cities both large and small. With majestic staircases, high ceilings, and broad counters, these post offices are impressive civic spaces. Under the New Deal, many were decorated with artwork portraying American life and documenting important events in local and national history. "These murals and sculptures constitute a great national treasure," stated James H. Bruns, former director of the National Postal Museum, "comprising a comprehensive public collection of artworks that portray the diverse culture and character of the American people during this period; and the buildings that house these works represent a valuable and important American asset." It was not commercialism that produced such national treasures.[39]

The most outlandish example of commercialization at the Postal Service may involve the 2014 film *Amazing Spider-Man 2*. The agency announced it would be "teaming up with Sony Pictures for the release of the highly anticipated motion picture." The ensuing "high-profile, multi-channel marketing campaign" involved plastering images of Spider-Man on postal shipping boxes, inside post offices, and across postal vehicles. "Our Priority Mail products share many qualities with a Super Hero of Spider-Man's caliber, namely those of speed, agility, and reliability," gushed Nagise Manabe, chief marketing and sales officer. Perhaps the oddest aspect of the episode was the title on the press release trumpeting this "wide-ranging promotion," which proclaimed, "Priority Mail gets amazing endorsement from Spider-Man."[40]

One of the Postal Service's greatest assets is the trust of the American people. In 2019, Gallup polling found the Postal Service was the top-rated federal agency: 74 percent of Americans stated it was doing an "excellent" or "good" job. Auctioning off its reputation to the highest bidder is a short-sighted approach to revenue creation. The Postal Service's high public standing will exist only so long as Americans perceive it to embody higher values—notably public service—which are above the commercial considerations that drive advertising. And the more the Postal Service allows itself to be corrupted by commercialism, the more it looks like yet another commercial institution, and the less logic there is to maintaining its privileged status. Such an outcome would be consistent with the pro-corporate agenda for the Postal Service. Ruskin believes public institutions "exist to promote the public good, and when there's corporatization of public institutions . . . a tremendous number of conflicts of interest [follow], and it ends up degrading public institutions and civic participation in the life of our nation."[41]

Proposals to commercialize the postal system are desperate attempts to obtain negligible revenues and appear "businesslike." Postal management should never have faced a predicament where financial shortfalls appeared to demand stooping to this level. For decades, the Postal Service failed to offer, expand, and improve a number of services that were directly relevant to its mission and would have generated significant revenues. The American people would have benefited from a more extensive Postal Service. In some cases, postal officials who lacked faith in the institution were at fault. There were even instances when agency executives disapproved of the Postal Service's public service mission. More generally, corporate sector lobbying undermined the broader public interest in order to further the narrow self-interest of various firms. Contrary to assertions of the Postal Service's adversaries, the agency should offer the American people additional and improved services.

SEVEN

WORKERS

In recent decades, American workers have faced a redefinition of employment norms. Large numbers of Americans experienced a shift away from an employment model based on fair compensation to a low-wage model. It used to be much more common for workers to expect that full-time employment meant economic security. But wages and earnings have been cut, health-care benefits have been slashed, and pension and retirement plans have been terminated or depleted. Well-paying jobs have been exported in search of cheaper labor; the expansion of foreign trade has undercut the prices of American-made products; the minimum wage has declined in real terms; monetary policy has favored employers; mass immigration has increased the supply of low-wage labor; corporate outsourcing has disempowered workers; and government policies have weakened unions.[1]

The Postal Service occupies an important role in this low-wage economic environment as a source of fair compensation and stable employment. As the country's third-largest civilian employer with more than 600,000 workers, it serves as a model that has positive impact on individuals, families, communities, and the nation as a whole. The postal workplace has its share of flaws and should not be idealized, but during a period when employers increasingly do not compensate workers at levels that were once considered basic American standards, the Postal Service continues to serve as a significant source of middle-class jobs. Postal employment runs counter to the alarming rise in inequality that has produced a second Gilded Age that harms working people and undermines democracy itself.[2]

POSTAL HEROES

Postal workers are essential workers. Their hard work keeps the U.S. Mail moving day in and day out. Not only do postal workers deliver over 472 million pieces of mail every day, their presence in neighborhoods and streets across America benefits the nation in many ways that do not show up when the Postal Service computes its earnings and losses. Recently retired rural letter carrier Keith Fletcher was greatly appreciated along his route in Franklin County, New York. Local postmaster Priscilla McCabe revealed that Fletcher would "search and search to find the proper individual to receive an item of mail that had been sent without a complete address." He kept an eye on the local community, making sure to check on residents and passing out candy to children when they collected the mail. "I am saddened to think this caring gentleman will not be part of our daily lives after this week," one local resident said immediately prior to Fletcher's retirement.[3]

"We help people daily, weekly, and yearly and we do more than deliver mail," remarked Peter Monteleone, a letter carrier in Westchester County, New York. "We look out for the communities." On many occasions, a heroic letter carrier's presence has meant the difference between life and death for the people they serve. Robert J. McLennan, president of National Association of Letter Carriers Branch 3 in Buffalo, observed: "We don't get much publicity for this, but virtually every week there is a carrier to help some kid in trouble, or an elderly person who falls down and needs help." Letter carriers' familiarity with their routes and patrons allows them to recognize when something is amiss. In Berkeley Heights, New Jersey, Principelina "Princess" Mendes saw a wide-open front door at the home of an elderly man on her route and suspected something was wrong. After calling out and receiving no response, Mendes dialed 911. Emergency responders arrived and aided the unconscious resident. "Our family does not have the words to express our deep appreciation for her," a relative stated.[4]

Joshua H. Hefta had started hand delivering the mail to a ninety-four-year-old woman on his rural route in Walsh County, North Dakota, since she was having difficulty collecting the mail from her box. But one cold day in January, she failed to answer the door. The woman had fallen hours earlier. Knowing the mail arrived around 12:45 p.m., she gathered her strength to call out for help. Hefta broke down the door and summoned medical aid. "He saved my life," she said. Justin Hull was delivering mail at the right place at the right time in Canandaigua, New York, to notice a man who was passed out on his porch. He called 911, and first responders rushed the man to the hospital. "My uncle is very grateful," a relative stated. "Justin literally saved his life." Rural carrier Amanda Nalley noticed that a patron on her Forsyth County, Georgia, route was not collecting his mail. The deputies who responded to her 911 call found the eighty-four-year-old man passed out on his bedroom floor. "They said if he had been there another hour," she reported, "he would have passed away."[5]

Postal workers never know what situations they will encounter while making their daily rounds. City carrier German Osorio happened upon a disturbing message attached to a mailbox on his route in Corpus Christi, Texas. He immediately called his supervisor Corisa Ruiz to report the suicide note. Ruiz contacted emergency responders who found the patron unresponsive following an attempt to take his own life. "He was unconscious, but they saved his life," Osorio reported. In Moundsville, West Virginia, Randy Caldwell heard yelling while delivering mail. Caldwell discovered a mobile home that had slipped from a jack, pinning a man underneath. He notified the police and made sure they brought equipment to lift the trailer off the man, who later recovered in the local hospital.[6]

Letter carriers often encounter situations that cannot wait for emergency responders. Fortunately for residents of West Bloomfield Township, Michigan, letter carrier Brandon Franklin did not hesitate when he saw a Jeep careening toward a school zone with a woman slumped over the steering wheel. Franklin sprinted after the runaway Jeep, dived headfirst through the open driver's side window, and steered the vehicle to safety. When Joseph Moskal "heard the most blood-curdling scream you could ever imagine," he rushed to restrain a man with mental health issues randomly attacking a girl along his route on Buffalo's West Side. While delivering mail in Norwalk, California, Fernando Garcia heard a call for help. He found a man on the ground who accidentally had wounded his arm with a chainsaw. Garcia used his belt as a tourniquet until paramedics arrived.[7]

When a pit bull attacked a woman walking her dog in Syracuse's Tipperary Hill neighborhood, Richard W. Blasland Jr. had just started his delivery route. Blasland tried kicking the pit bull, then emptied an entire can of mace on it, but the vicious dog remained a threat. So Blasland guided the woman and her dog to a nearby enclosed porch, barricaded it with lawn furniture, and called 911. "I just did what anyone else would do," he said. Joseph J. Clark was completing his rural route in Pittston Township, Pennsylvania, when he learned a venomous copperhead snake had just bitten one of his patrons. The 911 dispatcher recommended sucking the venom out of the wound. "I did what I had to do," Clark affirmed. The patron made a full recovery.[8]

Letter carriers will double as firefighters, discovering flames that threaten property damage, injury, or even death. While delivering mail on her Akron, Ohio, route, Kizzy Spaulding smelled smoke coming from a house, so she looked through a window and saw that the resident was unconscious. Spaulding entered the home, identified that the stove was on fire, doused the flames with water, and remained with the woman until medical help arrived. Daniel P. Maguire smelled smoke on his Revere, Massachusetts, route and decided to investigate. Upon locating a fire spreading to a building from a bed of mulch he started yelling and banging on the door, which alerted three teenagers on the second floor to evacuate. "You saved my life, man," said one, "so glad you stopped!" When Matthew Lamb is on his Johnstown, Pennsylvania, route, he will help carry groceries, change a tire, or move a refrigerator. But on one extraordinary day, Lamb guided an elderly resident to safety after seeing flames rising from her house. Then he doubled back for the woman's grandson, who was trapped on the second floor. By this point, the fire had grown so intense that it was impossible to enter the house. "I told him to jump out of the window and I'd catch him," Lamb said. "He had to just let himself fall, and I was able to catch him." Once the fire department arrived, Lamb continued the rest of his route.[9]

Letter carriers making their rounds create safer communities even when there is no emergency. The celebrated urban theorist Jane Jacobs pointed out that "eyes belonging to those we might call the natural proprietors of the street" make communities safer. Letter carriers are such persons, and they also strengthen community bonds. Ric Zassenhaus was a "living legend" on the route where he delivered mail for over thirty years in Olympia, Washington. "He really cares about the people on his route," resident Carolyn von Gohren said. "You can really tell people thought of him as not just a mailman, but a friend," stressed Carl See, president of the local neighborhood association. When Hank Martin retired from walking his ten-mile route in Lebanon, Pennsylvania, Richard Wertz, owner of a downtown candy shop, called him "a ray of sunshine." Wertz added, "We're going to miss him." Senator Shelley Moore Capito (R-W.Va.) acknowledged: "I know at certain times in my life I felt like if I did not see my friendly mailman or mailwoman at my door, I felt like I did not have a friend in the world."[10]

Postal workers historically have demonstrated great dedication to government service. In recent decades, less than 2 percent of career employees have resigned from the Postal Service each year. It is in our national interest for postal employees to have a high degree of dedication to their jobs, because they are entrusted with the U.S. Mail. Americans expect that the postal system will operate securely and efficiently. Replacing fairly compensated postal employees with low-wage workers would degrade service. During 2001's anthrax scare, Senator Barbara Mikulski (D-Md.) stated: "I really want to compliment the nation's postal workers for staying on the job [and] for their steadfastness, their loyalty, their bravery, and really their patriotism."[11]

More recently, despite the risk of COVID-19 exposure, postal employees remained on the job, providing a lifeline during a period when millions of people in the United States sheltered at home. In the early stages of the pandemic, Courtney Jenkins, a Baltimore postal clerk, acknowledged: "I and many of my co-workers are terrified to go to work; with mail coming from all over the world, we have a heightened potential to be exposed to the virus." Despite justified fear of contracting the disease, postal workers kept the U.S. Mail moving. The nation depended on the postal system for the delivery of prescription drugs, social security and pension checks, and numerous important items that were not readily available. Package delivery boomed as more of the population avoided exposing themselves to the virus in stores by shopping online. Many people found solace in still-open post offices and the familiar rhythms of mail delivery. "We are the 'normal' that the American people look forward to," observed letter carrier Samuel H. Farley of Elyria, Ohio. "Among my anchors are family, friends, faith, home, and historic American institutions, like the United States Postal Service," stated Jack McDonald of Nashua, New Hampshire. "I am thankful for their work and the bit of trusted stability they add to my life. . . . We are blessed by their service and we are reassured by their daily presence."[12]

THE POSTAL WORKPLACE

Since the early 1970s, wage growth has stagnated even as productivity has risen. At the same time, employer-sponsored health care and retirement plans often are either inadequate or nonexistent.

Despite a labor market that offers fewer pathways to economic security, career employees at the Postal Service continue to earn enough to maintain a middle-class living standard. In 2019, the median annual earnings of postal workers was $52,060. Postal workers receive the level of benefits that American employers traditionally offered their employees in the decades following World War II. They participate in a defined benefit pension plan and are covered by the Federal Employees Health Benefits Program, which allows federal employees to choose from a wide selection of health plans.[13]

Low wages and inadequate benefits produce high employee turnover, while employers that offer fair treatment attract better-qualified and more-dedicated workers. Most career postal workers make a thirty-year commitment to the agency. Billions of pieces of mail containing financial and health records, identification numbers and passwords, checks and bills, and a host of other items that need to remain secure and confidential, pass through the postal system each year. Meanwhile, the number of packages containing valuable articles is increasing all the time. There is a well-founded confidence that these items will not be tampered with and will reach their destination.[14]

Postal jobs are particularly important in rural areas and especially consequential for veterans. Nancy Pope, former chief curator of the National Postal Museum, stated that in small towns serving as postmaster has ranked right next to being the mayor. "It was the job to have," she attested. The Institute for Policy Studies reports that in rural states the Postal Service is "a critical source of decent jobs." Ronnie W. Stutts, president of the National Rural Letter Carriers' Association, stresses that "in smaller communities postal jobs are really good jobs," especially in today's economic environment. Moreover, he points out, "You don't need a college education" to work for the Postal Service.[15]

The basic framework of veterans' preference was established during World War II. "I believe that the Federal Government, functioning in its capacity as an employer," President Franklin D. Roosevelt stated, "should take the lead in assuring those who are in the armed services that when they return special consideration will be given to them in their efforts to obtain employment." Veterans receive preference points on their passing postal exam score. The American Legion affirms the importance of this benefit, declaring "all lawmakers . . . are urged to oppose any and all efforts to repeal or circumvent veterans' preference in government hiring practices." In 2020, the almost 100,000 veterans working at the Postal Service accounted for around one in six employees, significantly higher than the approximately 6 percent representation of veterans throughout the civilian labor force.[16]

Postal employment has notable social and economic importance within black communities. Black workers first secured postal jobs following the Civil War. Due to discrimination, postal employment opportunities were relatively better than those that private employers typically offered. By the 1920s, there were sizable numbers of black employees in a number of large northern post offices, including Chicago, Detroit, and New York City. Historian Philip F. Rubio emphasized that these postal jobs served "as launching pads for social mobility." Black postal workers played a notable part in the post–World War II southern civil rights movement, because they were economically independent of local employers who supported Jim Crow. Black employees celebrate this tradition of government service. "I am a proud postal worker," said Rachel Walthall, a national business agent of the American Postal Workers Union. "I take what we do as postal workers very seriously. We take the oath to protect the sanctity of the mail."[17]

Advocates of dismantling the Postal Service through privatization and deregulation want a postal system that possesses a signal "efficiency": low-wage workers. "Postal workers are under the gun," stated Wilbur L. Duncan, president of the National Alliance of Postal and Federal Employees. "There are those who wish to limit, even erase, any or all of the benefits that postal employees now enjoy." The belief that postal workers should not earn an income that allows for a middle-class living standard has long prevailed at the Cato Institute. In 1988, James P. Bovard complained that postal workers were "overpaid" and "underworked." Moreover, he characterized the Postal Service as a source of "lifetime overpaid jobs." At the American Enterprise Institute, R. Richard Geddes has grumbled about a "postal wage premium." David Ditch of the Heritage Foundation recently objected to what he alleged were "extraordinarily generous retirement benefits." In 2016, Chris R. Edwards of the Cato Institute criticized the Postal Service for employing "a costly union-dominated workforce." He thinks it would be best to "remove collective bargaining from the USPS altogether."[18]

The economic security that postal workers receive in return for their labor is a product of their unions. Around 90 percent of all postal employees are members of either the American Postal Workers Union (APWU), National Association of Letter Carriers (NALC), National Rural Letter Carriers' Association, or National Postal Mail Handlers Union. These unions all began as associations that could lobby Congress and the Post Office Department but had no collective bargaining rights. In 1889, letter carriers attending a convention in Milwaukee formed the NALC, the first enduring postal union, which had been preceded five years earlier by the first national organization of postal clerks. Like other employers during this time period, postal management opposed unionization. The initial focus of postal unions was reducing the long hours of work that were standard practice at the department, with letter carriers laboring through ten-to-twelve-hour shifts six, and even seven, days a week. Shortly after the NALC's establishment, the union achieved a major victory in 1893 when its efforts won letter carriers the eight-hour day.[19]

This reduced workday did not apply to postal clerks, however, for whom twelve hours was standard, and sixteen hours was a common shift during the busy period before Christmas.

Clerks processing mail were surrounded by constant noise from conveyor belts and unhealthy clouds of paper dust. Amid filthy post office work spaces, tuberculosis was an occupational disease: among postal workers it was called "clerk's sickness." Railway postal clerks risked serious injury and even death while sorting mail aboard rickety wooden cars. Railroad corporations insisted on placing mail cars directly behind the locomotive—to better buffer passengers from ash and smoke—sandwiching these frail carriages between steel cars and the locomotive itself. The significant damage inflicted on mail cars in wrecks left 5 percent of all railway mail clerks working between 1905 and 1910 either dead or seriously injured.[20]

The growing assertiveness of postal workers led the federal government to issue a series of "gag" orders starting in 1902 that forbade employees from making efforts to improve pay and working conditions, "on penalty of dismissal." During this same decade, a new group of workers organized a union when Rural Free Delivery was made a permanent service. Following its establishment in 1903, the National Rural Letter Carriers' Association grew rapidly. Rural carriers made less money than their city counterparts but shouldered significant job-related equipment expenses, including blacksmith, veterinary, and feed bills for their horses. Black workers formed the National Alliance of Postal Employees in 1913 to combat workplace discrimination. At the time, Postmaster General Albert S. Burleson—a southern segregationist—was implementing a policy of Jim Crow in the department. In his book *There's Always Work at the Post Office*, Philip F. Rubio documented the union's ensuing achievements, stating that "the National Alliance advanced both civil rights and labor struggles."[21]

The gag orders ultimately failed to bridle postal workers. In January 1912, Oscar F. Nelson, president of the National Federation of Post Office Clerks, defied the gag rule by testifying before a congressional committee. Senator Robert M. La Follette Sr. (R-Wisc.)

attacked the gag orders and managed to rescind the oppressive policy that summer. Postal workers now had the right to organize labor unions and lobby Congress. Additional legislative victories included the stipulation that standard shifts would be eight hours of work, which could not be spread out over more than ten hours. Further achievements included a transition to safer steel railway mail cars and the establishment of Sunday as a holiday. Meanwhile, rural letter carriers won a series of pay increases that raised their salaries to the same level as city carriers.[22]

Although postal workers made gains during the early twentieth century, their lives remained financially precarious. In 1920, the *Tucson Citizen* editorialized that "Uncle Sam ought to pay his letter carriers a living wage." Still, laws enacted at the time created the first pensions for retired postal workers and finally provided employees with sick leave. Rural letter carriers started receiving allowances in 1925 to compensate for the expense of maintaining the automobiles, horses, and wagons they used for mail delivery. In 1931, postal workers won the forty-four-hour week when a half day of work on Saturday became standard. Over the next few years, the widespread unemployment of the Great Depression popularized the idea that reducing the hours of labor provided a means to create additional jobs. In 1935, President Franklin D. Roosevelt approved a bill that established the forty-hour week for postal workers. The Depression made the stability of postal employment surprisingly attractive during the 1930s, and President Harry S. Truman approved a string of pay increases in the 1940s. But the 1953 appointment of Postmaster General Arthur E. Summerfield—a Michigan automobile dealer and GOP operative—caused postal workers to lose ground. Due to his concern over postal deficits, upon taking office Summerfield instructed postal workers that "we must all tighten our belts" and proceeded to adopt a low-wage policy.[23]

Operating under tight budgetary constraints, by the 1960s the Post Office Department was clearly a substandard employer. In order to make ends meet, many employees worked second jobs. As many as 10 percent of full-time postal workers in New York City received welfare benefits. Federal employees are barred from striking, but on March 18, 1970, the city's letter carriers stopped delivering mail and other postal workers honored their picket line. The wildcat strike soon spread to Buffalo, Chicago, Cleveland, Denver, Detroit, Los Angeles, Minneapolis, and San Francisco. With more than 200,000 postal workers on strike, the movement of mail was disrupted nationwide. The strike's impact on commerce was immediate, since checks worth vast sums of money were frozen in transit. "It obviously cannot go on long," insisted Gabriel Hauge, president of Manufacturers Hanover Trust Company. Within days, President Richard M. Nixon acknowledged that "hundreds of thousands of fine Americans in the mail service . . . are underpaid and they have other legitimate grievances." When the administration agreed to negotiate, the striking workers began resuming their duties. Postal workers soon received a retroactive pay increase. In addition, the Postal Reorganization Act of 1970 awarded postal workers collective bargaining rights.[24]

Collective bargaining has provided career postal workers with financial security. But the gains postal workers won over decades of struggle have eroded in recent years as the Postal Service employs increasing numbers of "non-career" employees. In 1990, Bert Ely of the Cato Institute proposed that "part-time employees should be used to a much greater extent." At the time, Postmaster General Anthony M. Frank characterized attacks on the existing postal employment model as code for "union busting." But reducing the share of career employees is a goal that postal management has embraced in recent years. Following the 2008 financial crisis, the Postal Service established new categories of non-career employees. Workers in these classifications receive lower wages and reduced benefits and privileges. Gale R. Thames of the National Alliance of Postal and Federal Employees states that worsening conditions of employment—including long hours and unreasonable workloads—are driving away new hires. "Understaffing has really caused problems," Ronnie W. Stutts reports. "We're shorthanded on part-time people so they work them to death. It's a revolving door with the part-time workers."[25]

In 2016, 42.7 percent of non-career employees left the agency—including almost 60 percent of those delivering mail on city routes. Despite such high turnover, the number of non-career employees had risen to 182,000 by 2021 as compared to 493,500 career employees. "This model has undermined the stability of the workforce," observes Mark Dimondstein, president of the APWU, with negative operational and service consequences, because "workers don't learn the postal system overnight." Moreover, although changing mail usage and streamlined operations have altered labor needs since 2000, expanded numbers of non-career employees have not compensated for the 38 percent decrease in career employees over the past two decades. Postal workers have been stretched to their limits in recent years, and existing plans for more than 10,000 new career hires are not sufficient to remedy understaffing at the agency.[26]

As management slashes the workforce in an effort to reduce labor costs, working conditions have deteriorated. "This job isn't what it used to be," remarked Kurt M. Eckrem, president of the Washington Rural Letter Carriers' Association. The Postal Service's focus on "squeezing every possible penny," Eckrem stated, entails "violating its contractual obligations and mistreating its employees." In 2014, Lawrence Kania, president of NALC Branch 3 in Buffalo, attested that "life in the Postal Service has dramatically changed. Everyone is micro-managed. Some 'number' has become more important than the individual." Inadequate staffing has exacted a toll on postal workers. Kania emphasized that "years of forced overtime and 60-hour work weeks negatively impacted many of our members' lives." His predecessor, Robert J. McLennan, objected that management would "insult carriers by telling them it doesn't take any extra time to deliver the mail when

walking on ice and snow. They wonder about the street productivity when carriers are out there fumbling around in the dark." In
2019, Paul McKenna, president of APWU Local 3 in Milwaukee,
reported that due to inadequate staffing "our members work
longer hours and do more work with less employees." As a result,
he observed, "stress is worse today in most offices than it has ever
been in my career."[27]

The Postal Service also has outsourced mail sorting and processing to private employers that rely on low-wage labor. Following
the establishment of bulk mailing discounts under Postmaster
General Benjamin F. Bailar in 1976, pre-sort bureaus specializing
in processing mail for clients grew and prospered. "We must
recognize the principle," Bailar insisted, "that those who relieve
the Postal Service of some of its costs should be compensated
accordingly." Pre-sort bureaus profit from charging a small fee
for attaching bar-codes to letters and bundling the mail based on
its destination before presenting it to the Postal Service. "To be
diplomatic," *Forbes* once noted, the industry and postal management "don't call it privatization. They call it 'work sharing.'" The
initial discount for pre-sorted first-class mail was 1¢ per item. In
1977, the Carter administration recommended a special reduced
postage rate for personal letters. But large mailers successfully
opposed this "citizens' rate" discount. Currently, residential mail
users receive no discount even when they mail automation-ready
return envelopes. Meanwhile, discounts for bulk mail have
increased over time.[28]

The pre-sort bureaus have made handsome profits thanks to
the core of the industry's business model: a low-wage workforce.
At one time, these employees were largely students and retirees.
More recently, growing numbers of immigrant workers ranging
from Russians and Poles in Massachusetts to Mexicans in Colorado have staffed many of these low-wage jobs. Industrial relations
expert Sarah F. Ryan reported that "the evidence is overwhelming
that wages [at pre-sort bureaus] are very low, and the industry

boasts that it pays far below wages paid to USPS workers for virtually identical work." These operations have fought to maintain the low-wage model by opposing their employees' attempts to unionize. Although the Postal Service's own career employees earn fair wages, through offering deep pre-sort discounts the agency created a low-wage industry.[29]

Controversy has arisen around discounts awarded to bulk mailers that exceed the cost savings of pre-sorting to the Postal Service. When discounts are larger than the agency's avoided costs, other postal users have to absorb the shortfall. In 2003, Michael J. Riley, former chief financial officer of the Postal Service, reported that excessive discounts had negatively impacted the agency's financial situation. Moreover, since 1976 the Postal Service has invested billions of dollars in automation. Yet the Postal Service still hands out bulk discounts, even though its own infrastructure could be doing this work instead. Morris A. "Moe" Biller, former president of the APWU, once observed that pre-sorting was just "creating jobs . . . in the private sector that the Postal Service used to do itself."[30]

RISING INEQUALITY

Although postal employment standards are under pressure, the middle-class compensation that career postal workers receive runs counter to the low-wage employment model that fuels rising economic inequality. Comparing the nation's largest civilian employer—Walmart Inc.—with the Postal Service reveals two substantially different models and illustrates the importance of equitable employment standards. Walmart adheres to a set of policies that oppose postal employment practices. The giant discount retailer's employment model rests on shifting the cost of its employees onto the communities where it operates and maintaining a virulently anti-union shop. And with 1.5 million employees working in more than 5,300 stores throughout the

United States, Walmart is an economic force whose influence is felt nationwide and extends internationally.[31]

Meager wages and benefits at Walmart force large numbers of its American employees to resort to government welfare programs. A 2020 Government Accountability Office study revealed that thousands of workers at the giant corporation rely on Medicaid to obtain health care and the Supplemental Nutrition Assistance Program to pay for food. Representative Martin Olav Sabo (DFL-Minn.) expressed a widely held belief when he stated that "full-time working Americans should make enough money to get by without government assistance." In 2014, Americans for Tax Fairness estimated that public assistance payments to Walmart's workers amounted to a corporate subsidy totaling over $6.2 billion per year.[32]

Walmart's absolute opposition to unions has prevented its employees from gaining the necessary bargaining power to improve their working conditions and terms of employment. In a leaked memorandum sent to managers at a distribution center the corporation laid out its anti-union philosophy in no uncertain terms: "Wal-Mart is opposed to unionization of its associates. Any suggestion that the Company is neutral on the subject or that it encourages associates to join labor organizations is not true." This document went on to state, "Staying union free is a full-time commitment" that "must exist at all levels of management." Walmart corporate headquarters has dispatched union-busting experts around the country to intimidate employees whenever and wherever there is any hint of union activity. A few organizing drives have succeeded despite this intense anti-union offensive, prompting Walmart management to take extreme measures. In 2000, butchers at its Jacksonville, Texas, store voted to unionize, so their department was eliminated and the chain shifted to prepackaged meat in all of its stores. When an entire Walmart in Quebec organized in 2005, the corporation simply closed that store.[33]

Comparing the compensation of cashiers and stockers at Walmart with its executives presents a glaring example of a disturbing development in the way corporations conduct business. Back in 1965, the average chief executive officer received compensation that was twenty-one times higher than the typical employee's earnings. By 2019, this ratio had ballooned to the point that average CEO compensation was 320 times what the typical worker earned. The total annual compensation of Walmart's CEO, C. Douglas McMillon, was $22.1 million, and the compensation a number of other executives received also reached eight figures. While such enormous differentials in pay play a notable role in driving economic inequality to today's historic heights, the compensation top postal officials receive is more in line with the salary conventions of the 1960s. In 2018, for example, federal law generally limited Postal Service compensation to $210,700. Twenty-two executives did receive additional bonus payments, however, which topped out at $80,795 for the postmaster general.[34]

In the post–World War II era, Americans envisioned the United States to be a middle-class society. "The America I grew up in— the America of the 1950s and 1960s—was a middle-class society, both in reality and in feel," economist Paul R. Krugman recalled. Historian Lizabeth Cohen documented that during this period millions of Americans benefited materially from a "commitment to deliver equality and democracy through mass prosperity." Times have changed. In 2002, Krugman concluded that "the middle-class America of my youth was another country." Even as the far-reaching consequences of this transformation reshaped American society, the Postal Service has maintained fundamental features of the employment practices that forged a middle-class nation.[35]

Unequal societies experience economic problems as a consequence of the underutilization and diversion of resources from productive activities. "A burgeoning empirical literature," economist Robert H. Frank noted, "has found a negative correlation between various measures of income inequality and economic growth in cross-national data." The eminent economic historian R. H. Tawney once observed that "as long as a minority has so large an income that part of it . . . must be spent on trivialities, so long will part of the human energy and mechanical equipment of the nation be diverted from serious work, which enriches it, to making trivialities, which impoverishes it, since they can only be made at the cost of making other things." A further consequence of inequality is the destruction of democracy itself. Justice Louis D. Brandeis—a prominent witness to inequality in the first Gilded Age—famously stated: "We may have democracy, or we may have wealth concentrated in the hands of a few, but we can't have both." It is in our national interest to promote equality, and the employment model the Postal Service has fashioned in partnership with its workers' unions upholds this principle.[36]

EIGHT

GOVERNANCE

Americans had high expectations of the old Post Office Department. Historian Wayne E. Fuller recounted how generations of Americans made "demands for postal routes, post offices, cheaper postage, and quicker service." The postal network grew in response to citizen advocacy, spreading across a continent, reaching across oceans to foreign shores, and expanding in entirely new directions to fulfill unmet needs. "No branch of government would be so intimately associated with the demands of the people as the Post Office Department," Fuller observed, "and none would be so twisted and shaped by the petitions and promptings of the people. In a way, the people themselves built the postal system." This direct relationship between citizen and government came to an end in 1971 when the U.S. Postal Service was born. Modeled on a business corporation, the new postal structure was designed to check the responsiveness to citizens that made the postal system such a remarkable institution in the first place.[2]

REORGANIZATION

The Postal Reorganization Act of 1970 empowered postal executives at the expense of elected officials and the American public. Although millions of residential postal patrons collectively own the Postal Service, they lack adequate representation when important decisions are made about this essential government service. The drive for postal reorganization began after October 1966, when mail processing at the main post office in Chicago—a massive thirteen-story structure containing sixty acres of work

141

space—came to a standstill. A department task force found that the breakdown in Chicago "resulted from an unexpectedly sharp increase in mail volume, abnormal employee absenteeism, hiring limitation in a tight labor market, and repairs that made unavailable one of the building's big loading docks. In addition, a new postmaster had taken over at the same time that high volumes were testing the facility's limits."[2]

Yet the logjam of mail in Chicago reflected broader physical infrastructure and mail distribution challenges. The Railway Mail Service that sorted mail en route was vital to the postal system, but use of trains had declined alongside falling passenger traffic after World War II, which shifted additional processing into overburdened central post offices in large cities. The rapid growth of suburbs following the war only compounded the Post Office's mail transportation and processing difficulties. The crisis in Chicago was the justification given for the formation of a presidential commission in 1967—largely composed of corporate executives—that was assigned the task of reforming the Post Office Department.[3]

Although new challenges in collecting, transporting, sorting, and delivering the mail were bound to pose problems and create a need for adjustments, the commission determined that the Post Office Department suffered from systemic problems due to its structure, and recommended that the institution be transformed into a self-funded government corporation—the U.S. Postal Service. "The possibility remains of private ownership at some future time," the commission's report added. Postmaster General Winton M. Blount Jr.—a wealthy Alabama businessman—strongly supported the idea of transforming his department into a "businesslike" operation, and joined forces with corporate interests—including large mailers—in the push for reorganization. Such corporations as Bank of America, General Foods Corp., McGraw-Hill Inc., Montgomery Ward & Co., Pitney-Bowes Inc., Sears, Roebuck and Co., Standard Oil Company of New Jersey, and Time Inc., formed a lobbying organization called the

Citizens Committee for Postal Reform to promote creation of a government corporation. The National Rural Letter Carriers' Association observed this development with apprehension and advised postal workers to brace themselves for "stormy weather."[4]

Critics of reorganization thought the best course of action was to address the particular logistical problems the Chicago episode exposed instead of altering the Post Office's entire organizational structure. J. Edward Day, postmaster general during the Kennedy administration, stated that using the problems the Chicago situation revealed to condemn the entire postal system was "just as unfair as it would be to take the isolated case of the Consolidated Edison power blackout in New York a few years ago and to conclude from that that the entire privately operated electric utility system in the country was poorly managed and on the verge of catastrophe." Pro-corporate ideologues have long claimed misleadingly that only the profit motive can stimulate organizations to operate efficiently. Yet as economist Frederick C. Thayer pointed out: "the ability of a private corporation to make a profit tells us nothing of its efficiency, but demonstrates only that it can set prices high enough to cover any and all inefficiencies." In 1993, Nobel Prize–winning economist Joseph E. Stiglitz observed that "knocking the post office is part of a deep-rooted suspicion about the inefficiencies of government." But Stiglitz stressed that "the post office has become an American leader in productivity gains. Clearly, if led and managed appropriately, a government agency is no barrier to dramatic gains in productivity." Importantly, efficient operation of the postal system means efficiency within the bounds of providing an essential government service, not a circumscribed view of efficiency that adopts narrow commercial model parameters that are inapplicable to the agency.[5]

Polling in 1967 found that the public was satisfied with the Post Office: a vast majority of Americans—95 percent—were either "completely satisfied with postal service" (76 percent) or "fairly well satisfied" (19 percent). "Reform is not spelled c-o-r-p-o-r-a-t-i-o-n," objected Senator Ralph W. Yarborough (D-Tex.). He argued that this proposed transformation "substitutes a corporation bookkeeping profit-oriented system for the public service concept installed by Benjamin Franklin." The concept behind reorganization was in the tradition of President Calvin Coolidge, an advocate of "trickle-down" economics who maintained "the taxpayers are the stockholders of the business corporation of the United States" and pushed for a self-funded postal system.[6]

Postal workers initially opposed reorganization, but agreed to the plan once it was tied to a much needed wage increase. At the same time that the Post Office's troubles had been mounting, members of Congress were losing interest in the institution. The numerous improvements to the postal system over the course of the nineteenth and early twentieth centuries meant there were no longer large numbers of constituents petitioning Congress about extending the service, and civil service reforms meant that postal employment was no longer the important political tool of the past. "It appears that many of the members did not entirely know what they were doing," explained Gerald Cullinan, a retired assistant postmaster general. "They were in favor of reform . . . but some never bothered to learn what was really involved in the bill for which they voted." On August 12, 1970, President Richard M. Nixon signed the Postal Reorganization Act into law. "No longer was the Post Office to be the people's homespun Post Office, to be used as an instrument of government policy for whatever purposes Americans desired," Wayne E. Fuller concluded. "And no longer was the basic postal policy to be service first and a balanced postal budget afterward."[7]

POSTAL GOVERNANCE

Reorganization proponents placed great emphasis on their claim that this reform would make the postal system apolitical. While reorganization notably ended patronage in the form of postmaster appointments, a congressional subcommittee's investigation into the first bonds the new Postal Service issued found that investment bank Dillon, Read & Co. received a portion of the business due to connections inside the Nixon administration. Partisan allegiance is an explicit factor when selecting members of the Postal Regulatory Commission (PRC)—no more than three members may be affiliated with the same political party—and the typical professional experience among commissioners has been a career in politics. Instead of occurring openly in Congress, political debates over postal rates and services now take place within an obscure framework of rate cases and administrative hearings. In 1970, Representative H. R. Gross (R-Iowa) warned that reorganization would not remove politics from postal management. "For the first time ever," he predicted, "we will have a bureaucratic head of a major Government service, appointed by and serving at the pleasure of a politically-oriented parttime commission." As with the PRC, selections for the Board of Governors, too, are explicitly political: partisan allegiance is a specific criterion when nominating governors, since no more than five can belong to a single political party.[8]

Postal expert Douglas F. Carlson observes that too often members of the Board of Governors "have not had a postal background or expertise or interest about postal issues." Governors generally have backgrounds as partisan functionaries and business executives. Notably, representatives with ties to consumer and labor groups have been scarce over the past fifty years. An examination of the individuals who served as chair of the board during the previous fifteen years illustrates this pattern. Former New York City public advocate Mark J. Green once called James C. Miller III "a pro-corporate cheerleader." An early champion of postal privatization who had described the agency as a "monstrosity," Miller became chairman of the Board of Governors in 2005. The nomination to serve on the Board of Governors came as a shock to Miller. "When I got the call from the White House I said, 'Do you know who you're talking to?'" Previously, Miller had served as chairman of the Federal Trade Commission and director of the Office of Management and Budget under President Ronald Reagan, and held a series of positions at such pro-corporate think tanks as the Hoover Institution, American Enterprise Institute, Citizens for a Sound Economy, and Center for Study of Public Choice at George Mason University. In 2008, Democrat Alan C. Kessler took over for Miller, a Republican. Kessler was a corporate lawyer at Wolf, Block, Schorr & Solis-Cohen in Philadelphia and a Democratic Party donor, fundraiser, and presidential convention delegate. He also served as finance vice chair of the Democratic National Committee and was a member of the Clinton-Gore transition team, as well as national vice chair for Gore 2000.[9]

The chair returned to a Republican in 2009, when Carolyn Lewis Gallagher of Austin, Texas, succeeded Kessler. Gallagher owned a furniture manufacturing company, and was a director of the Austin Chamber of Commerce, a Republican Party donor, and a serial George W. Bush appointee, including to the 2003 postal commission. The next chair came to the Postal Service after a lengthy career at ITT Industries Inc. that culminated in the positions of chairman and chief executive officer. Louis J. Giuliano subsequently became a senior advisor to the Carlyle Group, an investment bank. Giuliano was a member of the Business Roundtable and a Republican Party donor. In 2011, a Democrat again occupied the position when Thurgood Marshall Jr. became chair. Marshall was a corporate lawyer at Bingham McCutchen in Washington, D.C. A Democratic Party donor, he worked for the 1992 Clinton-Gore campaign and subsequently held a series of positions in the Clinton administration. Marshall also served on the board of the Corrections Corporation of America—the largest owner and operator of private prisons in the nation—and as a board member and trustee for the pro-corporate Democratic Party think tank Third Way.[10]

In 2012, a seasoned political operative became chair. Mickey D.

Barnett was a corporate lawyer and Republican Party fundraiser, donor, and presidential convention delegate. Formerly, Barnett had been a staff member at the Heritage Foundation, a New Mexico state senator, a national committeeman for the Republican Party of New Mexico, and chairman of the Republican Party of Bernalillo County, New Mexico. He was known in Washington, D.C., as host of a weekly luncheon meeting for Grover G. Norquist's Americans for Tax Reform. Barnett demanded a recount in New Mexico after the 2000 presidential election on behalf of GOP officials. He had lobbied in support of electric and telephone deregulation, gambling interests, the payday loan industry, and the Corrections Corporation of America. In 1977, Barnett organized New Mexico Citizens for Right to Work, and in 1999 he intervened on behalf of the National Right to Work Foundation in a casino unionization case.[11]

The position returned to a Democrat when James H. Bilbray became acting chairman. He was a corporate lawyer at Kaempfer Crowell in Las Vegas, Nevada, and a former Democratic member of the U.S. House of Representatives and Nevada state senate. In 2018, Robert M. Duncan Sr.—the chairman and chief executive officer of Inez Deposit Bank—took over as chair. Over a long career in Republican Party politics both in Kentucky and nationally, Duncan served as treasurer, general counsel, chairman, and chief executive officer of the Republican National Committee. Lastly, Ron A. Bloom was named chairman in 2021 just weeks after the Biden administration took office. A Democratic Party donor and Obama administration official, Bloom has a professional background in both finance and organized labor. His past union employment is a notable departure from the norm for governors.[12]

Reorganization did not establish governance in the public interest free from the influence of political commitments and ideologies that benefit particular special interests. Mark Dimondstein, president of the American Postal Workers Union (APWU), affirms that current governors "look at things through the prism of the business world because they have a business mentality not a service mentality." Not only do the members of the Board of Governors have their own biases and beliefs, their very selection arises from political considerations. The creation of a government corporation has made the postal system less accountable to the public, because its workings are further removed from citizen inquiry, scrutiny, and debate. Following reorganization, postal management operated more autonomously from Congress. Political scientist John T. Tierney stated that turning the Post Office Department into the Postal Service was "essentially an attempt to secure managerial autonomy." (Senator Yarborough pointed out that reorganization also awarded postal executives higher compensation.) Reforms ostensibly designed to make governance less political commonly involve taking power from elected representatives and placing it in the hands of unelected officials who are no less political than their predecessors, but less accountable and more responsive to small constituencies that are powerful and well-organized. Following reorganization, corporate interests increased their influence over postal policies.[13]

The current arrangement of providing an essential service in a "businesslike" manner presents postal officials with the conundrum of balancing two competing objectives. Management has the contradictory task of operating a public service on a break-even basis. Legal scholar Risa L. Lieberwitz has noted instructively that a "spectrum" of organizations exists. "Institutions at the public pole are democratic structures that provide goods and services in the public interest," she stated. "For-profit institutions function through unilateral managerial decision-making to promote their profit-making goals." The nature of government corporations poses fundamental problems. Ronald C. Moe of the Congressional Research Service explained that "the mission[s] of governmental agencies and private corporations are inherently different and often in conflict. The purpose of a government agency and its management is to implement the laws and policies set by

Congress. These laws and policies may or may not include values determined principally by the marketplace."[14]

Providing an essential service differs from running a business. There is a different calculus involved, different values. Private corporations exist to generate profits. But making money is not the purpose of government service. "The activity of accumulation, which is the guiding principle in business," the noted educator Liberty Hyde Bailey affirmed, "is not the motive of public service." The agency's current organizational structure has tended to subordinate its public service mission, because the backgrounds of members of the unelected Board of Governors have not disposed them to represent the interests of residential patrons, especially when the concerns of average citizens conflict with the competing priorities of "businesslike" practices and corporate interest groups. Robert M. Levi of the National Association of Postal Supervisors wants more consideration given to "the skill set we want on the Board of Governors." "Governors with no experience in public service won't have a public service outlook," he explains. "The skill sets of the governors create the outlook that guides the direction of the Postal Service." The agency's public service mandate requires a governing body with public service backgrounds.[15]

GOVERNANCE REFORM

During its 179 years of existence, the Post Office Department was under the control of Congress. Members of Congress determined postal salaries, set postage rates, and allocated appropriations to fund the department. But congressional interest in postal affairs waned in the mid-twentieth century as the federal government shouldered more responsibilities and the postal system's period of rapid expansion came to a close. Responsibility for the Post Office also forced members to contend with troublesome budgetary and labor issues. Postal expert Kathleen Conkey surmised that immediately prior to reorganization, Congress had been particularly "eager to rid itself of the responsibility of postal employees." This reform significantly reduced congressional involvement with the postal system. Although Congress maintained the authority to oversee postal operations, the attention legislators devoted to the agency diminished further over the following years. In 1977, the Senate simply eliminated the Post Office and Civil Service Committee. Representative James M. Hanley (D-N.Y.) bemoaned "an abdication of responsibility on the part of the Senate." "The idea has been to float this institution off into the sea," he said. "Why? It's one less thing to worry about."[16]

By the mid-1970s, reorganization's negative consequences were prompting rising criticism of the new structure of postal governance. "We recommend," the National Farmers Union resolved in 1977, "that mail service . . . be restored to the status which prevailed before the abolition of the U.S. Post Office as a federal Cabinet department." The AFL-CIO wanted to dissolve the Postal Rate Commission and instead have "congressional review of rate increases and service cutbacks." Hanley had concluded the governance structure of the Postal Service was a failure because "the principle of accountability to the people . . . has been lost under the current system." He dismissed the Board of Governors as a puppet—"a sounding board and ratifier for the plans of the postmaster general"—and proposed to abolish this body and make the postmaster general a presidential appointee once again. In addition, Hanley planned to "pursue various methods to re-involve Congress in the postal rate-making process." In 1977, he introduced legislation that awarded elected officials a larger role in the Postal Service's governance, empowering Congress to veto proposed rate and service changes, eliminating the Board of Governors, allowing the president to name the postmaster general, and establishing a regular public service appropriation set at the level Congress determined necessary after reviewing postal operations. Postal unions approved of the reforms and mailers hoped the measure would hold down postage rates.[17]

Service reductions and rate increases had produced significant agreement in the House that the Postal Service functioned poorly and the institution should more closely resemble the former Post Office Department. Representative William V. Alexander Jr. (D-Ark.) was "convinced" of the need to "remove the heavily added insulation of independence that surrounds the Postal Service and make its management fully accountable to the U.S. Congress and to the people." While Hanley's bill passed overwhelmingly in the House, postal management opposed the measure and the Carter administration worried it would negatively impact the federal budget. The Senate had not acted on similar legislation introduced by Quentin N. Burdick (D-N.Dak.), George S. McGovern (D-S.Dak.), and John Melcher (D-Mont.), and Hanley's bill met with the same fate in the upper chamber. No significant effort was made to reform the structure of postal governance over the following decades. Although Roger H. Davidson of the Congressional Research Service noted its "waning appeal" to members, the House maintained a postal committee until the 1994 congressional election gave the Republican Party its first majority in forty years. The GOP immediately implemented reforms of the House committee system that included eliminating the Post Office and Civil Service Committee.[18]

Six years after reorganization, investigative journalist Morton Mintz and attorney Jerry S. Cohen concluded, "Under the old system, postal revenues went into the Treasury. Congress—535 bosses—then annually appropriated monies needed by the Post Office Department. Whatever may be said of it, the system at least had some residual *potential* for accountability," while the Postal Service's governance afforded "near-zero accountability." The Postal Service would be more responsive to the public if policy was formulated openly in Congress. "The Post Office is so much the people's business," argued Gerald Cullinan, "that it always should be immediately supervised by the people's elected representatives."[19]

The Postal Reorganization Act included a mechanism for public representation in postal governance that no longer exists: the

Postal Service Advisory Council, which top postal officials were supposed to "consult with and receive the advice of . . . regarding all aspects of postal operations." The members of the council included four representatives of the major mailers, four representatives of postal unions, and three representatives of the public, plus the postmaster general and deputy postmaster general. But the council never fulfilled its intended role. In fact, the Board of Governors failed to ever meet with the council. Because no subsequent congressional action reenacted the council, it was eliminated in 1975 under a federal law designed to reduce the number of "advisory bodies that are duplicative, inefficient, and costly." The 1977 Commission on Postal Service recommended establishing a new ten-member advisory council composed of three presidential appointees representing postal unions, three presidential appointees representing mailers, two members representing the public appointed by the Speaker of the House, and two members representing the public appointed by the president pro tempore of the Senate. Postal governors would be required to meet with this council at least four times a year. The law that created the Postal Service included an advisory council in order to provide various interests—notably residential patrons—input on governing the agency. This rationale for an advisory committee remains compelling today.[20]

Ongoing financial issues may require Congress to assume a larger role in overseeing the Postal Service. The agency's primary commitment is to be universally available. Making availability the priority instead of revenue necessitates offering economically inefficient services. The Post Office Department typically generated sufficient revenues to cover around 85 percent of its expenses. Only surging mail volume at the end of the twentieth century made using postage to fully fund the agency feasible, and when the Postal Service did generate surpluses, major mailers argued that the agency's revenues were too high and postage rates ought to be reduced. As Postmaster General John E. Potter explained, the post-reorganization mandate to break even "means there is no cushion of retained earnings to carry you through the tough times." Although the oppressive pre-funding mandate is the overriding source of recent financial strain, maintaining an adequate level of service warrants serious consideration of regular congressional appropriations. Michael J. Riley, former chief financial officer of the Postal Service, observed that "the Postal Service has been scrimping on capital spending for its entire life." This predicament negatively impacts the agency's ability to improve and extend service. "By focusing excessively on short-term cost reductions while absorbing costs that Congress continued to legislate," Riley explained, "it allowed facilities to deteriorate and the infrastructure to become outdated." The financial troubles of the past decade have made long-range planning particularly difficult.[21]

While postal operations should be efficient within the universal service framework, the Postal Service does not exist to meet financial objectives. "I have always felt that the word service in the name implies just that," Representative J. Donald Fuqua (D-Fla.) attested. "We don't look upon our fire department or our police department or other services to turn a profit. We look at them to provide a service." Using appropriations from the U.S. Treasury to support government services is standard practice. A modest postal appropriation would require Congress to assume a more active role in overseeing the agency, which would invite citizens to be more engaged in postal issues, yielding the benefit of greater public influence over postal policy. Consumer advocate Ralph Nader has pointed out that a postal subsidy would serve the public interest and be "minuscule compared with the special interest subsidies to industry and commerce in this country."[22]

The public good of passenger railroad service exists in the United States due to the National Railroad Passenger Corporation (Amtrak)—a government-owned transportation network that does not show a profit. Amtrak operates both profitable trains that run through the densely populated area between Boston and

Washington, D.C., and unprofitable long-distance routes that serve sparsely populated expanses of the West. Passenger ticket revenues fund a majority of Amtrak's expenses, but federal appropriations have ensured the operation of a nationwide rail network that extends over 21,400 miles. Of course, this same combination of user fees and federal funding is the way the Post Office Department operated. However, congressional appropriations to supplement the Postal Service's revenues should not be allowed to create a two-tiered system that separates profitable and nonprofitable services, fracturing the agency and stigmatizing services that are not self-supporting.[23]

POST OFFICE CONSUMER ACTION GROUP

Residential postal patrons lack a dedicated advocate when postal policy and legislation are before Congress. "One-person, one-vote," Senator Robert C. Byrd (D-W.Va.) pointed out, "does not apply when the great body of citizens is underrepresented in the halls of Congress compared to the well-financed, highly organized special interest groups." The undue power that corporate interests exercise over postal policies is even more pronounced in regard to the PRC and the Postal Service itself. Corporations generally dominate PRC proceedings, and developing meaningful testimony is difficult without extensive knowledge of postal operations. Likewise, the Postal Service sponsors the Mailers Technical Advisory Council that offers major mailers direct access to the agency's officials. In order to obtain their rightful representation, citizens need their own full-time advocates, economists, researchers, organizers, and lobbyists as well. A long-proposed organization called the Post Office Consumer Action Group (POCAG) is designed to give individual patrons greater influence over national and local postal policies.[24]

POCAG is based on a concept that dates back to 1974, when Ralph Nader promoted the consumer check-off as a means for empowering residential utility consumers. The check-off allows consumers to join an advocacy group by checking a box on a form indicating they want to pay membership dues to the organization. "Imagine," Nader urged, "the impact of an action group in your state challenging the utilities on rate increases which reflect padding, inefficiencies, and profligate promotional spending." Nader recognized that the check-off offered a practical, straightforward means for consumers to organize and fund their own action groups. The check-off has been widely employed because it provides an effective means for individuals to voluntarily join together for the purpose of taking collective action. There are currently numerous examples of check-off programs in practice, including the Presidential Election Campaign Fund on federal income tax returns and charitable payroll deductions such as the Combined Federal Campaign.[25]

Currently existing Citizens' Utility Boards (CUBs) provide a model for a postal consumer organization. CUBs represent energy, telecommunications, and water utility ratepayers before regulatory boards and legislatures. They are voluntarily funded by utility consumers who choose to pay dues to join the CUB. These members vote for the governing board that hires the staff who advocate on behalf of the membership. This democratic structure is designed to make CUBs accountable to their members. In 1979, the Wisconsin state legislature authorized the first CUB. By 1984, Wisconsin's CUB had saved ratepayers in the state $100 for every $1 paid in membership dues. CUBs subsequently were established on a statewide basis in Illinois and Oregon, and locally in San Diego County, California. Informational notices enclosed in mailed utility bills were the primary means that CUBs used to communicate with ratepayers. But in 1986, the Supreme Court ruled that these inserts violated the free speech rights of utility companies, impeding the formation of additional CUBs. Still, by mobilizing the collective power of consumers, CUBs have saved ratepayers billions of dollars over the past forty years.[26]

In 1975, Ralph Nader first proposed an advocacy organization for "residential and small business users of the mails." POCAG would provide a practical means for individual postal patrons to obtain representation by joining together. "It is possible," economist Albert O. Hirschman observed, "to create entirely new channels of communication for groups, such as consumers, which have had notorious difficulties in making their voices heard, in comparison to other interest groups." As an independent, nonprofit organization, a member-elected board would oversee POCAG and establish the group's policies and goals. The organization's staff would advocate on behalf of members before the PRC, Board of Governors, and Congress. POCAG also would serve as a resource that postal patrons could seek assistance from when issues arise on the local level. "POCAG would provide a needed voice for residential postal consumers," Nader has stated, "and make the Postal Service more open and responsive."[27]

The present lack of consumer participation in postal affairs was obvious when the 2003 postal commission issued sweeping recommendations designed to reduce service levels. The commission invited testimony from dozens of business representatives, while only three individuals who claimed to speak for consumers appeared as witnesses. Philip A. Tabbita of the American Postal Workers Union said this process "focused on the business side of the Postal Service with little input from associations representing consumer groups and recipients of mail." In 2005, William H. Burrus Jr., president of the APWU, raised this issue when he endorsed POCAG. "The American public needs a voice.... There is nobody to speak for the average citizen. The public needs an advocate to speak on their behalf in terms of costs and service." "Other postal stakeholders—businesses and third-class mailers and their ilk—are well organized, why not residential postal users too?" agrees Edmund Mierzwinski, senior director of federal consumer programs at U.S. Public Interest Research

Group. "Consumers deserve real representation so postal service and rates remain fair. POCAG would give consumers the power they lack and the ability to make consumer voices heard in postal decision-making."[28]

The major impediment to making POCAG a reality is reaching inexpensively in postal context the more than 300 million Americans who use the Postal Service. It is very difficult just to contact such a large, diverse, and dispersed group of people, much less organize them. Fortunately, the Postal Service is the one institution in the nation that contacts every household on a regular basis. Letter carriers should be authorized to deliver a postcard to residential addresses four times a year with information about POCAG and how to join the organization. The past experience of CUBs suggests that POCAG would attain sufficient public support to become an effective, membership-supported consumer advocate for postal patrons.[29]

However, interest in POCAG in Washington has proven to be limited. When a push for POCAG was made in the early 1980s, the Reagan administration opposed the idea. A series of postmasters general rejected POCAG as well. Postal management has not demonstrated concern about proper representation for individual mail users. The great sociologist Max Weber once noted: "Bureaucratic administration always tends to exclude the public, to hide its knowledge and action from criticism as well as it can." If established, POCAG would erect the institutional framework for a more responsive Postal Service. "I would lay it down as a basic principle of human organization," civic leader John W. Gardner stated, "that the individuals who hold the reins of power in any enterprise cannot trust themselves to be adequately self-critical."[30]

POCAG would provide residential patrons with a watchdog to guard their interests and act as an advisor to postal management—offering officials a direct connection to the citizens they serve. "All Americans need and depend on postal service," Representative Patsy Mink (D-Hawaii) once observed, "and it belongs to us—not some faceless board members in a corporation." An organization of postal patrons that communicates regularly with postal officials would allow the agency to move from a consumer affairs model based on defensively reacting to complaints to a pro-active posture that takes the initiative on consumer issues. "The Postal Service is insular . . . not skilled at knowing what the public thinks and doesn't engage with the public in a collaborative way," Douglas F. Carlson notes. "The Postal Service should openly and honestly engage with the public." The American people are the Postal Service's owners, and POCAG would be an advocacy organization with the resources and standing to give citizens a true voice in shaping the agency's priorities and policies.[31]

To government, individuals are citizens and constituents who wield the authority of the ballot box, but to business we are just another dollar of revenue dwarfed by the magnitude of so many other dollars, with no recognized claim to be heard, and liable to be denied service at any time. Operating the Postal Service in the public interest demands a more open and democratic governance structure that recognizes the inherently political nature of a large organization with numerous interested stakeholders. A Board of Governors whose members have public service backgrounds would uphold the agency's public service mission. An advisory council with consumer representatives would oblige postal officials to give more consideration to residential patrons. An effective consumer organization—such as POCAG—would provide patrons with their own advocate. Citizens would exert greater influence over postal policies if Congress exercised more control over the agency—as the Constitution instructs.

NINE

THE FUTURE

In recent decades, presidents have shown little interest in the postal system. Postmaster General Anthony M. Frank once revealed that lack of White House interest in the Postal Service "has been one of my biggest disappointments." True to form, Donald J. Trump disrupted this norm. But the result of this newfound presidential engagement was not what Frank would have imagined. By his final year in office, Trump's belittling of the Postal Service included dismissing the agency as "a joke." In fact, the Postal Service is a great public enterprise that plays a vital role in American society. Mark Dimondstein, president of the American Postal Workers Union, foresees "expanding the civic and democratic role of the Postal Service in people's lives." The Postal Service can and should provide citizens with numerous additional services, and the decisions that we make about how to expand this historic institution will have a bearing on the future of all Americans.[1]

Even as Trump denigrated the Postal Service in April 2020, the importance of its delivery capacity to the nation has recently become unmistakable due to COVID-19. Amazon.com Inc. had acknowledged this strength back in 2013 when it signed a special deal to have letter carriers deliver its packages. As the Postal Service's largest commercial customer, Amazon has extended significant revenues to the agency while also placing significant strain on its infrastructure and workforce. The massive corporation is busily constructing its own delivery system, however, and emerging as a competitor to UPS and FedEx, making its future use of the postal network unclear. Amazon's enormous market power raises additional questions. The corporation is coming under increasing antitrust scrutiny that ultimately could alter the entire structure of the firm.[2]

The Postal Service's association with Amazon—given its monopolistic practices, mistreatment of workers, and other troubling corporate conduct—is a source of concern. With electronic commerce assuming a central role in contemporary life, a number of observers have warned that Amazon is too vital to remain under private ownership and should be brought under public control and combined with the Postal Service. "Nationalize the infrastructure of the digital age—including Amazon and private delivery services," social critic Mike Davis has proposed. The centrality of logistics operations to present-day society demands an open-minded examination of how such distribution networks should be structured.[3]

It would be relatively easy for the Postal Service to offer an online platform where small retailers could market their products. Argentina's national post office recently launched an electronic commerce division that may provide insight on operating such a service. Similarly, the Postal Service could provide fast, inexpensive delivery for small businesses modeled on an existing program with CVS Pharmacy that conducts all processing and transportation locally. Letter carriers pick up prescriptions from local CVS drugstores for delivery to residents within the same zip code. This localized delivery arrangement has broader potential. James W. Sauber of the National Association of Letter Carriers points out that local businesses in particular could benefit from an expansion of this delivery model. The Postal Service can also reintroduce the direct farm-to-consumer delivery service it operated in the early twentieth century. The World Wildlife Fund stated such deliveries would "reach a broad range of consumers with affordable, accessible, and nutritious produce while reducing environmental impacts through efficient logistics and food loss reduction."[4]

ESSENTIAL INFRASTRUCTURE

The Postal Service has been a Rock of Gibraltar amid the chaos and tragedy of natural disasters. Hours after wildfires devastated sections of northern California in 2017, letter carriers delivered mail to the homes of burned-out residents retrieving personal items who requested this service. Other residents who evacuated or lost their homes recovered some sense of normalcy from collecting their mail at local post offices. "We're all trying to continue to go about our business," one woman stated. When Hurricane Katrina struck the Gulf Coast with winds of up to 140 miles per hour in 2005, the Postal Service already had moved its delivery vehicles to higher ground, placed holds on mail headed for vulnerable areas, and updated postal workers' emergency contact information. Once the storm had passed, the U.S. Mail was being delivered before electricity and running water were fully restored. "The mail becomes such a critical component to a sense of normalcy, especially in catastrophic events like this," said Irene Lericos, the postal official who directed the agency's communications efforts during Katrina. With radio and television stations not broadcasting due to damaged transmitters, letter carriers distributed flyers making residents aware of Federal Emergency Management Agency services. The Postal Service later used its change-of-address directory to help the Department of Justice reunite missing children with their families.[5]

The postal network has a unique national security role. As an essential infrastructure with thousands of post offices, hundreds of sorting facilities, and a fleet of more than 200,000 vehicles, the postal system has the unique ability to contact every household and business in the nation daily. This indispensable physical connection between the American people and the federal government makes continuous postal operations a matter of national security. The 2001 terrorist attacks, subsequent anthrax scare, and COVID-19 pandemic all underscored the agency's health-security function. Federal health and security officials have tapped the Postal Service to deliver health-related materials and communications in the event of emergencies. In 2008, Secretary of Health and Human Services Michael O. Leavitt stated: "We have found letter carriers to be the federal government's quickest and surest way of getting pills to whole communities." Volunteer letter carriers already had completed successful medicine distribution dry runs in Boston, Philadelphia, and Seattle.[6]

In 2009, President Barack H. Obama issued an executive order to create a blueprint for postal workers to distribute medicine door to door in the event of a public health emergency. A small congressional appropriation allowed the Postal Service to partner with the Department of Health and Human Services, state and local health departments, and law enforcement agencies to conduct pilot programs that gave letter carriers the necessary training to complete this life-or-death assignment. When COVID-19 struck in 2020, the Department of Health and Human Services recommended that the Postal Service deliver packets containing five reusable three-ply cotton masks—650 million in total—to every household in the country. The Federal Emergency Management Agency approved the plan unanimously, and a number of manufacturers—including Fruit of the Loom Inc. and Hanes Inc.—prepared to produce the masks. But aides of President Trump deduced from his negative opinion of the agency that the idea was a non-starter and nixed the plan. Other potential ways for the Postal Service to aid in combating the virus in 2020 went unexplored, and amid a national crisis the federal government failed to utilize the remarkable capabilities of this invaluable infrastructure. The pandemic has revealed grave shortcomings in our public health system that demand an extensive overhaul to prepare for future crises, which should include preparations to utilize the postal system for distributing such items as protective materials, testing equipment, and pharmaceuticals.[7]

The Postal Service can aid in the provision of health care during periods of normalcy as well. Ronnie W. Stutts, president of the National Rural Letter Carriers' Association, explains that in cases where relatives of elderly residents do not live nearby they often "depend on the rural letter carrier to keep an eye out as a community watch on their families." The scope of such beneficial informal arrangements could be extended. In Japan, postal workers visit with elderly residents for half an hour on a monthly basis in order to make note of any changes in their health or living conditions. In this country, a similar pilot program operated in the Detroit area. Letter carriers would check on discharged patients of the William Beaumont Hospital System convalescing in their homes. The carriers would make sure that medications were taken, a proper diet was being followed, and any health complications were reported. Readmissions decreased as a result. Making such a program a standard agency service could offer health benefits while exerting downward pressure on health-care costs.[8]

SPURRING INNOVATION

Despite its recent spell in the limelight thanks to the 2020 election, the postal system remains an underutilized national resource. It has pioneered and subsidized numerous technological innovations. Invigorating this traditional role of the Postal Service would benefit Americans living in the twenty-first century. The Post Office was at the center of transportation advances from the stagecoach to modern aviation. In the 1790s, postal officials adopted stagecoaches to transport mail, since these vehicles could not only carry more mail than a post rider on horseback but also shield the mail from mud and inclement weather. Almost all stagecoach lines had mail contracts, and Congress used these agreements to subsidize routes in many areas stagecoaches otherwise would have avoided due to their lack of profitability. By 1830, the Post Office had used mail contracts to establish a network of stagecoaches that reached most settled areas of the nation.[9]

As the steam locomotive emerged in the 1830s—ushering in a new age of transportation—the national government embarked on what would be massive subsidies to the costly process of building railroads. The U.S. Army even provided engineering services to railroad companies, including surveying and assisting construction of the pioneer common carrier rail line, the Baltimore & Ohio Railroad. Mail contracts were one of the tools that the federal government employed to support railroad construction. By the 1850s, railroads had a prominent role in the postal system, and in the 1860s mail started to be sorted in transit on railway post office routes. Following the Civil War, Congress offered the prospect of future mail contracts to help promote the construction of rail lines west of the Mississippi River. Expansion of the Railway Mail Service expedited the circulation of mail and newspapers, and between 1860 and 1900 the length of railroad mileage nationally grew more than sixfold.[10]

In the interest of fostering new communications technologies, in 1843 the national government provided the funding that Samuel F. B. Morse required to build an experimental telegraph line linking Baltimore with Washington, D.C. Until 1847, the Post Office Department operated this pioneer line. Postmaster General Cave Johnson urged Congress to approve purchase of the patent rights, arguing that the federal government should control this important new technology outright. But Congress was occupied with waging war against Mexico and uninterested in the subject. With no additional funding for the service forthcoming, the Post Office leased the line to a recently formed private telegraph company. As economic historian George Rogers Taylor observed, once "the money-making possibilities of the telegraph began to be sensed . . . private capital rapidly took over."[11]

At the end of the nineteenth century, the Post Office Department advanced yet another technological innovation when it experimented successfully with underground pneumatic tubes in major cities. In 1893, Philadelphia gained the distinction of the first pneumatic postal tube line in the United States. Within a few years, more than 90 percent of the city's letters were traveling through the tubes. Pneumatic tube carriers could hold six hundred letters and travel at speeds of up to thirty-five miles per hour. The Post Office used pneumatic tube networks until 1953, when mail trucks replaced them entirely.[12]

The development of aviation may owe more than any other technology to the Post Office Department's pioneering role. In 1918, the nation's first regularly scheduled air mail service was inaugurated between New York City and Washington, D.C. Unlike other means of mail transportation, the Aerial Mail Service did not contract out to private companies and instead used its own airplanes and pilots. In 1920, the first transcontinental air mail route began operating between New York City and San Francisco. The Post Office constructed a national aviation infrastructure of airports, emergency landing fields, navigational beacons, searchlights, and radio communications. Opponents of government enterprise and railroad corporations disapproved of the Post Office transporting mail itself, and in 1925 Congress enacted a law that turned the carriage of air mail over to private contractors. This new policy offered subsidies that allowed the first successful commercial airlines to begin operating in the United States. Only in 1935 did the passenger revenues of airlines begin to exceed their mail revenues.[13]

When the Post Office Department promoted new technologies, it assumed risks that for-profit businesses avoided. F. Robert Van der Linden, air transportation curator at the Smithsonian Institution's National Air and Space Museum, explained that "when private capital was unwilling to invest [in aviation] . . . the Post Office invest[ed] public funds . . . in a successful effort to demonstrate the possibilities of a new technology to revolutionize communications." Any postal activity that potentially competed with for-profit business generated controversy, so in addition to shouldering the initial risk, the Post Office insulated businesses with subsidies while allowing them to capture the resulting revenues once a new industry became profitable. "The Post Office," historian Wayne E. Fuller observed, "was given numerous unprofitable assignments to help the private sector of the economy at the same time as it was forbidden to engage in business ventures from which it might have profited."[14]

In the early twentieth century, Rural Free Delivery stimulated road improvements in rural areas nationwide because the Post Office would not deliver mail on low-quality roads. Richard F. Weingroff of the Federal Highway Administration called RFD the "program that finally convinced the nation's farmers of the value of good roads and brought them into the Good Roads Movement." Unlike other means of transportation, the automobile was a technology that the Post Office ultimately did not outsource to private contractors. When postal officials enthusiastically introduced motor vehicles to carry mail, they initially contracted for delivery vehicles with companies that boosted their profits by adding unnecessary delivery runs and charging exorbitant amounts. Carl H. Scheele, curator in charge of the Smithsonian Institution's Division of Philately and Postal History, reported that once the Post Office discovered this chicanery, "the abandonment of contract service between 1914 and 1918 was pursued as fast as trucks could be purchased."[15]

Today, the Postal Service owns and operates more than 200,000 delivery and collection vehicles, including Dodge ProMaster vans, Ford Windstar minivans, and most notably Grumman Long Life Vehicles, which account for more than two-thirds of the entire fleet. Assembled in Montgomery, Pennsylvania, and designed specifically for postal use, these trucks were produced by Grumman between 1987 and 1994. Although the Long Life Vehicle has proved durable, they have outlived their thirty-year operating life spans. Not only are breakdowns occurring frequently, fires in the engine compartment have become all too familiar events. An additional shortcoming of the current postal fleet is the need for larger trucks designed to accommodate the growing number of packages that letter carriers are delivering.[16]

Environmentalists urge the Postal Service to transition to plug-in electric trucks. Postal vehicles currently travel more than 1.3 billion miles every year. Using electricity instead of gasoline to power postal trucks would reduce harmful emissions, lower fuel expenses, and decrease maintenance costs, since electric automobiles have fewer moving parts. The National Resource Defense Council, Public Citizen, Sierra Club, Union of Concerned Scientists, and other environmental organizations emphasize that "adopting lower-emission delivery trucks will position USPS as an innovative leader by showing how large government and private fleets can travel on nearly every type of road in the United States while emitting little to no harmful pollutants into our air." The Postal Service has a lengthy history of experimenting with electric vehicles. In 1899, Buffalo's superintendent of city delivery first tested an electric car, and the agency has undertaken a number of successful experiments with these vehicles since the 1973 oil crisis.[17]

When the Postal Service accepted bids for a contract to replace its existing fleet, the declining cost of electric automobiles created a real opportunity to advance the development of this industry in the United States. In February 2021, postal officials selected a manufacturer: Oshkosh, Wisconsin–based Oshkosh Corp., which will produce customized trucks equipped with either fuel-efficient internal combustion engines or electric batteries. The impact of selecting a fully electric fleet would have been greater. The Sierra Club urges the agency "to prioritize clean air and climate action in this critical moment of change for America's mail trucks by committing to a 100% all-electric fleet." The federal government is using only a fraction of its purchasing leverage to promote the necessary transition to an environmentally sustainable economy. "This contract is a multibillion-dollar opportunity to reimagine the federal fleet and develop this critical domestic supply line," objected Representative Marcy Kaptur (D-Ohio). "We can't fumble this opportunity." At least the federal government is using some purchasing leverage to promote the necessary transition to an environmentally sustainable economy. By acquiring electric vehicles, the Postal Service can promote this industry just as federal procurement once nurtured the airbag industry. In 1984, the General Services Administration prompted Ford Motor Company to produce this safety feature when it purchased airbag-equipped Ford Tempos. The safety benefits of airbags proved impressive, and they became a standard feature of automobiles in the 1990s.[18]

The Postal Service can further uphold its tradition of harnessing technological innovation to serve the public interest by promoting internet access. The internet is less available in rural America than urban and suburban areas: around one-quarter of rural residents call lack of access to high-speed internet a "major problem." This situation recalls the early twentieth century, when power lines did not extend into most of the countryside. In the early 1930s, only one in ten farms had electricity, and in parts of the Midwest and the South less than 1 percent of farms were electrified. Among other disadvantages, this absence consigned rural Americans to devote over ten hours every week to pumping and carrying water. Meanwhile, in some European nations—where public ownership bolstered rural electrification—90 percent of farms had electricity. Privately owned utility companies in the United States eschewed serving farms because they thought rural electrification would prove unprofitable. One North Carolina woman reported the local electric utility "wouldn't even consider" extending a power line to her farm. "They wouldn't even listen to us," she remembered.[19]

In 1935, the New Deal intervened decisively, forming the Rural Electrification Administration to fund the extension of power lines into rural areas lacking electricity. For-profit electric utilities bitterly resisted this federal action. Yet the threat of public power spurred utility companies to make new efforts to extend power lines. Around one million farms obtained electricity in the first five years that the REA was in operation, more than had been electrified during the previous half century. The technology rapidly became a standard feature of rural life: by 1946 a majority of farms had electricity, and seven years later over 90 percent were electrified. In 1961, cooperative movement leader H. Jerry Voorhis observed that without government action "America's countryside would probably still be using candle and lantern light." Rural electrification increased agricultural productivity and introduced a host of new amenities to rural life that extended well beyond electric lights to include indoor plumbing, hot water, and refrigeration. "It was almost too good to believe," one woman said. "It was a transformation," agreed another.[20]

The same profit calculus that directed electric utilities not to serve farms in the early twentieth century applies to internet access in rural America today. Government once again can serve as the equalizer, therefore, with the Postal Service potentially helping spearhead an overdue push to extend broadband into the countryside. Such a role would continue the postal system's historic mission of making communications services universally available. The Postal Service could provide internet service itself or partner with municipalities and cooperatives to offer broadband connections on the local level. There would be social benefits to the Postal Service providing internet service beyond rural areas as well. Since a handful of corporations dominate internet access, the resulting lack of competition has meant Americans receive worse service and pay higher prices than residents of other economically developed nations. In addition, the business practices and lobbying agendas of these corporations threaten consumer privacy and net neutrality. A 2018 poll found that 56 percent of Americans supported a public option for internet access.[21]

Providing internet service is not the only way the Postal Service could help Americans access electronic communications. The Postal Service should offer both secure public search engine services and email accounts. As the core of their business models, technology corporations habitually surveil and collect data from users. Legal scholar Arthur S. Hayes explained how the Postal Service's statutory obligation to preserve the privacy of correspondence could protect consumers from such abuse, proposing that the agency "fill a void by providing e-mail and browser-search engine services to shield users from advertisers' online behavioral marketing tracking and profiling and unauthorized government metadata collection." Videoconferencing and social media platforms potentially could find a place alongside a postal search engine and postal email accounts. Offering electronic communications services would allow the Postal Service to better fulfill its mission of transmitting news, information, and personal messages.[22]

TOMORROW'S POST OFFICES

The Postal Service is in the unique position of operating physical locations in thousands of communities across the nation, and the services these post offices provide extend well beyond stamps and shipping. Patrons can apply for a passport, register for the draft, request a burial flag for a veteran, purchase duck stamps, obtain philatelic sales materials, use photocopiers, and buy greeting cards. Still, a number of courtesies and services that post offices traditionally offered have disappeared in recent years. Changes in telephone policy reveal the motivation behind the push to eliminate these services. In 1996, the Postal Service started deleting the telephone numbers of post offices from local phone books in order to divert patrons' calls to regional centers staffed by non-postal employees. This decision was variously attributed to conforming with "the wave of the future" and preventing postal workers from making personal calls during work hours. "This distant phone policy makes no sense," columnist Elliott E. Brack complained. "You can do better than this, post office." The underlying reason for the change was that although answering the telephone benefited patrons, these conversations did not produce immediate revenues.[23]

One traditional service that post offices no longer offer is making income tax forms available. These materials used to be standard items in post office lobbies prior to tax day, but the Postal Service now makes a point of not supplying them. Products of the U.S. Mint are not available to coin collectors through post offices anymore either. Shortly before the 2020 election, management's push to curtail the services that post offices provide created problems for voters in the Houston area. The League of Women Voters protested that it was "very concerned" about the removal of voter registration and vote-by-mail applications from post office lobbies. A local Postal Service spokeswoman, Kanickewa Johnson, claimed regulations prohibited "depositing or posting of handbills, flyers, pamphlets, signs, posters, placards, or other literature." Press attention and congressional inquiries produced guidance from postal headquarters that affirmed postmasters in fact were authorized to supply voting materials "provided there is adequate space available." "It always is refreshing when things are corrected," Representative Alexander N. Green (D-Tex.) remarked.[24]

Questions about the legitimacy of distributing government forms and information in post office lobbies should never arise in the first place. These federal spaces are widely recognized as places where public notices are displayed. In 1980, journalist Richard J. Margolis reported that two bulletin boards were standard in rural post offices—one for official government communications and one for local community announcements. A typical post office in Maine featured notices about the town's newly enacted anti-pollution ordinance, the county conservation district, YMCA swimming lessons, a concert, and a nursery school rummage and bake sale, plus employment solicitations from a babysitter and a local fishing guide. Similar bulletin boards are still found in numerous post offices today. Yet a misguided emphasis on businesslike efficiency can interfere with such basic services as providing voter registration forms or offering space for public announcements. As the *Chicago Tribune* observed: "It takes time to put FBI Wanted posters on the bulletin board in the lobby. It takes time to check the Internal Revenue Service forms and order the missing items from Washington."[25]

Among the possible new services that post offices could offer, health care is a field with significant potential benefits to society, especially in rural areas. In 2020, polling found that one in five Americans were receiving medications through the mail. The Veterans Administration alone ships 120 million prescriptions a year, with 90 percent traveling through the U.S. Mail. Many small towns lack pharmacies, so residents depend on mailed prescriptions. But leaving prescriptions in mailboxes risks damaging the contents. Carol Miller, founder of the Frontier Education Center, stated that when the post office in her New Mexico community closed, the mail started being delivered to a cluster-box unit that was exposed to the elements. With post office boxes no longer available, she reported, "medications can be out there in freezing weather or in the heat, they can get wet or be stolen." Steve D. LeNoir, former president of the National League of Postmasters, proposes that post offices act as "repositories to hold medicine for pickup, which could prevent its exposure to adverse weather conditions." He adds that post offices should "maintain a supply of equipment used by Medicare patients." The USPS Office of Inspector General suggested that post offices offer health kiosks and serve as outlets where wellness organizations can reach clients. "This is especially beneficial," the inspector general noted, "for those in rural and remote areas, who find it challenging to travel to a government or nonprofit office not located in their town."[26]

In addition to assisting with Medicare and other health-care programs, post offices should become access points to government services more generally, at the local, state, and national levels. Duck stamps sold through post offices are required for hunting migratory waterfowl, and post offices ought to offer state hunting and fishing licenses as well. Public knowledge of Government Publishing Office publications covering countless subjects could be heightened through a partnership with post offices—including by offering a means to obtain printed copies. There are numerous federal programs that post offices should help administer. For example, since 2000 the Social Security Administration has closed more than a hundred field offices. "The closure of Social Security field offices around the country," noted Nancy Altman, president of Social Security Works, "makes the lives of all of us more difficult." The percentage of visitors to Social Security offices who waited longer than an hour to be served doubled between 2010 and 2019. Although post offices would not offer all of the services available at Social Security offices, they could extend assistance with the basics. Employing a similar approach, the Postal Service should help to make government at all levels more transparent and accessible to citizens. Many Americans are not aware of the full spectrum of services that government provides. Post offices have the potential to help millions of citizens learn about and access government services.[27]

For years, postmasters have been eager to see the agency take full advantage of the many opportunities that post offices offer. "Through our post offices we have an infrastructure that no one else has," LeNoir said, "and I truly think that we have underutilized the infrastructure we have in place." Post offices could supply notary public services; packing, printing, and copying services; office supplies; merchandise pick-up and storage lockers; public pay phones; and wireless public internet. Charging stations at post offices for electric postal trucks could be made available for public use during the daytime. Food and clothing drives need centrally located sites to collect and distribute these necessities, and post offices could support such community events. Similarly, post offices could provide space for local recycling efforts and for disposing of difficult-to-recycle items. Experimentation can identify numerous creative ways to employ these public spaces to the benefit of local communities. "Let's put a suggestion box in every post office," recommends Steven Hutkins of Save the Post Office, "so that people can help the Postal Service learn more about what each community wants and needs."[28]

POSTAL BANKING

Since the nineteenth century, post offices have offered Americans access to financial services. The postal money order debuted during the Civil War to help Union servicemen and their families exchange money. Post offices sell over $20 billion of money orders annually and were formerly retail outlets for savings bonds as well. Savings bonds are issued in small denominations with no fees, offering a low-risk strategy for middle- and lower-income earners to accumulate savings. Upon their introduction in 1935, the only way to purchase savings bonds—other than directly from the Office of the Treasurer—was at post offices. When the savings bond program boomed during World War II, the Post Office did its part to help finance the fight against fascism, extending window service into weekday evenings and on Saturday afternoons to help increase bond sales. Among the purchasers were children who handed clerks and postmasters milk bottles and paper bags filled with pennies.[29]

Savings bonds were a prominent form of thrift in the second half of the twentieth century, but in 2003 the Department of the Treasury closed forty-one regional marketing offices. Treasury officials and their congressional allies claimed the program was too costly to administer, and pushed to replace paper bonds with online accounts. However, economist Peter Tufano and sociologist Daniel J. Schneider argued the savings bond program "needs to be reinvigorated to enhance its role in supporting family saving." In 2012, the Treasury stopped issuing paper bonds, although they still can be obtained through federal income tax refunds. Tufano and Schneider have stated

"post offices . . . could again serve as an ideal location for the
sale of savings bonds." Selling paper savings bonds at post offices
would increase awareness of the program and offer small savers
greater access to this safe means to build assets and "take stock in
America."[30]

Approximately one in five American households are classi-
fied as either "unbanked" or "underbanked." Over eight million
unbanked households lack a bank account entirely, while approximately 24 million households have accounts but are underserved,
causing many to use high-cost "fringe banks" such as pawnshops, payday lenders, and check-cashing outlets. Fringe banking
emerged as a major financial factor in the 1980s due to the
deteriorating economic situation of millions of Americans and
financial deregulation that favored banks and other lenders over
consumers. Most underserved consumers are low income: among
families with incomes under $15,000 more than one-quarter are
unbanked, as compared to less than 2 percent with incomes over
$50,000. Savings account usage is particularly low. Less than half
of households in the two lowest income quintiles maintain this
basic means of setting aside emergency funds. The absence of a
financial cushion among the unbanked magnifies their vulnerability to income fluctuations, unexpected expenses, setbacks, and
misfortune, while also reducing their ability to take advantage of
career, educational, and other opportunities. Importantly, at all
income levels Americans with bank accounts are more likely to
save than those without accounts.[31]

Simply opening a bank account presents a major hurdle to
many low-income Americans, since minimum account balance
requirements necessitate setting aside a sizable cash reserve, and a
majority of unbanked households report lacking "enough money
to keep in an account." Becoming a bank customer also involves
financial risk, because banks have relied increasingly on exacting
fees from their customers to generate profits. In addition, banks
have deliberately used punitive fees to drive off customers who do

not generate "adequate returns." Among other fees hidden away in fine print contracts, those for account "maintenance," ATM withdrawals, debit card swipes, wire transfers, and overdrafts are unpredictable and add up quickly. Moreover, with dwindling numbers of bank branches, it is increasingly difficult to find a conveniently located bank in many rural and urban areas.[32]

As an alternative to banks, millions of Americans have turned to fringe banking services, and, as one Philadelphia journalist learned firsthand, fees for these transactions are high: he was assessed $16 to cash a paycheck at a pawnshop and $24 at a check-cashing outlet. Yet fringe banks hand their customers cash on the spot, unlike banks, which can make consumers wait for days until a check clears. And although fees for simple transactions at fringe banks are high, unwelcome financial surprises are minimal since costs are communicated clearly and paid up front. Still, in 2018 underserved consumers spent almost $17 billion on fees to access basic financial services. Such outlays make accumulating savings all the more difficult, and due to lack of a financial reserve many low-income households depend heavily on expensive loans from fringe banks. The Pew Charitable Trusts has reported that approximately twelve million consumers spend $9 billion in fees on small, short-term loans every year. Another Pew study found the average borrower spent $520 annually on interest payments to take out eight payday loans of $375 apiece.[33]

The Post Office Department once promoted access to basic banking services. From 1911 to 1966, Americans could walk into their local post office and open a savings account. During the Gilded Age, privately owned banks focused on businesses and affluent customers. Not only did banks neglect to serve working people adequately, bank failures were frequent occurrences. Frustrated farmers and workers agitated politically on behalf of numerous plans for remaking the banking system. One of the more prominent of these reforms was the idea that the Post Office should operate its own bank. A number of postal officials—including Postmaster General

John Wanamaker—embraced postal savings as well.[34]

A major banking panic in 1907 that caused an economic depression made financial reform a national political issue. At that moment, grassroots pressure for postal banking was intense. Bankers vigorously lobbied in opposition to this reform, but strong public demand for legislation secured the establishment of a postal savings bank. The Postal Savings System was a groundbreaking government service, but also the product of compromise with banking interests. Working people had imagined postal banks that extended loans and competed directly with the private banking system, but the Post Office was only allowed to operate a basic savings bank that offered patrons a noncompetitive 2 percent interest rate on their deposits. The Postal Savings System grew despite its encumbrances, however, particularly during the Great Depression, when more than one-fifth of the nation's banks failed and Americans sought safety with the government's savings bank.[35]

During the 1950s, a convergence of developments placed the Postal Savings System in jeopardy. The strong public interest in banking policy that suffused grassroots politics in the early twentieth century had waned, even as bankers remained committed to eliminating the service. The establishment of the Federal Deposit Insurance Corporation in 1934 had insured depositors against bank failures, doing away with this competitive advantage of postal savings. And inside the Post Office Department itself, officials who were "concerned about the future of the private enterprise system" wanted to discontinue the service. Although more than one million Americans used the Postal Savings System, patronage was declining in large part due to its low 2 percent interest rate, which compared unfavorably to the more than 3 percent depositors received at other savings institutions by the end of the 1950s. The banking lobby launched the final push to eliminate the service in the 1960s, with savings and loan associations playing a prominent role. One of the most active postal savings antagonists in Congress—Representative Edward J. Derwinski

(R-Ill.)—was president of a savings and loan. He argued that "in keeping with the principle of . . . free enterprise" it was necessary to "terminate the Postal Savings System." Postal unions were the only organized group to defend the institution. In 1966, Congress passed legislation that discontinued the service.[36]

The death of postal savings eliminated this potential alternative to fringe banks. For years, occasional proposals to revive postal banking kept the idea alive, but failed to gain traction.[37] However, in 2014—following extraordinary revelations about the misfeasance of banks associated with the 2008 financial crisis—the USPS Office of Inspector General issued a white paper endorsing the idea.[38] A flurry of interest in progressive political circles followed, including from Senator Elizabeth Warren (D-Mass.). "We need innovative ways to create pathways for struggling families to build economic security," she stated, "and this is an idea that falls in that category."[39] Postal banking proposals emphasize tailoring services to meet the needs of the unbanked by offering low-balance checking and savings accounts, inexpensive payment services, and small-dollar loans. In 2020, the push for postal banking attained a milestone when the Biden presidential campaign endorsed the idea. In April 2021, congressional supporters called for funding to launch postal banking pilot programs.[40]

There are three important dimensions of the Postal Service that make the agency uniquely suited to help underserved Americans access financial services. First, almost one-third of unbanked households state that lack of trust in banks is a reason they do not have an account, while 91 percent of Americans view the Postal Service favorably—the highest rating of any federal agency. Second, the Postal Service operates more than 30,000 post offices that are close at hand whether one lives in a big city or a remote hamlet. In fact, approximately 38 percent of post offices are located in zip codes with no banks. Third, the Postal Service does not have shareholders demanding business practices that target the most profitable customers and maximize earnings through more fees and reduced services. Instead of operating under the constraints of quarterly profit statements, postal officials would have the flexibility to offer services that meet the needs of underserved Americans.[41]

A twenty-first-century postal bank should offer affordable services that allow patrons to save, send, receive, convert, and transact funds. The service should provide ready access to currency—as opposed to only offering non-cash payment systems like stored-value cards. Affordable loans with generous grace periods would present a needed alternative to costly payday lenders. While postal banking ought to prioritize meeting the needs of underserved Americans over producing revenue, this service does present an opportunity to generate additional income for the agency. The USPS Office of Inspector General estimated that financial services could add $8.9 billion to the Postal Service's annual revenues. Alongside the opportunities that a revived postal bank presents, there are pitfalls to avoid. Contracting out services to banks or other corporations would subvert the purpose of this reform. The existing for-profit model has failed to provide millions of Americans with adequate financial access, and duplicating this incentive structure at post offices would similarly impair postal banking.[42]

Strong grassroots demand—not banker acquiescence—will be necessary to secure true postal banking. Concessions to the banks compromised postal banking in the twentieth century. A non-competitive interest rate, lack of publicity, and minimal services undermined the original Postal Savings System, ultimately leading to its demise. All of these unhelpful policies were attempts at conciliation. Banks lobbied against the Postal Savings System during its entire existence nevertheless. When designing postal banking the emphasis should not be on protecting existing banks in the hope of placating this powerful special interest group. Banks are not entitled to their customers. Postal banking should be attractive to a variety of prospective patrons, including those who are not unbanked. Millions of Americans with bank accounts have endured poor service, mercenary fees, account fraud scandals, and other consumer abuses. A postal bank that welcomes a range of patrons will remain viable and potentially exert new pressure on banks to improve their business practices. The campaign for an effective postal bank rests on mobilizing broad support among citizens who would benefit from this socially beneficial idea.

OUR POSTAL COMMONWEALTH

In the early twentieth century, Speaker Joseph G. Cannon (R-Ill.) captured the significance of the postal system: "The Post Office Department is like a great root spreading many feet underground and nourishing the mighty oak. It is the tap root of civilization." Today, there is no less need for first-class public service in the fields of communications, media, transportation, materials handling, and finance. In order for the Postal Service to fulfill its public service mission, reform efforts must focus on prudently enhancing services to the American people. "There is no question that the Postal Service needs to become more entrepreneurial to meet the changing needs of the digital revolution," Senator Bernard Sanders (I-Vt.) affirmed. Numerous innovative ideas point toward what the Postal Service can become. Still, Fredric V. Rolando, president of the National Association of Letter Carriers, advises approaching postal reform with "caution and humility." After all, as Niels Bohr once observed, "Prediction is very difficult, especially about the future." A democratic process that prioritizes involving the American people in this discussion will introduce the necessary diversity of knowledge and perspectives required to secure the people's post office.[43]

At the time of postal reorganization, Representative Patsy Mink (D-Hawaii) warned, "Decisions on what services to offer and what rates to charge will be made by administrators not responsible to the people and instead meeting behind closed [doors in] corporate boardrooms." The political push over the subsequent half century to restrict the agency's services and roll back its operations reflects an underlying pro-corporate bias. This shift toward commercial purposes and centralized corporate sector governance must be reversed if the Postal Service is to serve the public interest first. Greater congressional engagement in postal policy would insert a healthy dose of democracy when policies are debated. An effective organization of residential postal patrons will be necessary to ensure the public shapes future policy decisions. Only civic activism can resist the corporate threat to the Postal Service.[44]

We the people of the United States have inherited the Postal Service. The postal system is part of our "commonwealth"—the shared heritage we collectively own—that includes such mutual assets as public lands and their resources, knowledge not privatized by copyrighting, and essential infrastructures like highways and broadcast airwaves. We have a responsibility to steward the Postal Service so that future generations will have use of this great resource as well. The Postal Service is a national treasure that unifies the American people. "For more than two centuries, the mail has united us during times of social upheaval, economic change and world war," Postmaster General Marvin T. Runyon stated. "Suburban, urban and rural, north, south, east and west; the mail has been an enduring shared experience binding us together."[45] This legacy handed down to us generation after generation from our nation's founding should serve the uncompromised needs of the American people. We must be citizens worthy of our custodianship of this great American institution and decisively and creatively claim our commonwealth.

NOTES

INTRODUCTION

1. House Committee on Oversight and Reform, *Protecting the Timely Delivery of Mail, Medicine, and Mail-In Ballots*, 116th Congress, second session (Washington, D.C.: Government Publishing Office, 2021), 57; Steven Hutkins, "Do It Now: A Timeline of the Postal Service's Work Hour Reduction Plan," Save the Post Office, October 1, 2020, https://www.savethepostoffice.com/do-it-now-a-timeline-of-the-postal-services-work-hour-reduction-plan/.
2. House Committee on Oversight and Reform, *Protecting the Timely Delivery of Mail, Medicine, and Mail-In Ballots*, 23.
3. John Busby and Julia Tanberk, "FCC Reports Broadband Unavailable to 21.3 Million Americans, BroadbandNow Study Indicates 42 Million Do Not Have Access," *BroadbandNow*, February 3, 2020, https://broadbandnow.com/research/fcc-underestimates-unserved-by-50-percent. On "reserve technologies," see David E.H. Edgerton, *The Shock of the Old: Technology and Global History since 1900* (New York: Oxford University Press, 2007), 10-11.
4. Steven Hutkins, "How the Postal Service Began Prefunding Retiree Health Care and Fell Into a Deep Hole," Save the Post Office, January 2, 2013, https://www.savethepostoffice.com/how-postal-service-began-prefunding-retiree-health-care-and-fell-deep-hole/.
5. *CBS News*, August 20, 2020, https://www.cbsnews.com/news/us-postal-service-best-year-since-2015-mail-in-voting/.
6. Nicole C. Kirk, *Wanamaker's Temple: The Business of Religion in an Iconic Department Store* (New York: New York University Press, 2018), 76; Post Office Department, *Annual Report of the Postmaster-General, 1890* (Washington, D.C.: Government Printing Office, 1890), 9; Herbert Adams Gibbons, *John Wanamaker*, 2 vols. (New York: Harper & Brothers, 1926), 1:276-320.
7. Christopher W. Shaw, "The U.S. Postal Service Was Designed to Serve Democracy," *Foreign Affairs*, October 27, 2020, https://www.foreignaffairs.com/articles/united-states/2020-10-27/us-postal-service-was-designed-serve-democracy.

CHAPTER ONE: Privatization

1. Charles T. Goodsell, *The Case for Bureaucracy: A Public Administration Polemic*, 4th ed. (Washington, D.C.: CQ Press, 2004), 4-5, 33-34.
2. *Congressional Record*, 91st Congress, first session, 1969, 115, 23606; Jon C. Rogowski, John E. Gerring, Matthew Maguire, and Lee L. Cojocaru, "Public Infrastructure and Economic Development: Evidence from Postal Systems," *American Journal of Political Science* (forthcoming).
3. *U.S. Code* 18 (2018), §§1693-1699; *U.S. Code* 39 (2018), §§601-606; U.S. Postal Service, *Understanding the Private Express Statutes*, Publication No. 542 (June 1998), 1.
4. In director Oliver Stone's 1987 film *Wall Street*, investment banker Gordon Gekko (Michael Douglas) makes the following statement: "Greed—for lack of a better word—is good. Greed is right. Greed works. Greed clarifies, cuts through, and captures the essence of the evolutionary spirit." Laissez-faire, contrary to claims of its proponents, as Karl Polanyi observed, "was the product of deliberate state action" (*The Great Transformation* [Boston: Beacon Press, 1957], 141).

5. John B. Judis, *The Paradox of American Democracy: Elites, Special Interests, and the Betrayal of the Public Trust* (New York: Pantheon Books, 2000), 109-31; David J. Vogel, *Fluctuating Fortunes: The Political Power of Business in America* (New York: Basic Books, 1989), 220-26; Jason M. Stahl, *Right Moves: The Conservative Think Tank in American Political Culture since 1945* (Chapel Hill: University of North Carolina Press, 2016), 83-85, 90-92; Charles L. Heatherly, ed., *Mandate for Leadership: Policy Management in a Conservative Administration* (Washington, D.C.: Heritage Foundation, 1981), 827; *CQ Researcher* 6, no. 30 (1996): 703.

6. James C. Miller III, "End the Postal Monopoly," *Cato Journal* 5, no. 1 (1985): 149-55; Stuart M. Butler, "Isn't it Time to Sell the Postal Service?" *New York Times*, August 9, 1985, A27; Peter J. Ferrera, ed., *Free the Mail: Ending the Postal Monopoly* (Washington, D.C.: Cato Institute, 1990); J. Gregory Sidak and Daniel F. Spulber, *Protecting Competition from the Postal Monopoly* (Washington, D.C.: AEI Press, 1996); Edward L. Hudgins, ed., *The Last Monopoly: Privatizing the Postal Service for the Information Age* (Washington, D.C.: Cato Institute, 1996); Edward L. Hudgins, ed., *Mail @ the Millennium: Will the Postal Service Go Private?* (Washington, D.C.: Cato Institute, 2000); R. Richard Geddes, *Saving the Mail: How to Solve the Problems of the U.S. Postal Service* (Washington, D.C.: AEI Press, 2003); R. Richard Geddes, *Return to Sender: Reforms for the Failing Postal Service* (Washington, D.C.: AEI, 2011); Chris R. Edwards, "To Save the USPS, We Must Privatize It," *National Review*, May 8, 2019, https://www.nationalreview.com/2019/05/to-save-the-usps-we-must-privatize-it/; Chris R. Edwards, "Restructuring the U.S. Postal Service," *Cato Journal* 39, no. 3 (2019): 667-81; David Ditch, "Privatization Should Be on the Table," *Philadelphia Inquirer*, August 14, 2020, A11.

7. James L. Gattuso, "Privatize the U.S. Postal Service," *Capitalism Magazine*, August 25, 2003, https://www.capitalismmagazine.com/2003/08/privatize-the-us-postal-service/; Edwin J. Feulner, "Deliver Us," *Heritage Foundation Commentary*, September 18, 2003, https://www.heritage.org/government-regulation/commentary/deliver-us; Senate Committee on Governmental Affairs, *Postal Reform: Sustaining the Nine Million Jobs in the $900 Billion Mailing Industry*, 108th Congress, second session (Washington, D.C.: Government Printing Office, 2004), 159.

8. Cato Institute, *Cato Handbook for Policymakers*, 8th ed. (Washington, D.C.: Cato Institute, 2017), 465; Geddes, *Return to Sender*, 4; Bert Ely, "Privatizing the Postal Service: Why Do It; How to Do It," in Ferrera, *Free the Mail*, 117; Joseph A. Califano, Jr., "The Little Guy Will Get Hurt," *New York Times*, April 17, 1983, F2; *Philadelphia Inquirer*, June 1, 2020, B1.

9. Thomas Ferguson and Joel Rogers, *Right Turn: The Decline of the Democrats and the Future of American Politics* (New York: Hill & Wang, 1986), 3-10; Jacob S. Hacker and Paul Pierson, *Winner-Take-All Politics* (New York: Simon & Schuster, 2010), 180-82; *Washington Post*, June 23, 1997, A17; Elaine C. Kamarck, *Delaying the Inevitable: Political Stalemate and the U.S. Postal Service* (Washington, D.C.: Brookings Institute, 2015). Postal services include both "competitive" and "market-dominant" offerings—not all of the latter are monopoly-protected.

10. Douglass C. North, *Structure and Change in Economic History* (New York: W.W. Norton & Co., 1981), 201; Elliott D. Sclar, *You Don't Always Get What You Pay For: The Economics of Privatization* (Ithaca, N.Y.: Cornell University Press, 2000), 9.

11. John Kenneth Galbraith, *The Culture of Contentment* (Boston: Houghton Mifflin Company, 1992), 134; William Appleman Williams, *Americans in a Changing World: A History of the United States in the Twentieth Century* (New York: Harper & Row, 1978), xiv.

12. Wayne E. Fuller, *The American Mail: Enlarger of the Common Life* (Chicago: University of Chicago Press, 1972), 66; Post Office Department, *Annual Report to Congress, 1970* (Washington, D.C.: Government Printing Office, 1971), 146; Gerald Cullinan, *The Post Office Department* (New York: Frederick A. Praeger Publishers, 1968), 64; Julian P. Bretz, "Some Aspects of Postal Extension Into the West," in *Annual Report of the American Historical Association, 1909* (Washington, D.C.: Government Printing Office, 1911), 143; M. Clyde Kelly, *United States Postal Policy* (New York: D. Appleton and Company, 1932), 1; Anuj C. Desai, "Wiretapping Before the Wires: The Post Office and the Rebirth of Communications Privacy," *Stanford Law Review* 60, no. 2 (2007): 563-64; Winifred Gallagher, *How the Post Office Created America: A History* (New York: Penguin Books, 2016), 26-28; Ruth Lapham Butler, *Doctor Franklin, Postmaster General* (Garden City, N.Y.: Doubleday, Doran & Company, 1928), 162-65.

13. Kelly, *United States Postal Policy*, 21-22, 35-36; Jeffrey L. Brodie, "A Revolution by Mail: A New Post Office for a New Nation" (Ph.D. diss., George Washington University, 2005), 138-62; Wesley Everett Rich, *History of the United States Post Office to the Year 1829* (Cambridge, Mass.: Harvard University Press, 1924), 109; Pao Hsun Chu, "The Post Office of the United States" (Ph.D. diss., Columbia University, 1932), 127; Stuart M. Blumin, "The Social Implications of U.S. Economic Development," in *The Long Nineteenth Century*, vol. 2 of *The Cambridge Economic History of the United States*, ed. Stanley L. Engerman and Robert E. Gallman (New York: Cambridge University Press, 2000), 828; Albert Fishlow, *American Railroads and the Transformation of the Ante-Bellum Economy* (Cambridge, Mass.: Harvard University Press, 1965), 32; Fuller, *American Mail*, 42.

14. Richard B. Kielbowicz, *News in the Mail: The Press, Post Office, and Public Information, 1700-1860s* (New York: Greenwood Press, 1989), 83-88; David M. Henkin, *The Postal Age: The Emergence of Modern Communications in Nineteenth-Century America* (Chicago: University of Chicago Press, 2006), 2; Historian of the U.S. Postal Service, *Mail Collection Boxes: A Brief History* (Washington, D.C.: U.S.P.S., 2017), 1-2; Allan Nevins, *The Emergence of Modern America, 1865-78* (New York: The Macmillan Company, 1927), 87; Wayne E. Fuller, *Morality and the Mail in Nineteenth-Century America* (Urbana: University of Illinois Press, 2003), 62.

15. Wayne E. Fuller, *RFD: The Changing Face of Rural America* (Bloomington: Indiana University Press, 1964), 22-24, 41-43, 314; C. Vann Woodward, *Tom Watson, Agrarian Rebel* (New York: Rinehart & Company, Inc., 1955), 244-46; James H. Bruns and Donald James Bruns, *Reaching Rural America: The Evolution of Rural Free Delivery* (Washington, D.C.: Smithsonian Institution, 1998), 10-15; *Congressional Record*, 54th Congress, first session, 1896, 28, 2620; Kelly, *United States Postal Policy*, 111-13.

16. Peter Z. Grossman, "The Dynamics of a Stable Cartel: The Railroad Express, 1851-1913," *Economic Inquiry* 34, no. 2 (1996): 220-36; Fuller, *RFD*, 202-3; Richard B. Kielbowicz, "Testing the Boundaries of Postal Enterprise in the U.S. Free-Market Economy, 1880-1920," in *More than Words: Readings in Transport, Communication, and the History of Postal Communication*, ed. John Willis (Gatineau, Quebec: Canadian Museum of Civilization, 2007), 90.

17. Richard B. Kielbowicz, "Government Goes into Business: Parcel Post in the Nation's Political Economy, 1880-1915," *Studies in American Political Development* 8, no. 1 (1994): 156; Anthony H. Smith, "The Battle for Parcel Post: The Western Farmer vs. the Eastern Mercantile Interests," *Journal of the West* 13, no. 4 (1974): 79, 81-82, 87; Frank Parker Stockbridge, "When We Get the Parcels Post," *World's Work* 24, no. 2 (1912): 170; Fuller, *RFD*, 221-22; Senate Subcommittee on Parcel Post, *Parcel Post*, 62nd Congress, second session (Washington, D.C.: Government Printing Office, 1912), 4: 966-67.

18. Bruns and Bruns, *Reaching Rural America: The Evolution of Rural Free Delivery*, 95; Senate Subcommittee on Parcel Post, *Parcel Post*, 4:1092; William R. Leach, *Land of Desire: Merchants, Power, and the Rise of a New American Culture* (New York: Vintage Books, 1994), 184; Rae E. Rips, "An Introductory Study of the Role of the Mail Order Business in American History, 1872-1914" (master's thesis, University of Chicago, 1938), 108-11; Rita L. Moroney, *History of the U.S. Postal Service, 1775-1982* (Washington, D.C.: U.S.P.S., 1983), 6; Kelly, *United States Postal Policy*, 185; Hal S. Barron, *Mixed Harvest: The Second Great Transformation in the Rural North, 1870-1930* (Chapel Hill: University of North Carolina Press, 1997), 188.

19. James H. Bruns and Donald James Bruns, *Reaching Rural America: The Introduction of Rural Free Delivery and Parcel Post* (Washington, D.C.: Smithsonian Institution, 1994).

20. Susan Tolchin and Martin Tolchin, *Dismantling America: The Rush to Deregulate* (Boston: Houghton Mifflin Company, 1983), 5-8; Joel Bakan, *The Corporation: The Pathological Pursuit of Profit and Power* (New York: Free Press, 2004), 60-84; Russell Mokhiber and Robert Weissman, *Corporate Predators: The Hunt for Mega-Profits and the Attack on Democracy* (Monroe, Maine: Common Courage Press, 1999); Subcommittee on Consumer Affairs, Foreign Commerce, and Tourism of the Senate Committee on Commerce, Science, and Transportation, *Perspectives on Improving Corporate Responsibility and Consumer Protections*, 107th Congress, second session (Washington, D.C.: Government Printing Office, 2005), 24; Judis, *Paradox of American Democracy*, 124-25.

21. Michael Scherer, "The Soul of the New Machine," *Mother Jones* 29, no. 1 (2004): 44; Public Broadcasting Service, "Interviews: Grover Norquist," *Frontline*, http://www.pbs.org/wgbh/pages/frontline/shows/choice2004/interviews/norquist.html; Subcommittee of the Senate Committee on Appropriations, *Financial Security of the U.S. Postal Service*, 107th Congress, first session (Washington, D.C.: Government Printing Office, 2002), 32.

22. Peter L. Francia, "Do Unions Still Matter in U.S. Elections? Assessing Labor's Political Power and Significance," *The Forum* 10, no. 1 (2012): Article 3; James J. Feigenbaum, Alexander Hertel-Fernandez, and Vanessa Williamson, "From the Bargaining Table to the Ballot Box: Political Effects of Right to Work Laws," NBER Working Paper No. 24259 (2018): 1-70; Grover G. Norquist, "Why Republicans (and Trump) May Still Win Big in 2020," *Ozy*, May 27, 2017, https://www.ozy.com/news-and-politics/why-republicans-and-trump-may-still-win-big-in-2020-despite-everything/78775/; Grover G. Norquist, "Reducing the Government by Half," *The Insider*, May 2000; Scherer, "Soul of the New Machine," 47; Grover G. Norquist, letter to J. Dennis Hastert, June 1, 2005.

23. George L. Priest, "The History of the Postal Monopoly in the United States," *Journal of Law & Economics* 18, no. 1 (1975): 33-80; Rachel Egen, *Buying a Movement: Right-Wing Foundations and American Politics* (Washington, D.C.: People for the American Way, 1996), 19; Jane Mayer, *Dark Money: The Hidden History of the Billionaires Behind the Rise of the Radical Right* (New York: Anchor Books, 2017), 130-35; Alice O'Connor, "Financing the Counterrevolution," in *Rightward Bound: Making America Conservative in the 1970s*, ed. Bruce J. Schulman and Julian E. Zelizer (Cambridge, Mass.: Harvard University Press, 2008), 166-67; Barbara Moulton et al., *Justice for Sale: Shortchanging the Public Interest for Private Gain* (Washington, D.C.: Alliance for Justice, 1994), 23; David F. Linowes et al., *Privatization: Toward More Effective Government* (Washington, D.C.: President's Commission on Privatization, 1988), 126.

24. *National Rural Letter Carrier* 65, nos. 38 & 39 (1966): 710; George L. Priest, "Socialism, Eastern Europe, and the Question of the Postal Monopoly," in Sidak, *Governing the Postal Service*, 51-52.

25. Priest, "Socialism, Eastern Europe, and the Question of the Postal Monopoly," 50; R. Richard Geddes, "Politics Tied Up In Postal Monopoly," *Roanoke (Va.) Times*, May 22, 1990, A7.

26. James W. Brock, ed., *The Structure of American Industry*, 13th ed. (Long Grove, Ill.: Waveland Press, 2016); David Dayen, *Monopolized: Life in the Age of Corporate Power* (New York: New Press, 2020), 5; John Kenneth Galbraith, *American Capitalism: The Concept of Countervailing Power* (Boston: Houghton, Mifflin, 1952), 39.

27. *Washington Post*, June 22, 2018, A4; Office of Management and Budget, *Delivering Government Solutions in the 21st Century: Reform Plan and Reorganization Recommendations* (Washington, D.C.: OMB, 2018), 68-70; Margaret Weichert, "This Is How to Reshape American Government for the 21st Century," *The Hill*, June 21, 2018, https://thehill.com/opinion/white-house/393495-this-is-how-to-reshape-american-government-for-the-21st-century.

28. *Washington Post*, March 27, 2017, A1; *New York Times*, August 23, 2020, A1; Task Force on the United States Postal System, *United States Postal Service: A Sustainable Path Forward* (Washington, D.C.: Department of the Treasury, 2018). The Task Force's recommendations included reduced service standards, more contracting out, fewer post offices, higher package rates, and allowing private companies mailbox access for a fee.

29. *Washington Post*, December 17, 2020, A22; *St. Louis Post-Dispatch*, August 31, 2020, A1; *New York Times*, August 21, 2020, A24; Steven Hutkins, "Lawsuits Against DeJoy, USPS & Trump Over Mail Delays and Election Mail," Save the Post Office, November 6, 2020, https://www.savethepostoffice.com/lawsuits-against-dejoy-usps-trump/.

30. U.S. Postal Service, *Delivering for America: Our Vision and Ten-Year Plan to Achieve Financial Sustainability and Service Excellence* (Washington, D.C.: U.S.P.S., 2021), 2-3; Mark Dimondstein (president, APWU, Washington, D.C.), interview by author, April 10, 2021.

31. *San Francisco Examiner*, February 2, 1988, A1; *St. Petersburg (Fla.) Times*, April 17, 1988, 11.

CHAPTER TWO: Deregulation

1. Gerald R. Ford, *Public Papers of the Presidents of the United States: Gerald R. Ford, 1976-77*, 3 vols. (Washington, D.C.: Government Printing Office, 1979), 1:945.
2. John C. Panzar, "Is Postal Service a Natural Monopoly," in *Competition and Innovation in Postal Services*, ed. Michael A. Crew and Paul R. Kleindorfer (Boston: Kluwer Academic Publishers, 1991), 219; Thorstein Veblen, *The Theory of Business Enterprise* (New York: Charles Scribner's Sons, 1904), 84.
3. James Meek, *Private Island: Why Britain Now Belongs to Someone Else* (London: Verso, 2014), 35; National Academy of Public Administration, *Evaluation of the United States Postal Service* (Washington, D.C.: The Academy, 1982), 149.
4. Sclar, *You Don't Always Get What You Pay For*, 44; Michael A. Crew and Paul R. Kleindorfer, "Developing Policies for the Future of the United States Postal Service," in *Competitive Transformation of the Postal and Delivery Sector*, ed. Michael A. Crew and Paul R. Kleindorfer (Boston: Kluwer Academic Publishers, 2004), 344; Vincent R. Sombrotto, "Postal Service Delivers Even Unprofitable Mail," *New York Times*, July 1, 1986, A22; General Accounting Office, *Pricing Postal Service in a Competitive Environment*, GAO/GGD-92-49 (March 1992), 32; U.S. Postal Service, *The Household Diary Study: Mail Use & Attitudes in FY 2019* (Washington, D.C.: U.S.P.S., 2020), 17-22, 39-40, 50, 55-57; Marshall R. Kolin and Edward J. Smith, "Mail Goes Where the Money Is: A Study of Rural Mail Delivery in the United States," in *Emerging Competition in Postal and Delivery Services*, ed. Michael A. Crew and Paul R. Kleindorfer (Boston: Kluwer Academic Publishers, 1999), 159-79; USPS Office of Inspector General, *What's Up with Mail? How Mail Use Is Changing across the United States*, Report No. RARC-WP-17-006 (April 2017), 14-15.
5. Andrew Perrin, "Digital Gap Between Rural and Nonrural America Persists," Pew Research Center, May 31, 2019, https://www.pewresearch.org/fact-tank/2019/05/31/digital-gap-between-rural-and-nonrural-america-persists/; Monica Anderson, "Digital Divide Persists Even as Low-Income Americans Make Gains," Pew Research Center, May 7, 2019, https://www.pewresearch.org/fact-tank/2019/05/07/digital-divide-persists-even-as-lower-income-americans-make-gains-in-tech-adoption/; Steven P. Martin and John P. Robinson, "The Income Digital Divide: Trends and Predictions for Levels of Internet Use," *Social Problems* 54, no. 1 (2007): 1-22; Ruth Y. Goldway (commissioner, P.R.C., Washington, D.C.), interview by author, July 28, 2005.
6. Geddes, *Saving the Mail*, 103; José A. Gómez-Ibáñez and John R. Meyer, *Going Private: The International Experience with Transport Privatization* (Washington, D.C.: Brookings Institution, 1993), 196.
7. Transportation Research Board, *Winds of Change: Domestic Air Transport Since Deregulation* (Washington, D.C.: National Research Council, 1991), 26-28; Andrew R. Goetz and Timothy M. Vowles, "The Good, the Bad, and the Ugly: 30 Years of U.S. Airline Deregulation," *Journal of Transport Geography* 17, no. 4 (2009): 260; House Committee on Transportation and Infrastructure, *Oversight of U.S. Airline Customer Service*, 115th Congress, first session (Washington, D.C.: Government Publishing Office, 2017), 16; Bureau of Transportation Statistics, "Airline Domestic Market Share, July 2019-June 2020," *TranStats*, September 26, 2020, https://www.transtats.bts.gov; Donald L. Barlett and James B. Steele, *America: What Went Wrong?* (Kansas City: Andrews and McMeel, 1992), 109; *Multinational Monitor* 17, no. 6 (1996): 18; Walter Adams and James W. Brock, *The Bigness Complex: Industry, Labor, and Government in the American Economy*, 2nd ed. (Stanford, Calif.: Stanford University Press, 2004), 209-21; *St. Louis Post-Dispatch*, July 15, 2015, A12.
8. Goetz and Vowles, "The Good, the Bad, and the Ugly," 257-58; *New York Times*, June 9, 2005, C1; *Washington Post*, June 28, 2005, D1; Paul Stephen Dempsey, "Airline Deregulation and Laissez-Faire Mythology: Economic Theory in Turbulence," *Journal of Air Law and Commerce* 56, no. 2 (1990): 349-56; *Consumer Reports* 67, no. 7 (2002), 31-32.
9. General Accounting Office, *Air Service Trends at Small Communities since October 2000*, GAO-02-432 (March 2002), 28; Dempsey, "Airline Deregulation and Laissez-Faire Mythology," 347; *Chronicle of Higher Education*, September 30, 2005, A33; Office of Senator Olympia J. Snowe, press release, July 23, 2007; Government Accountability Office, *Effects of Changes to the Essential Air*

Service Program, and Stakeholders Views on Benefits, Challenges, and Potential Reforms, GAO-20-74 (December 2019), 16; Office of Representative David J. Trone, press release, September 11, 2020.

10. *New York Times*, October 3, 1982, A4; Frederick C. Thayer, *Rebuilding America: The Case for Economic Regulation* (New York: Praeger Publishers, 1984), 93; *U.S. News & World Report* 94, no. 15 (1983), 87; *Wall Street Journal*, August 4, 1988, 1; Richard J. Margolis, "A World Without Wheels," *New Leader* 73, no. 12 (1990): 15; *St. Louis Post-Dispatch*, February 25, 1995, 1A.

11. *Dallas Morning News*, July 3, 1987, 1D; *Virginian-Pilot* (Norfolk, Va.), October 8, 2005, D1; *Bismarck Tribune*, June 30, 2004, 6A; *San Francisco Chronicle*, April 2, 2005, A1; *Christian Science Monitor*, August 26, 2005, 1.

12. *Star-Ledger* (Newark, N.J.), June 17, 2014, 24; Joseph P. Schwieterman, Nicholas J. Klein, and Alexander Levin, "Direct to Your Destination: The Size, Scope, and Competitive Status of Express Coach Carriers in the United States," *Transportation* 46, no. 4 (2019): 1489; *Toledo (Ohio) Blade*, August 10, 2005, B1; Office of Representative John M. McHugh, press release, November 30, 2005.

13. Theresa Firestine (senior economist, Bureau of Transportation Statistics, Washington, D.C.), email to author, September 30, 2020; *Herald* (Sharon, Pa.), October 3, 2007, https://www.sharonherald.com/news/local_news/ex-rider-misses-the-bus-seeks-commissioners-help/article_92f26dee-9978-50c9-82c5-08f67b246f49.html; *Plain Dealer* (Cleveland), August 19, 2005, E1. In 2018, 21.2 percent of rural residents lived twenty-five miles or more from an intercity bus stop.

14. Christoph Hermann, "The Liberalization of European Postal Markets: The Response of Firms and Impacts on Employment and Service," *Competition and Change* 15, no. 4 (2011): 253-73.

15. Robert M. Campbell, *The Politics of Postal Transformation: Modernizing Postal Systems in the Electronic and Global World* (Montreal: McGill-Queen's University Press, 2002), 184-88; Tim Shoebridge, "Mail and Couriers," *Te Ara—The Encyclopedia of New Zealand*, March 11, 2010, https://teara.govt.nz/en/mail-and-couriers/page-4; David Russell (chief executive, Consumers' Institute, Wellington, New Zealand), interview by author, March 28, 2005.

16. Campbell, *Politics of Postal Transformation*, 188-90; Syndex/Uni Global, *The Economic and Social Consequences of Postal Services Liberalization* (Brussels, Belgium: Uni Global Union, 2018), 49; Russell, interview, March 28, 2005; *Tribune* (Palmerston North, N.Z.), September 20, 2017, 8; *Dominion Post*, (Wellington, N.Z.), December 4, 2017, 3; *Dominion Post* (Wellington, N.Z.), January 17, 2018, 8; *Time*, October 23, 2013, https://world.time.com/2013/10/23/new-zealand-cutting-back-mail-service/; *Press* (Christchurch, N.Z.), February 16, 2015, 12; Paul Charman, "Enhance NZ Post—Don't Destroy It," *New Zealand Herald* (Auckland), April 1, 2016, https://www.nzherald.co.nz/nz/paul-charman-enhance-nz-post-dont-destroy-it/2FEEKWORF6VC4WE2KBDX2DGUME/.

17. Campbell, *Politics of Postal Transformation*, 144-47; *Aberdeen (Scotland) Press & Journal*, March 13, 2002, 7; *Financial Times*, June 7, 2002, 8; U.K. Comptroller and Auditor General, *Opening the Post: Postcomm and Postal Services—The Risks and Opportunities* (London: The Stationery Office, 2002), 68; Sarah Ryan with Cornelia Broos, *Postal Liberalisation: The Issues, the Impact, and Union Responses* (Nyon, Switzerland: Uni Global Union, 2012), 26-27; Bengt Ingerstam (president, Swedish Consumer Coalition, Osby, Sweden), interview by author, March 30, 2005.

18. Syndex/Uni Global, *Economic and Social Consequences of Postal Services Liberalization*, 61-62; Post-Nord, *Annual and Sustainability Report, 2019* (n.p., 2020), 6, 10.

19. Posten Norge, press release, September 7, 2004; Posten Norge, press release, June 27, 2003; *Aftenposten* (Oslo), February 21, 2006, http://www.aftenposten.no/english/business/article1229754.ece.

20. George R. Lakey, *Viking Economics: How the Scandinavians Got it Right—and How We Can, Too* (Brooklyn: Melville House, 2017), 101-3; Rolf Danielsen et al., *Norway: A History from the Vikings to Our Own Times*, trans. Michael Drake (Oslo: Scandinavian University Press, 1995), 420-22; Arbeiderpartiet, Sosialistisk Venstreparti, and Senterpartiet, *Politisk Plattform for Flertallsregjeringen, 2009-2013* (n.p., 2009), 28; Posten Norge, *Quarterly Report, First Quarter 2016* (n.p., 2016), [9]; *Norsk Rikskringkasting*, February 12, 2019, https://www.nrk.no/tromsogfinnmark/ruth-far-12-timers-reise-for-a-hente-posten_-_-det-er-helt-forferdelig-1.14425884; Posten Norge, *Annual and Sustainability Report, 2019* (n.p., 2020), 132-33 (translations by the author).

21. *Guardian* (London), February 6, 1993, 40; Meek, *Private Island*, 8-9; *Times* (London), June 3, 1987, 8; *Guardian* (London), January 8, 1994, 36.

22. *Financial Times*, March 27, 2001, 20; *Guardian* (London), October 9, 2002, 21; *Guardian* (London), February 16, 2002, 22; *Sunday Express* (London), January 1, 2006, 14; Tony Benn, "The Post Office Test," *Guardian* (London), October 11, 2007, 32; *Which?*, January 2007, 13.

23. *Daily Mirror* (London), July 21, 2013, 22; *Guardian* (London), July 10, 2014, https://www.theguardian.com/uk-news/2014/jul/11/royal-mail-sale-lost-1bn-says-select-committee; Postal Services Act, 2011, c. 5; *Yorkshire Evening Post* (Leeds), September 3, 2016, https://www.yorkshireeveningpost.co.uk/news/investigation-reveals-40-yorkshire-post-offices-shut-down-614546; *Daily Record and Sunday Mail* (Glasgow), January 20, 2016, 19; Syndex/Uni Global, *Economic and Social Consequences of Postal Services Liberalization*, 66; *Scotsman* (Edinburgh), March 13, 2015, 14; *Independent* (London), July 11, 2020, 36; *Times* (London), February 22, 2020, 39.

24. Tim Walsh, *Delivering Economic Development: Postal Infrastructure and Sectoral Reform in Developing Countries* (London: Consignia plc., 2001), 26; James W. Sauber, "Privatizing the Post: The World Bank's Role in the Americas" (paper presented at the UNI-Americas Postal Conference, November 1, 2000); David Rock, "Racking Argentina," *New Left Review* 17 (2002): 68-70; Paul Cooney, "Argentina's Quarter Century Experiment with Neoliberalism: From Dictatorship to Depression," *Revista de Economia Contemporânea* 11 no. 1 (2007): 18-19; *Wall Street Journal*, May 23, 1997, A14.

25. Sauber, "Privatizing the Post"; "Supporting Postal Development," World Bank Group, http://info.worldbank.org/ict/policyPostalService.html; Werner Baer and Gabriel Montes-Rojas, "From Privatization to Re-Nationalization: What Went Wrong with Privatizations in Argentina?," *Oxford Development Studies* 36, no. 3 (2008): 334; *Miami Herald*, April 7, 2006, 9A.

26. U.K. Comptroller and Auditor General, *Opening the Post*, 6; Susan Christopherson, "Market Rules and Territorial Outcomes: The Case of the United States," *International Journal of Urban and Regional Research* 17, no. 2 (1993): 274.

27. Carl H. Scheele, *A Short History of the Mail Service* (Washington, D.C.: Smithsonian Institution Press, 1970), 83; Rodman W. Paul, *California Gold: The Beginning of Mining in the Far West* (Cambridge, Mass.: Harvard University Press, 1947), 23-25; J. S. Holliday, *The World Rushed In: The California Gold Rush Experience* (New York: Simon and Schuster, 1981), 310-11; Henkin, *Postal Age*, 124; Ernest A. Wiltsee, *The Pioneer Miner and the Pack Mule Express* (San Francisco: California Historical Society, 1931), 26; Post Office Department, *Report of the Postmaster General, 1859* (Washington, D.C.: Government Printing Office, 1859), 1408; Le Roy R. Hafen, *The Overland Mail, 1849-1869: Promoter of Settlement, Precursor of Railroads* (Cleveland: Arthur H. Clark Company, 1926), 103-4; Ray Allen Billington, *Westward Expansion: A History of the American Frontier* (New York: The Macmillan Company, 1949), 634-36.

28. George Rogers Taylor, *The Transportation Revolution, 1815-1860* (New York: Rinehart & Company, 1951), 149-50; Edward Hungerford, *The Modern Railroad* (Chicago: A. C. McClurg & Co., 1911), 370-72; Adams Express Company, *The Adams Express Company: 150 Years* (Baltimore: Adams Express Company, 2004), [1]; Gallagher, *How the Post Office Created America*, 80; Oliver W. Holmes and Peter T. Rohrbach, *Stagecoach East: Stagecoach Days in the East from the Colonial Period to the Civil War* (Washington, D.C.: Smithsonian Institution Press, 1983), 130; Henkin, *Postal Age*, 18, 21, 30; Fuller, *RFD*, 12-13.

29. House, *Cost of Mail Transportation and Receipts of Postages*, 30th Congress, first session (1848), H. Doc. 72; Fuller, *American Mail*, 163-65; U.S. Postal Service, *Universal Service and the Postal Monopoly: A Brief History* (Washington, D.C.: U.S.P.S., 2008), 4, 13-14.

30. Kelly B. Olds, "The Challenge to the U.S. Postal Monopoly, 1839-1851," *Cato Journal* 15, no. 1 (1995): 22; Richard R. John, Jr., "Private Mail Delivery In the United States during the Nineteenth Century; A Sketch," *Business and Economic History* 15 (1986): 143-44.

31. Catherine J. Golden, *Posting It: The Victorian Revolution in Letter Writing* (Gainesville: University Press of Florida, 2009), 43-82; Howard Robinson, *The British Post Office: A History* (Princeton, N.J.: Princeton University Press, 1948), 379-80; David L. Straight, "Cheap Postage: A Tool for Social Reform," in *The Winton M. Blount Postal History Symposia: Select Papers, 2006-2009*, ed. Thomas Lera (Washington, D.C.: Smithsonian Institution Scholarly Press, 2010), 155-64; Henkin, *Postal Age*, 9, 27-30.

32. Conrad Kalmbacher, "The Postal Service as a Source of Sectional Controversy" (master's thesis, University of Texas, El Paso, 1972), 175-76; U. B. Phillips, *The Life of Robert Toombs* (New York: The Macmillan Company, 1913), 131; Robin L. Einhorn, *American Taxation, American Slavery* (Chicago: University of Chicago Press, 2006); Romain D. Huret, *American Tax Resisters* (Cambridge, Mass.: Harvard University Press, 2014), 27-28; William C. Davis, *Look Away! A History of the Confederate States of America* (New York: The Free Press, 2002), 100.

33. Confederate Post Office Department, *Report of the Postmaster-General to the President, April 29, 1861* (n.p., 1865), 11; Ben H. Procter, *Not Without Honor: The Life of John H. Reagan* (Austin: University of Texas Press, 1962), 132; August Dietz, *The Postal Service of the Confederate States of America* (Richmond, Va.: Press of the Dietz Print Company, 1929), 12; John Nathan Anderson, "Money or Northing: Confederate Postal System Collapse during the Civil War," *American Journalism* 30, no. 1 (2013): 65-86.

34. Geddes, *Saving the Mail*, 21; Chris R. Edwards, "Privatizing the U.S. Postal Service," *Tax & Budget Bulletin*, no. 75 (2016): [4]; Peter J. Ferrera, "Postal Service Problems: The Need to Free the Mail," in Hudgins, *Last Monopoly*, 28; *Christian Science Monitor*, December 12, 2002, 8.

35. *Billings Gazette*, December 10, 1997, 1A; *Billings Gazette*, August 27, 1998, 1A; Patrick Judge, "Montana's Power Trap: Electric Deregulation, Consumers, and the Environment" (master's thesis, University of Montana, 2000); CBS News, *60 Minutes*, August 10, 2003; *Great Falls Tribune*, August 8, 2003, 8A.

36. *Mail on Sunday* (London), February 6, 2011, 8; Campbell, *Politics of Postal Transformation*, 52; Julian P. Boyd, ed., *The Papers of Thomas Jefferson*, 42 vols. (Princeton, N.J.: Princeton University Press, 1958), 14:221; Martin Tolchin and Susan Tolchin, *Buying Into America: How Foreign Money Is Changing the Face of Our Nation* (New York: Times Books, 1988), 269.

37. *Grand Forks (N. Dak.) Herald*, August 17, 2020, 1; Milton Friedman, *An Economist's Protest: Columns in Political Economy* (Glen Ridge, N.J.: T. Horton, 1975), 287; John Charles Daly, ed., *U.S. Postal System: Can it Deliver?* (Washington, D.C.: AEI, 1978), 16. On conservatism and the postal system, see Christopher W. Shaw, "The Conservative Case for the U.S. Postal Service," *The American Conservative*, May 26, 2020, https://www.theamericanconservative.com/articles/the-conservative-case-for-the-u-s-postal-service/.

CHAPTER THREE: Democracy

1. *Congressional Record*, 91st Congress, second session, 1970, 116, 20201; Brodie, "Revolution by Mail," 143-46.

2. Robert James Parks, *European Origins of the Economic Ideas of Alexander Hamilton* (New York: Arno Press, 1977), 67, 75; Barbara B. Oberg, ed., *The Papers of Thomas Jefferson*, 42 vols. (Princeton, N.J.: Princeton University Press, 2002), 29:7; Cullinan, *Post Office Department*, 19, 26-27, 31-32; Bretz, "Some Aspects of Postal Extension Into the West," 144; James Thomas Flexner, *Washington: The Indispensable Man* (Boston: Little, Brown and Company, 1974), 322.

3. Hafen, *Overland Mail*, 26-27; James Thomas Flexner, *George Washington and the New Nation, 1783-1793* (Boston: Little, Brown and Company, 1970), 350; Fuller, *American Mail*, 40; Fuller, *RFD*, 4-5.

4. Kelly, *United States Postal Policy*, 41; Fuller, *American Mail*, 41; Brodie, "Revolution by Mail," 205-15; Joyce Appleby, *Capitalism and a New Social Order: The Republican Vision of the 1790s* (New York: New York University Press, 1984), 76; Rich, *History of the United States Post Office to the Year 1829*, 182; Henkin, *Postal Age*, 16-17.

5. Fuller, *American Mail*, 42; Gallagher, *How the Post Office Created America*, 32; George Washington, *The Writings of George Washington*, ed. John C. Fitzpatrick (Washington, D.C.: Government Printing Office, 1939), 305; W.W. Abbot and Dorothy Twohig, eds., *The Papers of George Washington: Presidential Series*, 20 vols. (Charlottesville: University Press of Virginia, 1993), 4:545; Philander D. Chase, ed., *Papers of George Washington: Presidential Series*, 9:115.

6. Kielbowicz, *News in the Mail*, 34; Richard D. Brown, *The Strength of a People: The Idea of an Informed Citizenry in America, 1650-1870* (Chapel Hill: University of North Carolina Press, 1996), 36, 91; Joseph M. Adelman, *Revolutionary Networks: The Business and Politics of Printing the News, 1763-1789* (Baltimore: Johns Hopkins University Press, 2019), 201-2; Richard B. Kielbowicz, "Newsgath-

ering by Printers' Exchanges Before the Telegraph," *Journalism History* 9, no. 2 (1982): 43; Chase, *Papers of George Washington*, 11:346; *Annals of Congress*, 2nd Congress, second session, 1792, 678.

7. Holmes and Rohrbach, *Stagecoach East*, 130; Kielbowicz, *News in the Mail*, 182; Adelman, *Revolutionary Networks*, 203; Henkin, *Postal Age*, 21; Oberg, *Papers of Thomas Jefferson*, 36:60; Charles Maurice Wiltse, *The Jeffersonian Tradition in American Democracy* (Chapel Hill: University of North Carolina Press, 1935), 144; Charles Grier Sellers, Jr., *The Market Revolution: Jacksonian America, 1815-1846* (New York: Oxford University Press, 1991), 370; Fuller, *American Mail*, 146-47.

8. Fuller, *American Mail*, 112, 115; Carl Russell Fish, *The Rise of the Common Man, 1830-1850* (New York: The Macmillan Company, 1927), 151; Sellers, *Market Revolution*, 370; Alexis de Tocqueville, *Democracy in America*, ed. Phillips Bradley, trans. Henry Reeve and Francis Bowen, 2 vols. (New York: Alfred A. Knopf, 1945), 1:186; Ben H. Bagdikian, *The Media Monopoly*, 6th ed. (Boston: Beacon Press, 2000).

9. Richard B. Kielbowicz, "Modernization, Communication Policy, and the Geopolitics of News, 1820-1860," *Critical Studies in Media Communication* 3, no. 1 (1986): 23; Richard B. Kielbowicz and Linda Lawson, "Protecting the Small-Town Press: Community, Social Policy, and Postal Privileges, 1845-1970," *Canadian Review of American Studies* 19, no. 1 (1988): 25; Arthur E. Summerfield with Charles Hurd, *U.S. Mail: The Story of the United States Postal Service* (New York: Holt, Rinehart, and Winston, 1960), 64; Kelly, *United States Postal Policy*, 62-64; Fuller, *American Mail*, 65.

10. Historian of the U.S. Postal Service, *Postage Rates for Periodicals: A Narrative History* (Washington, D.C.: U.S.P.S., 2010), 3; Jane Kennedy, "Development of Postal Rates: 1845-1955," *Land Economics* 33, no. 2 (1957): 98-100; Fuller, *American Mail*, 140; H. Shelton Stromquist, *Reinventing "The People": The Progressive Movement, the Class Problem, and the Origins of Modern Liberalism* (Urbana: University of Illinois Press, 2006), 46-48; Louis Filler, *Crusaders for American Liberalism* (Yellow Springs, Ohio: Antioch Press, 1950).

11. Lawrence C. Goodwyn, *Democratic Promise: The Populist Moment in America* (New York: Oxford University Press, 1976), 357-59; Charles Postel, *The Populist Vision* (New York: Oxford University Press, 2007), 62-65; C. Vann Woodward, *Origins of the New South, 1877-1913* (Baton Rouge: Louisiana State University Press, 1951), 247-48; John D. Hicks, *The Populist Revolt: A History of the Farmers' Alliance and the People's Party* (Minneapolis: University of Minnesota Press, 1931), 130-32; Wayne E. Fuller, "The Populists and the Post Office," *Agricultural History* 65, no. 1 (1991): 1-16.

12. *Domestic Mail Manual* 207 (2020); Senate Committee on Homeland Security and Government Affairs, *Laying Out the Reality of the United States Postal Service*, 114th Congress, second session (Washington, D.C.: Government Printing Office, 2017), 46, 235-36; Victor Pickard, "Restructuring Democratic Infrastructures: A Policy Approach to the Journalism Crisis," *Digital Journalism* 8, no. 6 (2020): 708-10.

13. Penelope Muse Abernathy, *The Expanding News Desert* (Chapel Hill: University of North Carolina Press, 2018), 12; Erik Peterson, "Paper Cuts: How Reporting Resources Affect Political News Coverage," *American Journal of Political Science*, 65, no. 2 (2021): 443-59; Daniel W. Hayes III and Jennifer L. Lawless, "The Decline of Local News and Its Effects: New Evidence from Longitudinal Data," *Journal of Politics* 80, no. 1 (2017): 332-36; James M. Snyder, Jr., and David Strömberg, "Press Coverage and Political Accountability," *Journal of Political Economy* 118, no. 2 (2010): 355-408; Meghan E. Rubado and Jay T. Jennings, "Political Consequences of the Endangered Local Watchdog: Newspaper Decline and Mayoral Elections in the United States," *Urban Affairs Review* 56, no. 5 (2020): 1327-56; Pengjie Gao, Chang Joo Lee, and Dermot Murphy, "Financing Dies in Darkness? The Impact of Newspaper Closures on Public Finance," *Journal of Financial Economics* 135, no. 2 (2020): 445-67; "Help for Community Newspapers," National Newspaper Association, April 13, 2020, https://www.nna.org/issue-brief-help-for-community-newspapers; National Newspaper Association, press release, December 6, 2019.

14. Fuller, *American Mail*, 137-38; Raymond H. Shove, "Cheap Book Production in the United States, 1870 to 1901" (master's thesis, University of Illinois, 1937), 57-58; Fuller, *Morality and the Mail*, 160; *Congressional Record*, 53rd Congress, second session, 1894, 26, 4052; Richard B. Kielbowicz, "Mere Merchandise or Vessels of Culture? Books in the Mail, 1792-1942," *Papers of the Bibliographic Society of America* 82, no. 2 (1988): 183-85.

15. *Statutes at Large* 45 (1928): 943; Linda Lawson and Richard B. Kielbowicz, "Library Materials in the Mail: A Policy History," *Library Quarterly* 58, no. 1 (1988): 31-37.
16. Kielbowicz, "Mere Merchandise or Vessels of Culture?," 194-99; *Statutes at Large* 53 (1938): 2497-98; *Statutes at Large* 56 (1942): 462.
17. *Domestic Mail Manual* 273 (2020); Lawson and Kielbowicz, "Library Materials in the Mail," 38-43.
18. Dorothy Ganfield Fowler, *Unmailable: Congress and the Post Office* (Athens: University of Georgia Press, 1977), 109-25; Adrian N. Anderson, "Albert Sidney Burleson: A Southern Politician in the Progressive Era" (Ph.D. diss., Texas Technological College, 1967), 226-35; Alexander Stewart Leidholdt, "Dancing with Two Cork Legs: The American Post Office's Stumbling Surveillance of the Foreign-Language Press during World War I," *Journalism History* 46, no. 3 (2020): 227-47; Cullinan, *Post Office Department*, 201-2; Robert K. Murray, *Red Scare: A Study in National Hysteria, 1919-1920* (Minneapolis: University of Minnesota Press, 1955), 204.
19. *Statutes at Large* 40 (1917): 328; *Congressional Record*, 53rd Congress, second session, 1894, 26, 3488; Subcommittee of the Committee on Post Office and Civil Service, *Adjustment of Postal Rates*, 81st Congress, first session (Washington, D.C.: Government Printing Office, 1949), 701; Richard B. Kielbowicz and Linda Lawson, "Reduced-Rate Postage for Nonprofit Organizations: A Policy History, Critique, and Proposal," *Harvard Journal of Law & Public Policy* 11, no. 2 (1988): 350-58.
20. David J. Garrow, *Bearing the Cross: Martin Luther King, Jr., and the Southern Christian Leadership Conference* (New York: William Morrow and Company, 1986), 166, 225; James L. Farmer, Jr., *Lay Bare the Heart: An Autobiography of the Civil Rights Movement* (New York: Arbor House, 1985), 265; Thomas B. Allen, *Guardian of the Wild: The Story of the National Wildlife Federation, 1936-1986* (Bloomington: Indiana University Press, 1987), 48-49; James Morton Turner, *The Promise of Wilderness: American Environmental Politics since 1964* (Seattle: University of Washington Press, 2012), 65-66; Kirkpatrick Sale, *The Green Revolution: The American Environmental Movement, 1962-1992* (New York: Hill and Wang, 1993), 23; Frank S. Zelko, *Make It a Green Peace! The Rise of Countercultural Environmentalism* (New York: Oxford University Press, 2013), 304.
21. Colston E. Warne, *The Consumer Movement: Lectures* (Manhattan, Kans.: Family Economics Trust Press, 1993), 74; Jeffrey M. Berry, *Lobbying for the People: The Political Behavior of Public Interest Groups* (Princeton, N.J.: Princeton University Press, 1977), 29-30; Public Citizen, *Public Citizen: The Sentinel of Democracy* (Washington, D.C.: Public Citizen Foundation, 2016), 21, 26; *Democratic Left* 20, no. 1 (1992): 13; Vogel, *Fluctuating Fortunes*, 224; Will Nixon, "Are We Burying Ourselves in Junk Mail?," *E: The Environmental Magazine* 4, no. 6 (1993): 30.
22. *Domestic Mail Manual* 703.1.0 (2020); Special Panel on Postal Reform and Oversight of the House Committee on Government Reform, *Answering the Administration's Call for Postal Reform—Parts I, II, and III*, 108th Congress, second session (Washington, D.C.: Government Printing Office, 2004), 366-67; Patrick Sullivan, "Nonprofit Magazines: Being in Print Still Key to Donor Satisfaction," *Non-Profit Times* 29, no. 9 (2015): 14; Mark Hrywna, "March of Dimes Grappling as 80th Birthday Approaches," *Non-Profit Times* 31, no. 10 (2017): 1; *Non-Profit Times*, July 11, 2017, https://www.thenonprofittimes.com/npt_articles/study-donors-react-direct-mail-email/; USPS Office of Inspector General, *Enhancing the Value of Mail: The Human Response*, Report No. RARC-WP-15-012 (June 2015); Mark Hrywna, "Individuals Powered Giving to Record Level in 2016," *Non-Profit Times* 31, no. 8 (2017): 1.
23. Sullivan, "Nonprofit Magazines," 14; *Philadelphia Inquirer*, June 13, 1999, G1; Norman Isaac Silber, *Test and Protest: The Influence of Consumers Union* (New York: Holmes & Meier Publishers, 1983), 122-28.
24. Christopher W. Shaw, "'Of Great Benefit': The Origin of Postal Services for Blind Americans," *Kansas History* 38, no. 3 (2015): 180-91; Judith M. Dixon and Alfred D. Hagle, "Free Matter: Nearly a Century of Change," in *That All May Read: Library Service for the Blind and Physically Handicapped People*, National Library Service for the Blind and Physically Handicapped (Washington, D.C.: Government Printing Office, 1983), 425-29; *Domestic Mail Manual* 703.5.0 (2020).
25. Robert M. Levi (director of legislative and political affairs, NAPS, Alexandria, Va.), interview by author, February 1, 2021; Jonathan W. White, "Canvassing the Troops: The Federal Government and the Soldiers' Right to Vote," *Civil War History* 50, no. 3 (2004): 291-317; Randy H. Hamilton, "American All-Mail Balloting: A Decade's Experience," *Public Administration Review* 48, no. 5

(1988): 860-66; Oregon Legislative Fiscal Office, *Oregon Vote by Mail* (Salem: Legislative Fiscal Office, 2020), 1-2.

26. Daniel M. Thompson et al., "Universal Vote-by-Mail Has No Impact on Partisan Turnout or Vote Share," *Proceedings of the National Academy of Sciences* 117, no. 35 (2020): 14052-56; Michael Jay Barber and John B. Holbein, "The Participatory and Partisan Impacts of Mandatory Vote-by-Mail," *Science Advances* 6, no. 35 (2020): 1-7; Amber McReynolds and Charles Stewart III, "Let's Put the Vote-by-Mail 'Fraud' Myth to Rest," *The Hill*, April 28, 2020, https://thehill.com/opinion/campaign/494189-lets-put-the-vote-by-mail-fraud-myth-to-rest.

27. Hutkins, "Do It Now: A Timeline of the Postal Service's Work Hour Reduction Plan"; Paul V. Hogrogian, "COVID-19 Pandemic Has Devastating Effect," *Mail Handler*, Summer 2020, 6; NAACP, press release, August 14, 2020; MSNBC, *Deadline: White House*, August 21, 2020; Mark Jamison, "DeJoy's Fix for the Post Office: The Wrong Time, the Wrong Plan, the Wrong Man," Save the Post Office, August 29, 2020, https://www.savethepostoffice.com/dejoys-fix-for-the-post-office-the-wrong-time-the-wrong-plan-the-wrong-man/.

28. Hutkins, "Lawsuits Against DeJoy, USPS & Trump Over Mail Delays and Election Mail"; *CBS News*, November 2, 2020, https://www.cbsnews.com/news/usps-postal-service-delivery-rates-slower/; Jane Slaughter, "How Postal Workers Saved the Election," *Labor Notes*, no. 501 (2020): 7; U.S. Postal Service, *Delivering the Nation's Election Mail in an Extraordinary Year* (Washington, D.C.: U.S.P.S., 2021), 19; Jeanette Senecal, "Giving Thanks to the People Behind Our Elections in 2020," League of Women Voters, November 24, 2020, https://www.lwv.org/blog/giving-thanks-people-behind-our-elections-2020; Steven Hutkins, "The 2020 Mail Delays: Stats & Charts," Save the Post Office, February 14, 2021, https://www.savethepostoffice.com/2020-mail-delays-stats-charts/.

CHAPTER FOUR: Community

1. Subcommittee of the Senate Committee on Appropriations, *Financial Security of the U.S. Postal Service*, 30; Richard J. Margolis, *At the Crossroads: An Inquiry into Rural Post Offices and the Communities They Serve* (Washington, D.C.: Government Printing Office, 1980), 10.

2. *Federal Register* 67, no. 240 (2002): 76671-72; President's Commission on the United States Postal Service, *Embracing the Future: Making the Tough Choices to Preserve Universal Mail Service* (Washington, D.C.: Government Printing Office, 2003), 17; *Bismarck (N. Dak.) Tribune*, July 19, 2003, 6A; Office of Senator Harry Reid, press release, August 1, 2003.

3. Christopher W. Shaw, *Preserving the People's Post Office* (Washington, D.C.: Essential Books, 2006), 4-5; Senate Committee on Governmental Affairs, *U.S. Postal Service: What Can Be Done to Ensure Its Future Viability?*, 108th Congress, first session (Washington, D.C.: Government Printing Office, 2003), 7; President's Commission, *Embracing the Future*, 83, 153; *New York Times*, September 6, 2014, A16. Travelers and new arrivals to town also use general delivery.

4. Paul M. Weyrich, "The Next Conservatism #19: The Public Space," *Townhall*, February 13, 2006, https://townhall.com/columnists/paulweyrich/2006/02/13/the-next-conservatism-19-the-public-space-n1229502; Christopher Lasch, *The Revolt of the Elites: And the Betrayal of Democracy* (New York: W.W. Norton, 1995), 117.

5. Cameron B. Blevins, "The Postal West: Spatial Integration and the American West, 1865-1902" (Ph.D. diss., Stanford University, 2015), 135-36; Everett N. Dick, *The Sod-House Frontier, 1854-1890* (New York: D. Appleton-Century Company, 1937), 409.

6. *Abilene (Tex.) Reporter-News*, March 23, 2011, A4; *Atlanta Journal-Constitution*, June 25, 2002, 1A; *Central Wisconsin Sunday* (Wausau), August 17, 2003, 1A.

7. *Montgomery (Ala.) Advertiser*, March 21, 2006, 9; *Contra Costa Times* (Walnut Creek, Calif.), August 18, 2012, 1B; *Daily Courier-Observer* (Massena, N.Y.), May 12, 2012, 2; *Tribune-Democrat* (Johnstown, Pa.), December 6, 2005, 5; *Pittsburgh Post-Gazette*, May 11, 2012, A1.

8. Daniel M. Heins (national president, UPMA, Alexandria, Va.), interview by author, February 5, 2021; *Ithaca (N.Y.) Journal*, March 25, 2005, 12; *Kitsap Sun* (Bremerton, Wash.), June 2, 2001, A1.

9. Robert D. Putnam, *Bowling Alone: The Collapse and Revival of American Community* (New York: Simon & Schuster, 2000), 402; National Public Radio, *Morning Edition*, March 11, 1997; Sherry

Turkle, *Alone Together: Why We Expect More from Technology and Less from Each Other* (New York: Basic Books, 2011).

10. Commission on Postal Service, *Report of the Commission on Postal Service*, 3 vols. (Washington, D.C.: The Service, 1977), 3b:1382; *Statutes at Large* 84 (1970): 719; Steve D. LeNoir (president, National League of Postmasters, Alexandria, Va.), interview by author, July 21, 2005; Margolis, *At the Crossroads*, 21; *Daily Herald* (Arlington Heights, Ill.), August 17, 2003, 1; *Daily Oklahoman* (Oklahoma City, Okla.), June 9, 1997, 1; Robert M. Levi (director of government relations, NA-PUS, Alexandria, Va.), interview by author, May 18, 2005.

11. *Wall Street Journal*, May 9, 1977, 14; General Accounting Office, *$100 Million Could Be Saved Annually in Postal Operations in Rural America Without Affecting the Quality of Service*, GGD-75-87 (June 1975); Kathleen Conkey, *The Postal Precipice: Can the U.S. Postal Service Be Saved?* (Washington, D.C.: Center for Study of Responsive Law, 1983), 332-33; *Chicago Tribune*, February 27, 1976, 19; *New York Times*, March 30, 1976, 27.

12. Ford, *Gerald R. Ford, 1976-77*, 3:2321; *Statutes at Large* 90 (1976): 1303, 1310-11.

13. General Accounting Office, *Information on Post Office Closures, Appeals, and Affected Communities*, GAO/GGD-97-38BR (March 1997), 4; Steven Hutkins, "The Postal Service Runs Amok: How Not to Close a Post Office," Save the Post Office, October 22, 2011, https://www.savethepostoffice.com/postal-service-runs-amok-how-not-close-post-office/.

14. Senate, *Post Office Discontinuance Accountability Act of 2017*, 115th Congress, second session (2018), S. Rept. 115-329; PRC Public Representative, "Public Representative Comments," Docket No. PI2016-3, June 15, 2016.

15. *Wall Street Journal*, January 24, 2011, A1; Prairie City, S. Dak., Residents, "Letters from the Community Regarding the Closure," Docket No. PI2010-1, February 3, 2010; *Bismarck (N. Dak.) Tribune*, February 6, 2010, 1A.

16. Commission on Postal Service, *Report of the Commission*, 3b:1397; *Omaha World-Herald*, January 3, 2004, 1B.

17. General Accountability Office, *Expanding Nonpostal Products and Services at Retail Facilities Could Result in Benefits but May Have Limited Viability*, GAO-20-354 (2020), 12-13; David J. Frederickson, letter to Susan Collins, November 14, 2003.

18. John E. Potter, *Remarks By Postmaster General John E. Potter to the President's Commission on the Postal Service* (Washington, D.C.: U.S.P.S., 2003), 2; John E. Potter (postmaster general, U.S.P.S., Washington, D.C.), interview by Ralph Nader and author, July 21, 2005; Robert M. Levi, interview by author, July 29, 2005.

19. *Wall Street Journal*, January 24, 2011, A1.

20. *New York Times*, July 27, 2011, A13; *Chicago Tribune*, February 22, 2012, 6; *Wall Street Journal*, July 27, 2011, A19; *Buffalo News*, October 12, 2011, B3.

21. *Federal Times*, May 14, 2012, 6; J. Blake Perkins, *Hillbilly Hellraisers: Federal Power and Populist Defiance in the Ozarks* (Urbana: University of Illinois Press, 2017), 221; *Times-Leader* (Wilkes-Barre, Pa.), May 10, 2012, 1A.

22. *Federal Times*, May 14, 2012, 6; Steve D. LeNoir (postmaster, U.S.P.S., Wedgefield, S.C.), interview by author, March 10, 2021; Government Accountability Office, *Post Office Changes Suggest Cost Savings*, GAO-16-385 (April 2016), 8-10; *Watertown (N.Y.) Daily Times*, December 14, 2012, B2; *Grand Forks (N. Dak.) Herald*, October 19, 2012, 1B; *Manchester (N.H.) Union Leader*, June 14, 2012, 1.

23. *Portland (Maine) Press Herald*, August 22, 2003, 1A; *Worcester (Mass.) Telegram & Gazette*, September 24, 2003, B1; *Iowa City Press-Citizen*, August 10, 2002, 1A.

24. *Time* 149, no. 8 (1997): 33; *New York Times*, December 3, 1996, B9.

25. *Time* 149, no. 8 (1997): 33; Laura Skaggs and Kennedy Lawson Smith, "Wait a Minute, Mr. Postman!," *Main Street*, no. 131 (1997), 2; *Baltimore Sun*, November 29, 1999, 1B; Ryan Zigelbauer, Bill Ryan, and Steven H. Grabow, *The Importance of Government Facilities in Downtowns: An Analysis of Business Establishments in Wisconsin's County Seats* (Jefferson: University of Wisconsin—Extension, 2005), 3.

26. *New York Times*, July 10, 1988, 31; *Philadelphia Inquirer*, December 1, 1999, B5.

27. *Washington Post*, May 4, 1997, C1; Steven Hutkins, "The Annexation of the Post Office," Save the Post Office, July 26, 2012, https://www.savethepostoffice.com/annexation-post-office/; Steven Hutkins (founder, Save the Post Office, Rhinecliff, N.Y.), email to author, January 10, 2021.

28. Andres Duany, Elizabeth Plater-Zyberk, and Jeff Speck, *Suburban Nation: The Rise of Sprawl and the Decline of the American Dream* (New York: North Point Press, 2000), 115-33; Richard J. Jackson and Chris S. Kochtitzky, *Creating a Healthy Environment: The Impact of the Built Environment on Public Health* (Washington, D.C.: Sprawl Watch Clearinghouse, 2001), 12; Richard Retting, *Pedestrian Traffic Fatalities by State: 2019 Preliminary Data* (Washington, D.C.: Governors Highway Safety Association, 2020), 5; Reid H. Ewing, Richard A. Schieber, and Charles V. Zegeer, "Urban Sprawl as a Risk Factor in Motor Vehicle Occupant and Pedestrian Fatalities," *American Journal of Public Health* 93, no. 9 (2003): 1541-45; Michelle Ernst, *Mean Streets, 2004* (Washington, D.C.: Surface Transportation Policy Project, 2004), 16; Howard Frumkin, "Urban Sprawl and Public Health," *Public Health Reports* 117, no. 3 (2002): 201-17; Brian Stone, Jr., "Urban Sprawl and Air Quality in Large U.S. Cities," *Journal of Environmental Management* 86, no. 4 (2008): 688-98; Julia Freedgood et al., *Farms Under Threat: The State of the States* (Washington, D.C.: American Farmland Trust, 2020), 25; James Howard Kunstler, *The Geography of Nowhere: The Rise and Decline of America's Man-Made Landscape* (New York: Simon & Schuster, 1993), 10.

29. *Wall Street Journal*, August 30, 1993, B1; Jessica Oski et al., *A Local Official's Guide to Developing Better Community Post Offices* (n.p., 2001), [2-3].

30. James H. Bruns, *Great American Post Offices* (New York: John Wiley & Sons, 1998); Antoinette J. Lee, *Architects to the Nation: The Rise and Decline of the Supervising Architect's Office* (New York: Oxford University Press, 2000); U.S. Postal Service, *History of Post Office Construction, 1900-1940* (Washington, D.C.: U.S.P.S., 1982); U.S. Postal Service, *USPS Nationwide Historic Context Study: Postal Facilities Constructed or Occupied Between 1940 and 1971* (Washington, D.C.: U.S.P.S., 2012).

31. President's Commission, *Embracing the Future*, 98; Ditch, "Privatization Should Be on the Table"; Geddes, *Saving the Mail*, 124; Geddes, *Return to Sender*, 15-16; Bruns, *Great American Post Offices*, 130.

32. *New York Times*, February 2, 2013, A19; *New York Times*, February 5, 2014, A17; *New York Daily News*, January 14, 2014, 29; *Welcome2TheBronx*, October 31, 2018, https://welcome2thebronx.com/2018/10/31/exclusive-bronx-general-post-office-for-sale-again/.

33. *Berkeley (Calif.) Voice*, June 26, 2012, 1A; Citizens to Save the Berkeley Post Office, *Golden State Heritage: Saving a Legacy* (n.p., 2013); Barbara Lee, letter to Diana Alvarado, April 23, 2013; *Berkeley (Calif.) Voice*, July 15, 2016, 1A; *East Bay Times* (Oakland), May 17, 2018, 7B.

34. Peter Byrne, "Going Postal," *East Bay Express* (Oakland), September 18, 2013, https://www.eastbayexpress.com/oakland/going-postal/Content?oid=3713528&showFullText=true; USPS Office of Inspector General, *Postal Service Management of CBRE Real Estate Transactions*, Report No. SM-AR-15-003 (April 2015); Steven Hutkins, "The Postal Service Gets a New Real Estate Provider," Save the Post Office, January 30, 2018, https://www.savethepostoffice.com/the-postal-service-gets-a-new-real-estate-provider/. The chairman of CBRE Group, Inc., was Richard C. Blum—husband of Senator Dianne Feinstein (D-Calif.).

35. Advisory Council on Historic Preservation, *Preserving Historic Post Offices: A Report to Congress* (Washington, D.C.: Advisory Council on Historic Preservation, 2014). For examples of former post offices serving new civic roles, see Katherine Coffield, "Keeping Post Offices Public: Three Case Studies on the Disposal and Rehabilitation of Historic Post Offices" (master's thesis, Cornell University, 2013).

36. House, H.R. 5377, 113th Congress, second session (2014); National Trust for Historic Preservation, press release, August 1, 2014.

37. Robert D. Leighninger, Jr., *Long-Range Public Investment: The Forgotten Legacy of the New Deal* (Columbia: University of South Carolina Press, 2007); Bruns, *Great American Post Offices*, 94-97; *Congressional Record*, 90th Congress, second session, 1968, 114, 24095; U.S. Postal Service, *History of Post Office Construction, 1900-1940*, 31-32; William B. Rhoads, "Franklin D. Roosevelt and Dutch Colonial Architecture," *New York History* 59, no. 4 (1978): 430-64; Anthony P. Musso, *FDR and the Post Office: A Young Boy's Fascination, a World Leader's Passion* (n.p., 2006), 62-101.

CHAPTER FIVE: Cutbacks

1. *New York Times*, February 27, 1976, 9; *Reno (Nev.) Gazette-Journal*, April 7, 2002, 1A.
2. General Accounting Office, *Deteriorating Financial Outlook Increases Need for Transformation*, GAO-02-355 (February 2002), 45; *Time* 151, no. 2 (1998): 46; National Research Council, *Electronic Message Systems for the U.S. Postal Service* (Washington, D.C.: National Academy of Sciences, 1976), 12; Irwin Lebow, *Information Highways and Byways: From the Telegraph to the 21st Century* (New York: IEEE Press, 1995), 53; *Oregonian* (Portland), February 24, 2006, E1; Ronald R. Kline, *Consumers in the Country: Technology and Social Change in Rural America* (Baltimore: Johns Hopkins University Press, 2000), 66; Jonathan C. Coopersmith, *Faxed: The Rise and Fall of the Fax Machine* (Baltimore: Johns Hopkins University Press, 2015), 214.
3. Historian of the U.S. Postal Service, *First-Class Mail Volume since 1926* (Washington, D.C.: U.S.P.S., 2021); USPS Office of Inspector General, *What's Up with Mail? How Mail Use Is Changing Across the United States*, Report No. RARC-WP-17-006 (April 2017), 9-10.
4. Ruth Susswein, "Preserving Paper Choice," *Consumer Action News*, Winter 2018-2019, 1; *Sun Sentinel* (Fort Lauderdale, Fla.), December 10, 2018, 1; *Pittsburgh Post-Gazette*, February 20, 2019, B7; Judy T. Lin et al., *Investors in the United States, 2019* (Washington, D.C.: FINRA Investor Education Foundation, 2019), 17; Melissa Cuddington, "Feeling the Pressure to Go Paperless?," National Consumers League, June 17, 2018, https://nclnet.org/paperless_billing/; Alegna Howard, "Given the Choice, Consumers Prefer a Paper Trail," *Consumer Action News*, Winter 2018-2019, 1; Keep Me Posted, *Paper or Digital? Consumer Choice Is Being Removed by Corporations* (n.p., 2018); Joanne McNeish, "A Plea to Businesses: Don't Take Away Our Paper Bills," *The Conversation*, March 9, 2020, https://theconversation.com/a-plea-to-businesses-dont-take-away-our-paper-bills-131960.
5. U.S. Postal Service, *Postal Facts, 2020* (Washington, D.C.: U.S.P.S., 2020), 3; U.S. Postal Service, *Public Cost and Revenue Analysis, FY 2019* (Washington, D.C.: U.S.P.S., 2020).
6. Kirstin B. Blom and Katelin P. Isaacs, *U.S. Postal Service Retiree Health Benefits and Pension Funding Issues*, Congressional Research Service Report No. R43349 (January 2015); National Association of Letter Carriers, *Misdiagnosis: A Review of the Report of the White House Task Force on the Postal Service* (Washington, D.C.: NALC, 2019); James W. Sauber (chief of staff, NALC, Washington, D.C.), interview by author, February 12, 2021; Senate, S. 1720, 117th Congress, first session (2021); *Statutes at Large* 120 (2006): 3200, 3202.
7. Conkey, *Postal Precipice*, 91, 100; *Journal of Commerce*, March 9, 1976, 4; *New York Times*, March 30, 1976, 27.
8. *Postal Life* 13, no. 5 (1980): 7; *New York Herald Tribune*, April 19, 1950, 1; *Wall Street Journal*, March 11, 1976, 3; Historian of the U.S. Postal Service, *Deliveries per Day* (Washington, D.C.: U.S.P.S., 2005); Office of Technology Assessment, *Implications of Electronic Mail and Message Systems for the U.S. Postal Service* (Washington, D.C.: Government Printing Office, 1982), 15.
9. *Federal Register* 43, no. 193 (1978): 45839-42; Government Accountability Office, *Delivery Mode Conversions Could Yield Large Savings*, GAO-14-444 (May 2014), 11; Commission on Postal Service, *Report of the Commission*, 2:78; Lawrence F. O'Brien, interview by Michael L. Gillette, November 21, 1986, 6, Lyndon B. Johnson Presidential Library and Museum, Austin, Tex.; *Washington Post*, May 4, 1983, E21.
10. William S. Broomfield, "Let's Put 'Service' Back in Postal Service," *Christian Science Monitor*, November 12, 1991, 18; Shaw, *Preserving the People's Post Office*, 92; Douglas F. Carlson (postal expert, San Francisco, Calif.), interview by author, February 9, 2021; Douglas F. Carlson, "Correspondence with the Postal Service Concerning Nationwide Policy for Removal of Collection Boxes," Docket No. C2003-1, November 21, 2002.
11. *Philadelphia Inquirer*, October 8, 2007, B1.
12. *Chicago Tribune*, July 21, 2009, 27; *Morning Call* (Allentown, Pa.), August 31, 2004, A1; *San Francisco Chronicle*, November 29, 2002, A1.
13. *Morning Call* (Allentown, Pa.), June 7, 2005, B1; *Rockford (Ill.) Register Star*, July 26, 2014, 1; *Los Angeles Times*, March 18, 2009, A3; *Washington Post*, October 16, 2002, A23; *Newsday*, June 3, 2002, A27.

14. U.S. Postal Service, "Answer of the United States Postal Service," Docket No. C2003-1, December 20, 2002; U.S. Census Bureau, press release, July 23, 2020; Public Representative, "Public Representative Comments," Docket No. ACR2020, February 1, 2021; *Record* (Hackensack, N.J.), August 4, 1997, A1; *Times Union* (Albany, N.Y.), November 4, 2005, B1.

15. Government Accountability Office, *Delivery Mode Conversions Could Yield Large Savings*, 5-6; *Seattle Post-Intelligencer*, February 5, 1999, C1; *St. Petersburg (Fla.) Times*, July 25, 1999, 8; *St. Petersburg (Fla.) Times*, May 19, 1999, 1; *Chico (Calif.) Enterprise-Record*, January 16, 2016, 4; *Los Angeles Times*, May 24, 1999, B1; *Arlington (Tex.) Morning News*, November 27, 1998, 1C; *Press Democrat* (Santa Rosa, Calif.), November 5, 2010, B1.

16. *Orlando (Fla.) Sentinel*, March 15, 2005, B1; *Herald-Sun* (Durham, N.C.), August 15, 2005, A1; *News & Observer* (Raleigh, N.C.), April 25, 2005, A1; Office of Representative Susan Davis, press release, January 7, 2019.

17. *Columbian* (Vancouver, Wash.), November 10, 2017, C1; *Times-Herald* (Vallejo, Calif.), February 24, 2017, 1; *Modesto (Calif.) Bee*, August 27, 2016, 1A; *Albuquerque (N.M.) Journal*, March 4, 2008, 1; *Washington Post*, June 19, 2003, E1; *East Bay Times* (Oakland), April 5, 2017, 1B; *Redding (Calif.) Record Searchlight*, April 18, 2007, A6; Office of Representative Susan Davis, press release, January 7, 2019.

18. *Washington Post*, January 15, 2006, F1; *Santa Fe (N.M.) New Mexican*, January 10, 2006, A1; *Las Cruces (N.M.) Sun-News*, January 20, 2006, 1A; *Berkeley (Calif.) Daily Planet*, January 10-12, 2006, 1; WOAI-TV, January 9, 2021, https://news4sanantonio.com/news/trouble-shooters/postal-service-has-just-two-workers-repairing-vandalized-mailboxes-for-all-of-san-antonio; *Arizona Republic* (Phoenix), December 19, 2005, 1; *San Diego Union-Tribune*, December 18, 2005, A1; *Washington Times*, April 18, 2021, https://www.washingtontimes.com/news/2021/apr/18/dc-residents-frustrated-month-long-mail-delay/.

19. Carlson, interview, February 9, 2021; Mailers Technical Advisory Committee, *Membership Guide, 2020* (n.p., 2020); National Postal Forum, *Innovating the Journey: At Every Touchpoint* (n.p., 2019).

20. House Committee on Post Office and Civil Service, *The Postal Service Act of 1979*, 96th Congress, first session (Washington, D.C.: Government Printing Office, 1979), 151; Senate Committee on Governmental Affairs, *The Report of the Presidential Commission on the U.S. Postal Service: Preserving Access and Affordability*, 108th Congress, first session (Washington, D.C.: Government Printing Office, 2003), 200.

21. John Haldi and William J. Olson, *Postal Costing and Pricing: Top Down Discounts versus Bottom Up Surcharges* (n.p., 2004); Association for Postal Commerce, "Reply Comments," Docket No. ACR2013, February 14, 2014; Philip A. Tabbita (manager of contract negotiations and special projects, APWU, Washington, D.C.), interview by author, February 2, 2021; Special Panel on Postal Reform and Oversight of the House Committee on Government Reform, *Answering the Administration's Call for Postal Reform*, 134.

22. U.S. Postal Service, *Transformation Plan Progress Report* (Washington, D.C., U.S.P.S., 2004), 3; U.S. Postal Service, *Transformation Plan* (Washington, D.C., U.S.P.S., 2002), 14, 17.

23. U.S. Postal Service, *Transformation Plan*, v, x; Joint Hearing Before the House Committee on Government Reform and Senate Committee on Governmental Affairs, *The Postal Service in Crisis: A Joint Hearing on Principles for Meaningful Reform*, 108th Congress, second session (Washington, D.C.: Government Printing Office, 2004), 177; William B. Disbrow, *Statement to President's Commission on the United States Postal Service* (n.p., 2003) 12.

24. Valpak Direct Marketing Systems, Inc., "Initial Brief," Docket No. N2012-1, July 10, 2012; National Postal Policy Council and Major Mailers Association, "Comments," Docket No. N2012-1, July 10, 2012; Association for Postal Commerce, "Initial Comments," Docket No. ACR2014, February 2, 2015.

25. *Washington Post*, October 3, 2008, D3; Federal Financial Management, Government Information, Federal Services, and International Security Subcommittee of the Senate Committee on Homeland Security and Governmental Affairs, *The U.S. Postal Service in Crisis*, 111th Congress, first session (Washington, D.C.: Government Printing Office, 2010), 5, 22; *Washington Post*, August 26, 2009, A13.

26. *Washington Post*, March 2, 2010, A3; U.S. Postal Service, *Ensuring a Viable Postal Service for America: An Action Plan for the Future* (Washington, D.C.: U.S.P.S., 2010); McKinsey & Company, *USPS Future Business Model* (n.p., 2010), 32.

27. *Washington Post*, March 22, 2010, A15; *Washington Post*, May 10, 2010, A15; *Pittsburgh Post-Gazette*, March 11, 2010, A7; *Washington Post*, March 10, 2010, A22.

28. *Washington Post*, May 13, 2010, A14; *Wall Street Journal*, January 24, 2011, A1; *New York Times*, July 27, 2011, A13; *Christian Science Monitor*, September 6, 2011, https://www.csmonitor.com/USA/2011/0906/Crunch-time-at-US-Postal-Service-Five-questions-about-post-office-closings/Do-potential-closures-represent-a-failure-of-the-USPS-mission; *Washington Post*, March 25, 2011, B4.

29. *New York Times*, September 5, 2011, A1; House, H.R. 2309, 112th Congress, first session (2011); *Washington Post*, June 24, 2011, A14.

30. *Washington Post*, September 16, 2011, A10; National Newspaper Association, "Initial Brief," Docket No. N2012-1, July 10, 2012; National Postal Mail Handlers Union, "Brief," Docket No. N2012-1, July 11, 2012; National Postal Policy Council and Major Mailers Association, "Comments," Docket No. N2012-1, July 10, 2012; *Inside Tucson (Ariz.) Business* 21, no. 40 (2012): 5.

31. *New York Times*, December 6, 2011, B1; *Los Angeles Times*, December 6, 2011, B1; *Los Angeles Daily News*, December 6, 2011, A1; APWU Helena Local 649, "Complaint," Docket No. C2013-8, April 11, 2013.

32. *Chicago Tribune*, May 10, 2012, 5; U.S. Postal Service, press release, May 17, 2012; *Wall Street Journal*, May 18, 2012, A2; *New York Times*, May 18, 2012, A19; *New York Times*, May 27, 2012, A20.

33. *Washington Post*, October 5, 2012, B4 ; *Washington Post*, September 6, 2013, B4; Valpak Direct Marketing Systems, Inc., "Initial Brief," Docket No. N2012-1, July 10, 2012; *Washington Post*, February 7, 2013, A1; *San Francisco Chronicle*, March 22, 2013, A8; *The Hill*, April 11, 2013, 7.

34. U.S. Postal Service, press release, November 14, 2013; *Washington Post*, January 17, 2014, A13; American Postal Workers Union, "USPS Send Jobs, Work to Staples," *APWU News Bulletin*, November 26, 2013; *Wall Street Journal*, April 23, 2014, A3.

35. *Washington Post*, January 17, 2014, A13; *Retiree Record* 15, no. 12 (2020): 1; *Washington Post*, April 25, 2014, A16; *Los Angeles Times*, April 25, 2014, B2; American Federation of Teachers, press release, July 12, 2014; New York State United Teachers, press release, July 14, 2014; *California Teacher* 67, no. 4 (2014): 5.

36. *Washington Post*, January 1, 2015, A5; *Washington Post*, November 15, 2014, A5; R. Jon Tester et al., letter to Barbara Mikulski et al., August 14, 2014; David P. Joyce et al., letter to Hal D. Rogers et al., September 11, 2014; Ruth Y. Goldway, "Postal Service Cuts Ill-Considered," *The Hill*, January 13, 2015, https://thehill.com/blogs/congress-blog/economy-budget/229239-postal-service-cuts-ill-considered; Association for Postal Commerce, "Initial Comments," Docket No. ACR2014, February 2, 2015; *Arizona Daily Star* (Tucson), May 27, 2015, A2; USPS Office of Inspector General, *Operational Window Change Savings*, Report No. NO-AR-19-001 (October 2018).

37. Valpak Direct Marketing Systems, Inc., "Initial Brief," Docket No. N2012-1, July 10, 2012; *Linn's Stamp News*, January 21, 2016, https://www.linns.com/postal-updates/2016/january/usps-abandons-quest-to-end-saturday-mail-delivery.html; *New York Times*, November 11, 2013, B1; Satish Jindel, "Pressure Increases on Couriers for Seven-Day B2C Service," *Journal of Commerce*, January 3, 2018, https://www.joc.com/international-logistics/logistics-providers/pressure-increases-large-deliverers-7-day-b2b-service_20180103.html; House Committee on Oversight and Reform, *The Financial Condition of the Postal Service*, 116th Congress, first session (Washington, D.C.: Government Publishing Office, 2019), 11; Alexandra Bradbury, "Staples Removed," *Labor Notes*, no. 455 (2017): 1, 3-5.

38. Philip F. Rubio, *Undelivered: From the Great Postal Strike of 1970 to the Manufactured Crisis of the U.S. Postal Service* (Chapel Hill: University of North Carolina Press, 2020), 206; *Berkeleyside*, October 28, 2016, https://www.berkeleyside.com/2016/10/28/berkeley-mail-delivery-prompts-tidal-wave-of-complaints; *East Bay Times* (Oakland), December 23, 2016, 1A; Edward P. Fletcher (president, NALC Branch 1111, Richmond, Calif.), interview by author, February 10, 2021; *WJZY-TV*, April 1, 2021, http://www.fox46.com/news/postal-workers-protest-alleged-harassment-mistreatment-by-management/.

39. Hutkins, "The 2020 Mail Delays: Stats & Charts."

40. Pew Research Center, *Public Holds Broadly Favorable Views of Many Federal Agencies* (Philadelphia: Pew Research Center, 2020), 5; Chuck Zlatkin (legislative and political director, New York Metro Area Postal Union, New York, N.Y.), interview by author, February 23, 2021.

41. Oregon Rural Letter Carriers' Association, letter to President's Commission on the U.S. Postal Service, February 7, 2003; Potter, interview, July 21, 2005.

42. LeNoir, interview, March 10, 2021; *Boston Globe*, June 12, 2005, 1; USPS Office of Inspector General, *Modes of Delivery and Customer Engagement with Advertising Mail*, Report No. RARC-WP-15-009 (April 2015).

43. Commission on Postal Service, *Report of the Commission*, 3b:1274.

CHAPTER SIX: Competitors

1. *Journal of Commerce*, February 14, 2000, 1.

2. *Business Week*, October 16, 1948, 21; U.S. Postal Service, *The United States Postal Service: An American History, 1775-2002* (Washington, D.C.: U.S.P.S., 2003), 26; Cullinan, *Post Office Department*, 196, 245; *Business Week*, February 19, 1966, 32; Fuller, *American Mail*, 334-36; House, *Subcommittee Staff Report on the United States Postal Service's National Bulk Mail System*, 94th Congress, first session (1976), H. Com. Prt. 94-12, 2; Post Office Department, *Annual Report of the Postmaster General, 1966* (Washington, D.C.: Government Printing Office, 1966), 31-32; Post Office Department, *Annual Report of the Postmaster General, 1965* (Washington, D.C.: Government Printing Office, 1965), 173; Senate Committee on Post Office and Civil Service, *Postal Modernization*, 91st Congress, first session (Washington, D.C.: Government Printing Office, 1969), 722.

3. Gerald Cullinan, *The United States Postal Service* (New York: Praeger Publishers, 1973), 239; Government Accountability Office, *The Service's Strategy for Realigning Its Mail Processing Infrastructure Lacks Clarity, Criteria, and Accountability*, GAO-05-261 (April 2005), 16; Milton R. Moskowitz, Michael Katz, and Robert E. Levering, eds., *Everybody's Business—An Almanac: The Irreverent Guide to Corporate America* (San Francisco: Harper & Row Publishers, 1980), 655; *Wall Street Journal*, August 25, 1980, 1; Christopher H. Lovelock and Charles B. Weinberg, "The Role of Marketing in Improving Postal Service Effectiveness," in *The Future of the Postal Service*, ed. Joel L. Fleishman (New York: Praeger Publishers, 1983), 170-71; House, *Subcommittee Staff Report on the United States Postal Service's National Bulk Mail System*, 1; General Accounting Office, *Problems of the New National Bulk Mail System*, GGD-76-100 (December 1976), 1.

4. Conkey, *Postal Precipice*, 72-106, 353-66; *Postal Life* 2, no. 5 (1969): [i-1]; *San Francisco Chronicle*, January 9, 1975, 1; House, *Subcommittee Staff Report on the United States Postal Service's National Bulk Mail System*, 5; General Accounting Office, *Grim Outlook for the United States Postal Service's National Bulk Mail System*, GGD-78-59 (May 1978); Joel L. Fleishman, "Postal Policy and Public Accountability: Is the 1970 Bargain Coming Unglued?," in Fleishman, *Future of the Postal Service*, 94; *New York Times*, May 30, 1977, 1; *U.S. News & World Report* 85, no. 19 (1978): 87.

5. *Wall Street Journal*, July 13, 1970, 3; *San Francisco Examiner*, October 6, 1977, 14; *U.S. News & World Report* 92, no. 8 (1982): 53; General Accounting Office, *Pricing Postal Services in a Competitive Environment*, GGD-92-49 (March 1992), 26; *Philadelphia Inquirer*, January 12, 1968, 3; *Washington Post*, August 6, 2017, G5.

6. *New York Times*, February 21, 2005, C2; *Denver Post*, July 19, 2001, A1; *Oakland Tribune*, August 6, 2001, 7.

7. *New York Times*, August 6, 1985, B6; Bill McAllister, "Postal Service Drops Plan for Air Fleet," *Washington Post*, August 19, 1991, A15; Government Information, Justice, and Agriculture Subcommittee of the House Committee on Government Operations, *U.S. Postal Service Diversification Into Nonmail Activities*, 102nd Congress, first session (Washington, D.C.: Government Printing Office, 1993), 61.

8. Dimondstein, interview, April 10, 2021; Thomas J. Dlugolenski (president, NALC Branch 134, Syracuse, N.Y.), interview by author, February 1, 2021; Ruth Y. Goldway, interview by author, February 4, 2021.

9. *Wall Street Journal*, August 8, 1995, A14; Michael Steel, "FedEx Flies High," *National Journal* 33, no. 8 (2001): 555; "FedEx Corp.," Center for Responsive Politics, https://www.opensecrets.org/orgs/

fedex-corp/lobbying?id=d000000089 (visited October 16, 2020); *New York Times*, October 12, 1996, 37. For an excellent account of FedEx Corporation's political activities, see Jill E. Fisch, "How Do Corporations Play Politics? The FedEx Story," *Vanderbilt Law Review* 58, no. 5 (2005): 1495-1570.

10. *Financial World* 148, no. 6 (1979): 34; *New York Times*, August 6, 1985, B6; Fisch, "How Do Corporations Play Politics?," 1512-38; Steel, "FedEx Flies High," 558; *Commercial Appeal* (Memphis, Tenn.), August 27, 2004, A1; *Commercial Appeal* (Memphis, Tenn.), September 23, 2003, A1; *New York Times*, November 17, 2019, A1; Frederick W. Smith, "FedEx Delivers Billions to the Taxman," *Wall Street Journal*, November 21, 2019, A17.

11. *Commercial Appeal* (Memphis, Tenn.), November 15, 1993, A1; *Commercial Appeal* (Memphis, Tenn.), February 25, 1995, A1; Garrett Workman, *The Transatlantic Trade and Investment Partnership: Big Opportunities for Small Business* (Washington, D.C.: Atlantic Council, 2014); FedEx, press release, November 13, 2014; *Commercial Appeal* (Memphis, Tenn.), November 10, 2016, A7.

12. *Washington Post Magazine*, February 22, 1981, 10; Fisch, "How Do Corporations Play Politics?," 1538-47; *New York Times*, October 12, 1996, 37; *Wall Street Journal*, July 20, 2009, B1; *Commercial Appeal* (Memphis, Tenn.), March 11, 2010, A1; *Commercial Appeal* (Memphis, Tenn.), February 3, 2011, C4; Evan Mackinder, "Capital Rivals: FedEx vs. UPS," Center for Responsive Politics, April 20, 2011, https://www.opensecrets.org/news/2011/04/capital-rivals-fedex-vs-ups-1/.

13. *Wall Street Journal*, August 25, 1980, 1; *Washington Post*, September 22, 2000, A8; "United Parcel Service," Center for Responsive Politics, https://www.opensecrets.org/orgs/united-parcel-service/lobbying?id=D000000081 (visited October 16, 2020).

14. Micah L. Sifry and Nancy Watzman, *Is That a Politician in Your Pocket? Washington on $2 Million a Day* (New York: John Wiley & Sons, 2004), 146; Vernon Mogensen, "State or Society? The Rise and Repeal of OSHA's Ergonomics Standard," in *Worker Safety Under Siege: Labor, Capital, and the Politics of Workplace Safety in a Deregulated World*, ed. Vernon Mogensen (Armonk, N.Y.: M. E. Sharpe, 2006), 129; United Parcel Service, press release, June 6, 2003; *Atlanta Journal-Constitution*, August 17, 2016, A13.

15. Mackinder, "Capital Rivals"; *Wall Street Journal*, July 20, 2009, B1; *Commercial Appeal* (Memphis, Tenn.), May 16, 2010, C1; David P. Abney and Frederick W. Smith, "Business Rivals Agree on Policy," *Wall Street Journal*, August 14, 2017, A17; *Commercial Appeal* (Memphis, Tenn.), December 28, 1996, 1A.

16. *New York Times*, November 15, 1996, D5; *St. Louis Post-Dispatch*, May 17, 1982, 12A; *Philadelphia Inquirer*, October 12, 1982, 11C; Bill McAllister, "FedEx Delivers Blow to Ad Campaign by Postal Service," *Washington Post*, December 9, 1998, C11.

17. James P. Kelley, address to the National Press Club, April 14, 1998, Washington, D.C.; *Wall Street Journal*, July 30, 1997, A3; *APMU Newsletter* 5, no. 1 (1998), http://www.apmu.org/news/spr98.html; *APMU Newsletter* 5, no. 4 (1998), http://www.apmu.org/news/win98.html; *Atlanta Journal-Constitution*, July 16, 2000, 7F; *APMU Newsletter* 7, no. 3 (2000), http://www.apmu.org/news/mayoo.htm.

18. Commission on Postal Service, *Report of the Commission*, 3b:1044; Michael L. Eskew, *Written Statement of Mike Eskew, Chairman and CEO, UPS, Before the President's Commission on the Postal Service* (n.p., 2003), 3; Senate Committee on Governmental Affairs, *Postal Reform: Sustaining the Nine Million Jobs in the $900 Billing Mailing Industry*, 142; Frederick W. Smith, "Competing with the Postal Service," *Cato Policy Report* 21, no. 2 (1999): 1; Subcommittee on the Postal Service of the House Committee on Government Reform, *H.R. 22, The Postal Modernization Act of 1999*, 106th Congress, first session (Washington, D.C.: Government Printing Office, 1999), 338.

19. *Wall Street Journal*, January 11, 2001, A6; William J. Henderson, "End of the Route," *Washington Post*, September 2, 2001, B1.

20. *Commercial Appeal* (Memphis, Tenn.), February 24, 2017, A7; *Commercial Appeal* (Memphis, Tenn.), April 24, 2013, 1; "$365 Million Federal Contract Awarded to UPS Worldwide Forwarding," *Targeted News Service*, November 13, 2014; United Parcel Service, Inc., *2015 Annual Report on Form 10-K* (n.p., 2016), 37; *Atlanta Journal-Constitution*, June 29, 2006, C1; *Wall Street Journal*, April 14, 2018, A3; *Wall Street Journal*, August 5, 2014, B1; *Atlanta Journal-Constitution*, March 12, 2011, A10; *Wall Street Journal*, September 5, 2014, B1; *Commercial Appeal* (Memphis, Tenn.), September 9, 2014, 1; Steven Hutkins, "Court Turns Back Bid to Drive Up USPS Parcel Prices," Save the Post Office, May 29, 2018, https://www.savethepostoffice.com/court-turns-back-ups-bid-to-drive-up-

usps-parcel-prices/; Tabbita, interview, February 2, 2021; *Commercial Appeal* (Memphis, Tenn.), April 21, 2020, A13; FedEx Corporation, "Comments," Docket No. RM 2020-4, April 7, 2020.

21. Federal Trade Commission, *Accounting for Laws That Apply Differently to the United States Postal Service and Its Private Competitors* (Washington, D.C.: F.T.C., 2007), 64; Parcel Shippers Association, "Comments Pursuant to Commission Order No. 5337," Docket No. RM 2017-3, February 3, 2020; *Sacramento (Calif.) Bee*, December 22, 2018, 23; Public Broadcasting Service, *Nightly Business Report*, May 11, 2018.

22. *News Journal* (Wilmington, Del.), January 13, 2002, 1F; *Wall Street Journal*, January 24, 2019, B1; *Wall Street Journal*, August 12, 2003, D1; SJ Consulting Group, *Report on Measuring the Benefits of Rural Postal Service for PRC* (Sewickley, Pa.: SJ Consulting Group, 2011), 4-5; *Philadelphia Inquirer*, June 1, 2020, B1; Federal Trade Commission, *Shipping to Non-Foreign Areas: Federal Trade Commission Report to Congress* (Washington, D.C.: F.T.C., 2020), 9.

23. *Wall Street Journal*, May 28, 2003, A4; John C. Spychalski, "Transportation Policy: Precedent-Breaking Choices over Five Decades," *Transportation Journal* 50, no. 1 (2011): 17; Mark A. Glick, "Antitrust and Economic History: The Historic Failure of the Chicago School of Antitrust," *Antitrust Bulletin* 64, no. 3 (2019): 322-23; Warren P. Preston and John M. Connor, "An Economic Evaluation of Federal Antitrust Activity in the Manufacturing Industries: 1980-1985," *Antitrust Bulletin* 37, no. 4 (1992): 969-96; James W. Brock, "Competition Policy in America: The Anti-Antitrust Paradox," *Antitrust Bulletin* 42, no. 2 (1997): 420-21; Willard F. Mueller, "A New Attack on Antitrust: The Chicago Case," *Antitrust Law & Economics Review* 18, no. 1 (1986): 33; James C. Miller III (chairman, U.S.P.S. Board of Governors, Washington, D.C.), interview by Ralph Nader and author, July 22, 2005.

24. *U.S. News & World Report* 89, no. 22 (1980): 40; Nancy Pindus et al., *A Framework for Considering the Social Value of Postal Services* (Washington, D.C.: Urban Institute, 2010), 8-9; Rhonda Abrams, "Many Small Businesses Rely on the US Postal Service to Compete, Stay Afloat," *USA Today*, August 27, 2020, https://www.usatoday.com/story/money/usaandmain/2020/08/27/usps-small-businesses-feel-attacks-agency/5636807002/; *Washington Post Magazine*, February 22, 1981, 10; Special Panel on Postal Reform and Oversight of the House Committee on Government Reform, *Answering the Administration's Call for Postal Reform*, 537; Package Coalition, "Statement of the Package Coalition," House of Representatives Document Repository, April 30, 2019, https://docs.house.gov/meetings/GO/GO00/20190430/109353/HHRG-116-GO00-20190430-SD010.pdf.

25. *New York Times*, December 28, 1975, 25; *Minneapolis Star*, December 25, 1975, 8E; *San Francisco Examiner*, January 24, 1976, 4; *Wall Street Journal*, January 28, 1976, 7; *Congressional Quarterly Weekly Report* 34, no. 15 (1976): 216-17.

26. *San Diego Union-Tribune*, December 4, 1995, D1; *Washington Post*, December 20, 1996, A25; Marvin T. Runyon, address before the National Press Club, April 14, 1998, Washington, D.C.; *Nation's Business* 86, no. 9 (1998): 47; CBS News, *Evening News*, December 8, 1996; *Washington Post*, February 13, 1997, C2.

27. Scheele, *Short History of the Mail Service*, 184; Summerfield and Hurd, *U.S. Mail*, 203; Coopersmith, *Faxed*, 98-100.

28. Commission on Postal Service, *Report of the Commission*, 1:23; Subcommittee on Postal Personnel and Modernization of the House Committee on Post Office and Civil Service, *Postal Research and Development*, 95th Congress, second session (Washington, D.C.: Government Printing Office 1979), 2; Subcommittee on Postal Operations and Services of the House Committee on Post Office and Civil Service, *Recommendations of the Commission on Postal Service*, 95th Congress, first session (Washington, D.C.: Government Printing Office, 1977), 8; *Congressional Quarterly Weekly Report* 35, no. 17 (1977): 741-43; Subcommittee on Postal Operations and Services of the House Committee on Post Office and Civil Service, *Impact of Electronic Communications Systems on Postal Operations*, 95th Congress, first session (Washington, D.C.: Government Printing Office, 1978), 1.

29. Subcommittee on Postal Personnel and Modernization of the House Committee on Post Office and Civil Service, *Abolish USPS Board of Governors and Require Presidential Appointment of Postmaster General with Senate Confirmation*, 95th Congress, first session (Washington, D.C.: Government Printing Office, 1978), 74, 86; Commission on Postal Service, *Report of the Commission*, 3b:1275, 1279.

30. *Fortune* 99, no. 12 (1979): 94; *Wall Street Journal*, May 10, 1977, 22; *New York Times*, March 2, 1978, A16; Conkey, *Postal Precipice*, 455; Benjamin F. Bailar, "End the Postal Service Monopoly on Delivering First-Class Mail," *USA Today*, July 10, 1991, 10A.

31. Conkey, *Postal Precipice*, 429, 434-43, 452; Ryan N. Ellis, "The Premature Death of Electronic Mail: The United States Postal Service's E-COM Program, 1978-1985," *International Journal of Communication* 7 (2013): 1955-56.

32. Conkey, *Postal Precipice*, 429-34; Ellis, "Premature Death of Electronic Mail," 1956-61; *Business Week*, June 18, 1984, 32.

33. *Plain Dealer* (Cleveland), August 2, 2000, 1C; *Washington Post*, January 24, 2000, A1; *Atlanta Journal-Constitution*, October 7, 1998, 6F; *Federal Times*, July 11, 2005, 12; *Federal Times*, March 11, 2002, 11; President's Commission, *Embracing the Future*, 27; Subcommittee of the Senate Committee on Appropriations, *Departments of Transportation, Treasury and General Government, and Related Agencies Appropriations for Fiscal Year 2005*, 108th Congress, second session (Washington, D.C.: Government Printing Office, 2005), 135; *Statutes at Large* 120 (2006): 3200.

34. *New York Times*, August 27, 1981, D15; *Los Angeles Times*, February 24, 2001, A1.

35. *Newsday*, June 16, 2001, C2; *New York Times*, February 6, 2001, C6.

36. *New York Times*, February 6, 2001, C6; *South Bend (Ind.) Tribune*, March 11, 2005, A1; *Omaha (Neb.) World-Herald*, March 3, 2091, 54.

37. *South Bend (Ind.) Tribune*, March 11, 2005, A1; *Seattle Times*, December 25, 2000, D2; Jane Mackie, "Get Grinch Off My Letters," *Chicago Tribune*, December 2, 2000, 24.

38. *Link Online*, May 19, 2004, http://liteblue.usps.gov/news/link/2004may19_1.htm; *Postal Bulletin* 126, no. 22149 (2005): 59; Minnesota Public Radio, *Marketplace*, February 27, 2001.

39. Marlene Park and Gerald E. Markowitz, *Democratic Vistas: Post Offices and Public Art in the New Deal* (Philadelphia: Temple University Press, 1984); Karal Ann Marling, *Wall-to-Wall America: A Cultural History Post-Office Murals in the Great Depression* (Minneapolis: University of Minnesota Press, 1982); Bruns, *Great American Post Offices*, 97.

40. *Link Online*, April 22, 2014, https://liteblue.usps.gov/news/link/2014/04apr/news22s4.htm; *Link Online*, April 1, 2014, https://liteblue.usps.gov/news/link/2014/04apr/news01s4.htm; U.S. Postal Service, press release, March 17, 2014.

41. Lydia Saad, "Postal Service Still Americans' Favorite Federal Agency," Gallup, May 13, 2019, https://news.gallup.com/poll/257510/postal-service-americans-favorite-federal-agency.aspx?version=print; Minnesota Public Radio, *Marketplace*, February 27, 2001.

CHAPTER SEVEN: Workers

1. Donald L. Barlett and James B. Steele, *The Betrayal of the American Dream* (New York: Public Affairs, 2012), 161-90; Dean Baker, *The United States since 1980* (New York: Cambridge University Press, 2007), 29-43; Robert E. Scott, "The Effects of NAFTA on U.S. Trade, Jobs, and Investment, 1993-2013," *Review of Keynesian Economics* 2, no. 4 (2014): 429-41; K. Daron Acemoglu et al., "Import Competition and the Great U.S. Employment Sag of the 2000s," *Journal of Labor Economics* 34, no. 1 (2016): S141-98; Craig K. Elwell, *Inflation and the Real Minimum Wage*, Congressional Research Service Report No. R42973 (January 2014); Christopher W. Shaw, "The Money Question," *Harper's Magazine*, April 2020, 55-59; George J. Borjas, "The Labor Demand Curve *Is* Downward Sloping: Reexamining the Impact of Immigration on the Labor Market," *Quarterly Journal of Economics* 118, no. 4 (2003): 1335-74; Vernon M. Briggs, Jr., *Immigration and American Unionism* (Ithaca, N.Y.: Cornell University Press, 2001); Kate Andrias, "The New Labor Law," *Yale Law Journal* 126, no. 1 (2016): 2-100; James H. Peoples, Jr., "Deregulation and the Labor Market," *Journal of Economic Perspectives* 12, no. 3 (1998): 111-30; Eileen Appelbaum, "Domestic Outsourcing, Rent Seeking, and Increasing Inequality," *Review of Radical Political Economics* 49, no. 4 (2017): 513-28.

2. Claudia Goldin and Robert A. Margo, "The Great Compression: The Wage Structure in the United States at Mid-Century," *Quarterly Journal of Economics* 107, no. 1 (1992): 1-34; Thomas Piketty and Emmanuel Saez, "Income Inequality in the United States, 1913-1998," *Quarterly Journal of Economics* 118, no. 1 (2003): 1-39; Bruce P. Western and Jake Rosenfeld, "Unions, Norms, and the Rise in U.S. Wage Inequality," *American Sociological Review* 76, no. 4 (2011): 513-37; Martin Gilens, *Affluence and*

Influence: Economic Inequality and Political Power in America (Princeton, N.J.: Princeton University Press, 2012).

3. "One Day," U.S. Postal Service, January 4, 2021, https://facts.usps.com/one-day/; *Daily Courier-Observer* (Massena, N.Y.), May 27, 2020, A4.

4. *Postal Record* 131, no. 10 (2018): 25; *Buffalo News*, May 2, 2010, A1; *Star-Ledger* (Newark, N.J.), December 24, 2016, 8.

5. *Grand Forks (N. Dak.) Herald*, May 20, 2017, C5; *Link Online*, November 20, 2015, https://link.usps.com/heroes_corner/justin-hull-canandaigua-ny/; *Atlanta Journal-Constitution*, March 21, 2018, B3.

6. *Postal Record* 130, no. 2 (2017): 13; *Postal Record* 129, no. 11 (2016): 11.

7. *Detroit News*, September 24, 2018, A4; *Postal Record* 129, no. 9 (2016): 14-15; *Buffalo News*, April 17, 2016, 1; *KCBS-TV*, October 10, 2020, https://losangeles.cbslocal.com/2020/10/10/everyday-hero-postal-carrier-helps-norwalk-man-who-cut-himself-with-chainsaw/.

8. *Post-Standard* (Syracuse), November 20, 2014, A9; *Times Leader* (Wilkes-Barre, Pa.), May 18, 2010, 1A.

9. *Akron (Ohio) Beacon Journal*, October 9, 2015, A1; *Branch 34's Clan* 46, no. 1 (2017): 9; *Pittsburgh Post-Gazette*, October 4, 2017, B1.

10. Jane Jacobs, *The Death and Life of Great American Cities* (New York: Random House, 1961), 35; *Olympian* (Olympia, Wash.), March 31, 2016, 1A; *Daily News* (Lebanon, Pa.), October 30, 2019, A3; *Congressional Record*, 109th Congress, first session, 2005, 151, 17570.

11. USPS Office of Inspector General, *Flexibility at Work: Human Resource Strategies to Help the Postal Service*, Report No. RARC-WP-15-004 (January 2015), 12; Philip F. Rubio, "Organizing a Wildcat: The United States Postal Strike of 1970," *Labor History* 57, no. 5 (2016): 577; President's Commission, *Embracing the Future*, 109; Subcommittee of the Senate Committee on Appropriations, *Financial Security of the U.S. Postal Service*, 4.

12. Courtney Jenkins, "Don't Forget the Postal Workers During Coronavirus Pandemic," *Baltimore Sun*, April 14, 2020, https://www.baltimoresun.com/opinion/op-ed/bs-ed-op-0415-coronavirus-postal-workers-20200414-5cyktu55h5hpnkukcjjcg25wuu-story.html; *Postal Record* 133, no. 6 (2020): 15; Jack McDonald, "Amid Turmoil Let's Thank Our Postal Carriers," *New Hampshire Union Leader* (Manchester), August 21, 2020, A10.

13. Josh Bivens and Lawrence Mishel, *Understanding the Historic Divergence Between Productivity and a Typical Worker's Pay: Why It Matters and Why It's Real* (Washington, D.C.: Economic Policy Institute, 2015); Jacob S. Hacker, *The Great Risk Shift* (New York: Oxford University Press, 2006); Bureau of Labor Statistics, "Postal Service Workers," *Occupational Outlook Handbook*, September 1, 2020, https://www.bls.gov/ooh/office-and-administrative-support/postal-service-workers.htm.

14. John L. Cotton and Jeffrey M. Tuttle, "Employee Turnover: A Meta-Analysis and Review with Implications for Research," *Academy of Management Review* 11, no. 1 (1986): 55-70; Ernesto Dal Bo, Frederico Finan, and Martin A. Rossi, "Strengthening State Capabilities: The Role of Financial Incentives in the Call to Public Service," *Quarterly Journal of Economics* 128, no. 3 (2013): 1169-1218.

15. *Washington Post*, August 14, 2011, A2; Sarah Anderson et al., *The USPS and Rural America* (Washington, D.C.: Institute for Policy Studies, 2020), 1; Ronnie W. Stutts (president, National Rural Letter Carriers' Association, Alexandria, Va.), interview by author, April 30, 2021.

16. Thomas A. Rumer, *The American Legion: An Official History, 1919-1989* (New York: M. Evans & Company, Inc., 1990), 361-62; U.S. Civil Service Commission, *History of Veteran Preference in Federal Employment, 1865-1955* (Washington, D.C.: Civil Service Commission, 1956), 15-16; *American Legion Magazine* 176, no. 3 (2014): 22; American Legion, *The American Legion Legislative Agenda, 2020* (n.p., 2020), 18; American Legion, *Proceedings of the 98th Annual National Convention* (n.p., 2016), 212; U.S. Postal Service, *Postal Facts 2020 Companion* (Washington, D.C.: U.S.P.S., 2020), 3; Bureau of Labor Statistics, press release, March 19, 2020.

17. Philip F. Rubio, *There's Always Work at the Post Office: African American Postal Workers and the Fight for Jobs, Justice, and Equality* (Chapel Hill: University of North Carolina Press, 2010), 8, 20-27; Sterling D. Spero and Abram L. Harris, *The Black Worker: The Negro and the Labor Movement* (New York: Columbia University Press, 1931), 122; John A. Dittmer, *Local People: The Struggle for Civil Rights in Mississippi* (Urbana: University of Illinois Press, 1994), 30; Charles M. Payne, *I've Got the*

Light of Freedom: The Organizing Struggle for Civil Rights in Mississippi (Berkeley: University of California Press, 1995), 44; *Baltimore Sun*, October 30, 2020, 1.

18. Meek, *Private Island*, 53-54; Wilbur L. Duncan, "Mid-Term Elections," *NAPFE Newsletter* 10, no. 11 (2018): 1; James P. Bovard, "The Slow Death of the U.S. Postal Service," *Cato Institute Policy Analysis*, no. 102 (1988); R. Richard Geddes, "The U.S. Postal Service," in *Regulation, Deregulation, Reregulation: Institutional Perspectives*, ed. Claude Ménard and Michel Ghertman (Northampton, Mass.: Edward Elgar, 2010), 227; Rick Geddes, *Competing with the U.S. Postal Service: Effects on Consumers, Competitors, and Virginia State and Local Government* (Alexandria, Va.: TJIPP, 2004), 10; Rick Geddes, *Timid Steps Toward Postal Reform* (Washington, D.C.: AEI, 2004), 2; Ditch, "Privatization Should Be on the Table"; Chris R. Edwards, "Should the U.S. Postal Service Be Privatized?," *Costco Connection* 31, no. 2 (2016): 23; Edwards, "Restructuring the U.S. Postal Service," 672. Economist Monique Morrissey has presented evidence that postal workers are not "overpaid." See Monique Morrissey, *The War Against the Postal Service* (Washington, D.C.: Economic Policy Institute, 2020), 12, 34-36.

19. USPS Office of Inspector General, *Flexibility at Work*, 11; Karl H.W. Baarslag, *History of the National Federation of Post Office Clerks* (Washington, D.C.: National Federation of Post Office Clerks, 1945), 18; M. Brady Mikusko and F. John Miller, *Carriers in a Common Cause: A History of Letter Carriers and the NALC*, 2nd century ed. (Washington, D.C.: National Association of Letter Carriers, 2006), 10-12; Philip Taft, *Organized Labor in American History* (New York: Harper & Row, Publishers, 1964), 123-24; Cullinan, *Post Office Department*, 111.

20. Baarslag, *History of the National Federation of Post Office Clerks*, 25, 48, 56; Cullinan, *Post Office Department*, 109, 122; James H. Bruns, *Owney: Mascot of the Railway Mail Service* (Washington, D.C.: Smithsonian Institution, 2006), 17.

21. John Walsh and Garth L. Mangum, *Labor Struggle in the Post Office: From Selective Lobbying to Collective Bargaining* (Armonk, N.Y.: M. E. Sharpe, Inc., 1992), 74-77; Fuller, *RFD*, 132-33; Lester F. Miller, *The National Rural Letter Carriers' Association: A Centennial Portrait* (Encino, Calif.: Cherbo Publishing Group, 2003), 12, 16; A. L. Glenn, Sr., *History of the National Alliance of Postal Employees, 1913-1955* (Washington, D.C.: NAPE, 1956), 17, 101; Nicholas Patler, *Jim Crow and the Wilson Administration: Protesting Federal Segregation in the Early Twentieth Century* (Boulder: University Press of Colorado, 2004), 44-45; Rubio, *There's Always Work at the Post Office*, 128.

22. Baarslag, *History of the National Federation of Post Office Clerks*, 75; Belle Case La Follette and Fola La Follette, *Robert M. La Follette*, 2 vols. (New York: The Macmillan Company, 1953), 1:447; Mikusko and Miller, *Carriers in a Common Cause*, 24; Fuller, *RFD*, 134.

23. *Tucson (Ariz.) Citizen*, May 9, 1920, 4; Cullinan, *Post Office Department*, 128, 158-61; Miller, *National Rural Letter Carriers' Association*, 37, 49-50, 52-53; Kelly, *United States Postal Policy*, 200; Baarslag, *History of the National Federation of Post Office Clerks*, 188; Walsh and Mangum, *Labor Struggle in the Post Office*, 56-58; *National Rural Letter Carrier* 52, no. 35 (1953): 9; Mikusko and Miller, *Carriers in a Common Cause*, 55-58.

24. Cullinan, *United States Postal Service*, 6-7; Walsh and Mangum, *Labor Struggle in the Post Office*, 7, 24, 30-35; Mikusko and Miller, *Carriers in a Common Cause*, 72; Aaron Brenner, "Striking Against the State: The Postal Wildcat of 1970," *Labor's Heritage* 7, no. 4 (1996): 7; Joshua B. Freeman, *Working-Class New York: Life and Labor since World War II* (New York: New Press, 2000), 247-48; Rubio, *Undelivered*, 60-118; Thomas J. Germano, "Labor Relations in the United States Postal Service: A Sociological Perspective" (Ph.D. diss., City University of New York, 1983), 196-97; Richard M. Nixon, *Public Papers of the Presidents of the United States: Richard M. Nixon, 1970*, 6 vols. (Washington, D.C.: Government Printing Office, 1971), 2:299.

25. Ely, "Privatizing the Postal Service," 122; *Los Angeles Times*, April 1, 1990, D9; Government Accountability Office, *Additional Guidance Needed to Assess Effect of Changes to Employee Compensation*, GAO-20-140 (January 2020), 38-40; Gale R. Thames (national labor director, NAPFE, Washington, D.C.), interview by author, February 5, 2021; Stutts, interview, April 30, 2021.

26. USPS Office of Inspector General, *Non-Career Employee Turnover*, Report No. HR-AR-17-002 (December 2016), 6; U.S. Postal Service, *2020 Quarterly Report, Form 10-Q, December 31, 2020* (Washington, D.C.: U.S.P.S., 2021), 25; Kathryn A. Francis, *U.S. Postal Service Workforce Size and Employment Categories, FY1995-FY2014*, Congressional Research Service Report No. RS22864 (October 2015), 10;

Dimondstein, interview, April 10, 2021; Office of the Historian of the U.S. Postal Service, *Number of Postal Employees since 1926* (Washington, D.C.: U.S.P.S., 2021); Louis DeJoy, remarks at Board of Governors meeting, February 9, 2021, Washington, D.C.

27. Zlatkin, interview, February 23, 2021; Thames, interview, February 5, 2021; Kurt Eckrem, "Why Me?," *Washington Rural Carrier*, Spring 2020, 4; Lawrence Kania, "Somethings Never Change," *The Buzz* 68, no. 6 (2014): 3; Robert J. McLennan, "Management Creates Hostile Work Environment," *The Buzz* 63, no. 2 (2009): 1; Paul McKenna, "Disrespecting the Workforce," *The Hi-Lites* 41, no. 4 (2019): 2; Paul McKenna, "Hostile Working Conditions," *The Hi-Lites* 41, no. 3 (2019): 2.

28. *Wall Street Journal*, April 16, 1976, 3; Benjamin F. Bailar, address to the Comstock Club, Sacramento, Calif., February 7, 1977; *Forbes* 149, no. 9 (1992): 89; *Washington Post*, July 6, 1977, A2; *Los Angeles Times*, May 12, 1978, 1.

29. Conkey, *Postal Precipice*, 244; *Wall Street Journal*, June 5, 1989, B2; *New York Times*, February 4, 2001, 30; Sarah F. Ryan, "Understanding Postal Privatization: Corporations, Unions, and 'The Public Interest'" (master's thesis, Rutgers University, 1999), 73-75, 103-5; Tabbita, interview, February 2, 2021.

30. Subcommittee on Federal Workforce, Postal Service, and the District of the Columbia of the House Committee on Oversight and Government Reform, *The Price Is Right, or Is It? An Examination of USPS Workshare Discounts and Products That Do Not Cover Their Costs*, 111th Congress, second session (Washington, D.C.: Government Printing Office, 2010); American Postal Workers Union, "Comments of American Postal Workers Union, AFL-CIO," Docket No. RM2009-3, September 11, 2009; USPS Office of Inspector General, *Marketing Mail Letters Workshare Discounts*, Report No. CP-AR-18-006 (August 2018); Michael J. Riley, *The Challenge for the Presidential Commission* (n.p., 2003), 7; Walsh and Mangum, *Labor Struggle in the Post Office*, 237; *Postal Life* 25, no. 4 (1991): 3-5; Dimondstein, interview, April 10, 2021; Government Accountability Office, *Service's Strategy for Realigning Its Mail Processing Infrastructure Lacks Clarity, Criteria, and Accountability*, 18; Conkey, *Postal Precipice*, 244.

31. Nelson N. Lichtenstein, *The Retail Revolution: How Wal-Mart Created a Brave New World of Business* (New York: Picador, 2010), 9, 197-236, 286-87; Walmart, Inc., *2020 Annual Report* (n.p., 2020), 12, 24; Ted C. Fishman, *China, Inc.: How the Rise of the Next Superpower Challenges America and the World* (New York: Scribner, 2005), 152-58; Vincent A. Gallagher, *The True Cost of Low Prices: The Violence of Globalization* (Maryknoll, N.Y.: Orbis Books, 2006), 21-22; Clyde V. Prestowitz, Jr., *Three Billion New Capitalists: The Great Shift of Wealth and Power to the East* (New York: Basic Books, 2005), 67-69.

32. Byron L. Dorgan, *Take This Job and Ship It: How Corporate Greed and Brain-Dead Politics Are Selling Out America* (New York: Thomas Dunne Books, 2006), 139-42; Government Accountability Office, *Millions of Full-Time Workers Rely on Federal Health Care and Food Assistance Programs*, GAO-21-45 (October 2020); Office of Representative Martin Olav Sabo, press release, July 12, 2005; Americans for Tax Fairness, *Wal-Mart on Tax Day: How Taxpayers Subsidize America's Biggest Employer and Richest Family* (Washington, D.C.: ATF, 2014), 5.

33. Anthony Bianco, *The Bully of Bentonville: How the High Cost of Wal-Mart's Everyday Low Prices Is Hurting America* (New York: Currency/Doubleday, 2006), 109-34, 227-38; Lichtenstein, *Retail Revolution*, 156-96; Adam D. Reich and Peter S. Bearman, *Working for Respect: Community and Conflict at Walmart* (New York: Columbia University Press, 2018), 100; Orson Mason, *Labor Relations and You at the Wal-Mart Distribution Center #6022* (n.p., 1991).

34. Lawrence Mishel and Jori Kandra, *CEO Compensation Surged 14% in 2019 to $21.3 Million* (Washington, D.C.: Economic Policy Institute, 2020); Walmart, Inc., *Notice of 2020 Annual Shareholders' Meeting* (n.p., 2020), 68; Susan J. Stabile, "One for A, Two for B, and Four Hundred for C: The Widening Gap in Pay Between Executives and Rank and File Employees," *University of Michigan Journal of Law Reform* 36, no. 1 (2002): 154-55; Dean Baker, Josh Bivens, and Jessica Schieder, *Reining in CEO Compensation and Curbing the Rise of Inequality* (Washington, D.C.: Economic Policy Institute, 2019); Emmanuel Saez and Gabriel Zucman, "Wealth Inequality in the United States since 1913: Evidence from Capitalized Income Tax Data," *Quarterly Journal of Economics* 131, no. 2 (2016): 519-78; U.S. Postal Service, *Annual Report to Congress, 2019* (Washington. D.C.: U.S.P.S., 2019), 17.

35. John Kenneth Galbraith, *The Affluent Society* (Boston: Houghton Mifflin Company, 1958); Lester C. Thurow, "The Disappearance of the Middle Class," *New York Times*, February 5, 1984, F3; Paul R. Krugman, "For Richer," *New York Times Magazine*, October 20, 2002, 62; Lizabeth Cohen, *A Consumers' Republic: The Politics of Mass Consumption in Postwar America* (New York: Alfred A. Knopf, 2003), 152; George Packer, *The Unwinding* (New York: Farrar, Straus, and Giroux, 2013), 105.

36. Robert H. Frank, *Luxury Fever: Why Money Fails to Satisfy in an Era of Excess* (New York: Free Press, 1999), 243; R.H. Tawney, *The Acquisitive Society* (New York: Harcourt, Brace, and Howe, 1920), 38; Irving Dilliard, ed., *Mr. Justice Brandeis: Great American* (St. Louis: The Modern View Press, 1941), 42.

CHAPTER EIGHT: Governance

1. Fuller, *RFD*, 3; Bretz, "Some Aspects of Postal Extension Into the West," 150.

2. U.S. Postal Service, *United States Postal Service, 1775-2002*, 34; *Business Week*, November 5, 1966, 46-47; Conkey, *Postal Precipice*, 37-38.

3. *Postal Life* 1, no. 5 (1968): 9; Summerfield and Hurd, *U.S. Mail*, 194, 198; Fuller, *American Mail*, 334-36; Scheele, *Short History of the Mail Service*, 175-80; Commission on Postal Organization, *Towards Postal Excellence*, 5 vols. (Washington, D.C.: Government Printing Office, 1968), 1: ii.

4. John T. Tierney, *Postal Reorganization: Managing the Public's Business* (Boston: Auburn House Publishing Co., 1981), 12-20, 51; Commission on Postal Organization, *Towards Postal Excellence*, 1:2; Rubio, *Undelivered*, 36-37; Cullinan, *United States Postal Service*, 7-8; Miller, *National Rural Letter Carriers' Association*, 85.

5. Cullinan, *United States Postal Service*, 8; Miller, *National Rural Letter Carriers' Association*, 86; *Congressional Record*, 91st Congress, first session, 1969, 115, 26693; Frederick C. Thayer, "The President's Management 'Reforms': Theory X Triumphant," *Public Administration Review* 38, no. 4 (1978): 311; Joseph E. Stiglitz, *Economics* (New York: W.W. Norton, 1993), 188; Goodsell, *Case for Bureaucracy*, 119.

6. Commission on Postal Organization, *Towards Postal Excellence*, 3:12-63, 2-91, 2-93; *Congressional Record*, 91st Congress, second session, 1970, 116, 26693; Donald R. McCoy, *Calvin Coolidge: The Quiet President* (New York: The Macmillan Company, 1967), 202; Robert Sobel, *Calvin Coolidge: An American Enigma* (Washington, D.C.: Regnery Publishing, Inc., 1998), 279.

7. J. Joseph Loewenberg, "The Post Office Strike of 1970," in *Collective Bargaining in Government*, ed. J. Joseph Loewenberg and Michael H. Moskow (Englewood Cliffs, N.J.: Prentice-Hall, Inc., 1972), 200; Fuller, *American Mail*, 331-33; Cullinan, *United States Postal Service*, 230; *Evening Star* (Washington, D.C.), August 12, 1970, A13.

8. Rubio, *Undelivered*, 140; Morton Mintz and Jerry S. Cohen, *Power, Inc.: Public and Private Rulers and How to Make Them Accountable* (New York: Bantam Books, 1977), 409-10; Shaw, *Preserving the People's Post Office*, 190-91; Joseph W. Belluck, "Increasing Citizen Participation in U.S. Postal Service Policy Making: A Model Act to Create a Post Office Consumer Action Group," *Buffalo Law Review* 42, no. 1 (1994): 281-83; Conkey, *Postal Precipice*, 259-60; *Congressional Record*, 91st Congress, second session, 1970, 116, 27601; Cullinan, *United States Postal Service*, 231-32. In 2021, the postal regulatory commissioners included two former Republican congressional staff members, one former Republican National Committee staff member, and one former Democratic congressional staff member.

9. Carlson, interview, February 9, 2021; Senate Committee on Commerce, Science, and Transportation, *Nominations—Federal Trade Commission and Department of Commerce*, 97th Congress, first session (Washington, D.C.: Government Printing Office, 1981), 33; *Time* 131, no. 13 (1988): 50; Miller, interview, July 22, 2005; Miller, "End the Postal Monopoly"; James C. Miller III, "Stamping Out Postal Increases," *Washington Times*, January 11, 1999, A12; Ronald J. Brownstein and Nina Easton, *Reagan's Ruling Class: Portraits of the President's Top 100 Officials* (Washington, D.C.: Presidential Accountability Group, 1982), 413-25; Ian Gilbert, "The Deregulator Returns," *Public Citizen Magazine*, December 1985, 5; Senate Committee on Governmental Affairs, *Nominations of Clay Johnson, III, Albert Casey, and James C. Miller, III*, 108th Congress, first session (Washington, D.C.: Government Printing Office, 2003), 85-98; Lisa Graves, *The Billionaire Behind Efforts to Kill the U.S. Postal Service*

(Oakland: ITPI, 2020), 10-11; Senate Committee on Governmental Affairs, *Nominations of Alan C. Kessler and Carol Waller Pope*, 106th Congress, second session (Washington, D.C.: Government Printing Office, 2000), 15-39.

10. Senate Committee on Homeland Security and Governmental Affairs, *Nominations of Carolyn Lewis Gallagher, Louis J. Giuliano, and Tony Hammond*, 109th Congress, first session (Washington, D.C.: Government Printing Office, 2006), 24-28, 48-54; Carlyle Group, press release, May 31, 2005; Senate Committee on Homeland Security and Governmental Affairs, *Nominations of Hon. James H. Bilbray, Thurgood Marshall, Jr., and Hon. Dan G. Blair*, 109th Congress, second session (Washington, D.C.: Government Printing Office, 2007), 44-51; *Jet* 110, no. 16 (2006): 6; Lee Fang, "Third Way: 'Majority of Our Financial Support' from Wall Street, Business Executives," *Nation*, December 11, 2013, https://www.thenation.com/article/archive/third-way-majority-our-financial-support-wall-street-business-executives/.

11. Senate Committee on Homeland Security and Governmental Affairs, *Nominations of Mickey D. Barnett, Katherine C. Tobin, and Ellen C. Williams*, 109th Congress, second session (Washington, D.C.: Government Printing Office, 2007), 31-55; *New York Times*, December 3, 2000, 40; *Daily Labor Report*, January 22, 2002, E-1.

12. Senate Committee on Homeland Security and Governmental Affairs, *Nominations of Hon. James H. Bilbray, Thurgood Marshall, Jr., and Hon. Dan G. Blair*, 28-30; Senate Committee on Homeland Security and Governmental Affairs, *Nominations of Hon. David C. Williams, Hon. Robert M. Duncan, and Calvin R. Tucker to Be Governors, U.S. Postal Service*, 115th Congress, second session (Washington, D.C.: Government Publishing Office, 2019), 111-19; Senate Committee on Homeland Security and Governmental Affairs, *Nominations of Ron A. Bloom, Roman Martinez IV, James A. Crowell IV, and Jason Park*, 116th Congress, first session (Washington, D.C.: Government Publishing Office, 2019), 39-44; Noam Scheiber, "Manufacturing Bloom," *New Republic* 240, no. 22 (2009): 18-21.

13. Dimondstein, interview, April 10, 2021; Fleishman, "Postal Policy and Public Accountability," 49-51; Tierney, *Postal Reorganization*, 24; Conkey, *Postal Precipice*, 41.

14. Risa L. Lieberwitz, "The Corporatization of the University: Distance Learning at the Cost of Academic Freedom?," *Boston University Public Interest Law Journal* 12, no. 1 (2002): 109-10; Subcommittee on Space and Aeronautics of the House Committee on Science, *Range Privatization: How Fast, How Soon, and How Much?*, 106th Congress, second session (Washington, D.C.: Government Printing Office, 2001), 20.

15. Goodsell, *Case for Bureaucracy*, 50; Liberty Hyde Bailey, *What Is Democracy?* (Ithaca, N.Y.: Comstock Publishing Co., 1918), 87-88; Levi, interview, February 1, 2021.

16. Fuller, *American Mail*, 333; Charles G. Benda, "State Organization and Policy Formation: The 1970 Reorganization of the Post Office Department," *Politics & Society* 9, no. 2 (1980): 139; Conkey, *Postal Precipice*, 54, 61; Christopher J. Deering and Steven S. Smith, *Committees in Congress* (Washington, D.C.: CQ Press, 1997), 41; Senate, *Committee System Reorganization Amendments of 1977*, 95th Congress, first session (1977), S. Rept. 95-2, 39; *Congressional Record*, 95th Congress, first session, 1977, 123, 3691.

17. National Farmers Union, *1977 Policy of National Farmers Union* (n.p., 1977), 47-48; AFL-CIO *American Federationist* 84, no. 5 (1977): 17; *Washington Star*, February 18, 1977, B6; House, H.R. 7700, 95th Congress, first session (1977); House, *Postal Service Act of 1977*, 95th Congress, first session (1977), H. Rept. 95-808; Fleishman, "Postal Policy and Public Accountability," 82.

18. Subcommittee on Postal Personnel and Modernization of the House Committee on Post Office and Civil Service, *Abolish USPS Board of Governors and Require Presidential Appointment of Postmaster General with Senate Confirmation*, 18; *Congressional Record*, 95th Congress, second session, 1978, 124, 9079-80; Fleishman, "Postal Policy and Public Accountability," 81-82; Ann Mari May, "Fiscal Policy, Monetary Policy, and the Carter Presidency," *Presidential Studies Quarterly* 23, no. 4 (1993): 701; Erwin C. Hargrove, *Jimmy Carter as President: Leadership and the Politics of the Public Good* (Baton Rouge: Louisiana State University Press, 1988), 69-70; *Congressional Record*, 95th Congress, first session, 1977, 123, 18875; Senate, S. 1692, 95th Congress, first session (1977); Roger H. Davidson, "Congressional Committees as Moving Targets," in *The Modern American Congress, 1963-1989*, ed.

Joel H. Silbey, 3 vols. (Brooklyn: Carlson Publishing, 1991), 2:24; Deering and Smith, *Committees in Congress*, 48-50; *Philadelphia Inquirer*, January 8, 1995, C4.

19. Mintz and Cohen, *Power, Inc.*, 410-11; Cullinan, *Post Office Department*, 248.

20. *Statutes at Large* 84 (1970): 722; Senate, *The Federal Advisory Committee Act*, 92nd Congress, second session (1972), S. Rept. 92-1098, 5; *Congressional Record*, 92nd Congress, second session, 1972, 118, 30271-72; Commission on Postal Service, *Report of the Commission*, 1:77.

21. Cullinan, *United States Postal Service*, 257; Potter, *Remarks By Postmaster General John E. Potter to the President's Commission*, 2; Conkey, *Postal Precipice*, 481; Stephen M. Kearney, "How to Fix the U.S. Postal Service," *Roll Call*, August 27, 2020, https://www.rollcall.com/2020/08/27/how-to-fix-the-us-postal-service/; Riley, *Challenge for the Presidential Commission*, 6, 9; Goldway, interview, February 4, 2021.

22. Robert D. Behn, "Closing a Government Facility," *Public Administration Review* 38, no. 4 (1978): 333; Cullinan, *United States Postal Service*, 235-36; Ralph Nader, "Preface," in Conkey, *Postal Precipice*, xii; Ralph Nader, *Cutting Corporate Welfare* (New York: Seven Stories Press, 2000).

23. Elliott D. Sclar, *Amtrak Privatization: The Route to Failure* (Washington, D.C.: Economic Policy Institute, 2003); Ben Goldman, *Issues in the Reauthorization for Amtrak*, Congressional Research Service Report No. R45942 (January 2021), 5-9; Amtrak, *FY 2019 Company Profile* (Washington, D.C.: Amtrak, 2019), 3. Amtrak helped keep the U.S. Mail moving after the 2001 terrorist attacks (*Philadelphia Inquirer*, September 14, 2001, A13; *Washington Post*, September 21, 2001, A38).

24. Robert C. Byrd, *The Senate, 1789-1989*, 4 vols. (Washington, D.C.: Government Printing Office, 1991), 2:508; Harry R. Lewis, "Gone the Way of the 6¢ Stamp," *Public Citizen Magazine* 8, no. 4 (1988): 14, 20; Belluck, "Increasing Citizen Participation in U.S. Postal Service Policy Making"; Joseph W. Belluck, "Give Oversight of USPS Back to the People," *Times Union* (Albany, N.Y.), October 26, 2020, A10.

25. Ralph Nader, "A Self-Defense Plan for Utility Customers," *Newsday*, October 25, 1974, 77; Ralph Nader and Donald K. Ross, *Action for a Change: A Student's Manual for Public Interest Organizing* (New York: Grossman Publishers, 1972), 34-38; Andrew Sharpless and Sarah Gallup, *Banding Together: How Check-Offs Will Revolutionize the Consumer Movement* (Washington, D.C.: Center for Study of Responsive Law, 1981).

26. Robert B. Leflar and Martin H. Rogol, "Consumer Participation in the Regulation of Public Utilities: A Model Act," *Harvard Journal on Legislation* 13, no. 2 (1976): 235-97; Beth Givens, *Citizens' Utility Boards: Because Utilities Bear Watching* (San Diego: Center for Public Interest Law, 1991), 30, 33, 35-46; Pacific Gas & Electric Co. v. Public Utilities Commission of California et al., 475 U.S. 1 (1986); Alan L. Hirsch and Ralph Nader, "'The Corporate Conscience' and Other First Amendment Follies in *Pacific Gas & Electric*," *San Diego Law Review* 41, no. 2 (2004): 483-504; Nicholas J. Nesgos, "*Pacific Gas and Electric Co. v. Public Utilities Commission*: The Right to Hear in Corporate Negative and Affirmative Speech," *Cornell Law Review* 73, no. 5 (1988): 1080-1100; "Accomplishments," Citizens Utility Board, https://www.citizensutilityboard.org/accomplishments/; "About Us," Wisconsin Citizens' Utility Board, https://cubwi.org/about-us/; "CUB Accomplishments," Citizens' Utility Board of Oregon, https://oregoncub.org/about-us/accomplishments/; "About UCAN," Utility Consumers' Action Network, http://www.ucan.org/who-is-ucan/ (visited November 28, 2020).

27. Ralph Nader, "Mail Users Should Unite," *Washington Star*, April 19, 1975, B6; Albert O. Hirschman, *Exit, Voice, and Loyalty: Responses to Decline in Firms, Organizations, and States* (Cambridge, Mass.: Harvard University Press, 1970), 42; Ralph Nader, letter to President's Commission, July 26, 2003.

28. Philip A. Tabbita, address to the American Enterprise Institute, Washington, D.C., September 26, 2003; William H. Burrus, Jr. (president, APWU, Washington, D.C.), interview by author, July 19, 2005; Edmund Mierzwinski (senior director of federal consumer programs, U.S. PIRG, Washington, D.C.), email to author, February 18, 2021.

29. John Richard (director, Essential Information, Washington, D.C.), interview by author, January 15, 2021. The Utility Consumers' Action Network's first enclosure garnered a response rate of 4 percent (Givens, *Citizens' Utility Boards*, 54).

30. Ralph Nader, *The Ralph Nader Reader* (New York: Seven Stories Press, 2000), 226-27; Belluck, "Increasing Citizen Participation in U.S. Postal Service Policy Making," 292; Conkey, *Postal Precipice*, 511; Max Weber, *Economy and Society: An Outline of Interpretive Sociology*, ed. Guenther Roth and

Claus Wittich, trans. Ephraim Fischoff et al., 2 vols. (Berkeley: University of California Press, 1978), 2:992; John W. Gardner, "How to Prevent Organizational Dry Rot," *Harper's Magazine*, October 1965, 20.

31. *Congressional Record*, 91st Congress, second session, 1970, 116, 20497; Carlson, interview, February 9, 2021

CHAPTER NINE: The Future

1. *Fortune* 120, no. 4 (1989): 87; *Wall Street Journal*, April 25, 2020, A2; Dimondstein, interview, April 10, 2021.

2. *New York Times*, November 11, 2013, B1; *Washington Post*, September 19, 2020, A12; Jake Bittle, "Postal Service Workers Are Shouldering the Burden for Amazon," *Nation*, February 21, 2018, https://www.thenation.com/article/archive/postal-service-workers-are-shouldering-the-burden-for-amazon/; *Washington Post*, November 28, 2020, A1; Max B. Sawicky, *The U.S. Postal Service Is a National Asset: Don't Trash It* (Washington, D.C.: Center for Economic and Policy Research, 2020), 6; Stacy Mitchell, "The Empire of Everything," *Nation* 306, no. 7 (2018): 22-27, 33; House Subcommittee on Antitrust, Commercial, and Administrative Law, *Investigation of Competition in Digital Markets* (Washington, D.C.: Committee on the Judiciary, 2020), 247-329.

3. Jathan Sadowski, *Too Smart: How Digital Capitalism Is Extracting Data, Controlling Our Lives, and Taking Over the World* (Cambridge, Mass.: MIT Press, 2020), 25-35, 92-96; *Morning Call* (Allentown, Pa.), September 18, 2011, A1; Paris Marx, "To Fix the Looming Supply Chain Crisis, Nationalize Amazon," *In These Times*, March 27, 2020, https://inthesetimes.com/article/supply-chain-crisis-nationalize-amazon-coronavirus-covid-19; Mike Davis, "How to Save the Postal Service," *Nation* 310, no. 12 (2020): 20.

4. Cecilia Rikap, "What Would a State-Owned Amazon Look Like?," *Open Democracy*, November 24, 2020, https://www.opendemocracy.net/en/oureconomy/what-would-state-owned-amazon-look-ask-argentina/; *Wall Street Journal*, June 20, 2018, B2; Sauber, interview, February 12, 2021; Fuller, *RFD*, 234-47; World Wildlife Fund, *Farmers Post Produce Delivery* (Washington, D.C.: W.W.F., 2020), 8.

5. *National Public Radio*, October 12, 2017, https://www.npr.org/sections/thetwo-way/2017/10/12/557324350/neither-snow-nor-rain-nor-heat-watch-mail-carrier-deliver-to-burned-out-homes; *San Francisco Chronicle*, October 15, 2017, A9; Eric Katz, "How the Postal Service Managed a Remarkable Response During Katrina," *Government Executive*, August 28, 2015, https://www.govexec.com/management/2015/08/how-postal-service-managed-remarkable-response-during-katrina/119789/.

6. Christopher W. Shaw and Osamah F. Khalil, "The Postal Service Is Essential to National Security," *The Hill*, May 6, 2020, https://thehill.com/opinion/national-security/496349-the-postal-service-is-essential-to-national-security; *Washington Post*, October 2, 2008, A2; *St. Paul (Minn.) Pioneer-Press*, April 24, 2012, A5.

7. *Federal Register* 75, no. 3 (2010): 737-38; *Washington Post*, July 11, 2012, A15; *Washington Post*, September 18, 2020, A14; *Washington Post*, December 20, 2020, A1.

8. Stutts, interview, April 30, 2021; *Nikkei Asia*, November 18, 2016, https://asia.nikkei.com/Business/Postal-workers-to-deliver-senior-services-under-Japan-tie-up; Sauber, interview, February 12, 2021.

9. U.S. Postal Service, *United States Postal Service, 1775-2002*, 37-40; Kelly, *United States Postal Policy*, 120-21; Holmes and Rohrbach, *Stagecoach East*, 32, 74; Fuller, *American Mail*, 150, 157.

10. Lloyd J. Mercer, *Railroads and Land Grant Policy: A Study in Government Intervention* (New York: Academic Press, 1982); Forest G. Hill, *Roads, Rails, and Waterways: The Army Engineers and Early Transportation* (Norman: University of Oklahoma Press, 1957), 101-6; Sidney Ratner, James H. Soltow, and Richard E. Sylla, *The American Economy: Growth, Welfare, and Decision Making* (New York: Basic Books, 1979), 338; U.S. Postal Service, *United States Postal Service, 1775-2002*, 15-16; Carlos A. Schwantes, "Transportation and Politics," in *The Princeton Encyclopedia of American Political History*, ed. Michael Kazin, 2 vols. (Princeton, N.J.: Princeton University Press, 2010), 2:833-34; Fuller, *American Mail*, 166-68; William Cronon, *Nature's Metropolis: Chicago and the Great West* (New York: W.W. Norton & Company, 1991), 332-33; John F. Stover, *American Railroads*, 2nd ed. (Chicago: University of Chicago Press, 1997), 205.

11. C. L. Grant, "Cave Johnson: Postmaster General," *Tennessee Historical Quarterly* 20, no. 4 (1961): 333-34; Robert Luther Thompson, *Wiring a Continent: The History of the Telegraph Industry, 1832-1866* (Princeton, N.J.: Princeton University Press, 1947), 16-34; Taylor, *Transportation Revolution*, 369.

12. Scheele, *Short History of the Mail Service*, 131-35; Sandra Lach Arlinghaus, *Down the Mail Tubes: The Pressured Postal Era, 1853-1984* (Ann Arbor, Mich.: Institute of Mathematical Geography, 1985), 24, 26, 51; Nancy Pope, *Illustrated Guide to the National Postal Museum* (Washington, D.C.: Smithsonian Institution, 1998), 25.

13. William M. Leary, *Aerial Pioneers: The U.S. Air Mail Service, 1918-1927* (Washington, D.C.: Smithsonian Institution Press, 1985), 34-38, 124-25, 222-24; R.E.G. Davies, *Airlines of the United States since 1914* (London: Putnam & Company, 1972), 18, 33; U.S. Postal Service, *United States Postal Service, 1775-2002*, 29; F. Robert Van der Linden, *Airlines and Air Mail: The Post Office and the Birth of the Commercial Aviation Industry* (Lexington: University Press of Kentucky, 2002), 11; Bradley Behrman, "Civil Aeronautics Board," in *The Politics of Regulation*, ed. James Q. Wilson (New York: Basic Books, 1980), 79.

14. Van der Linden, *Airlines and Air Mail*, 8; Fuller, *American Mail*, 149.

15. Richard F. Weingroff, "A Peaceful Campaign of Progress and Reform: The Federal Highway Administration at 100," *Public Roads* 57, no. 2 (1993): 3; Peter J. Hugill, "Good Roads and the Automobile in the United States, 1880-1929," *Geographical Review* 72, no. 3 (1982): 330; Wayne E. Fuller, "Good Roads and Rural Free Delivery of Mail," *Mississippi Valley Historical Review* 42, no. 1 (1955): 67-83; Fuller, *RFD*, 194-95; Scheele, *Short History of the Mail Service*, 138.

16. USPS Office of Inspector General, *Delivery Vehicle Acquisition Strategy*, Report No. 19-002-R20 (August 2020), 4-5; *Grumman World* 6, no. 8 (1987): 1; *Postal Record* 130, no. 8 (2017): 15; Government Accountability Office, *Strategy Needed to Address Aging Delivery Fleet*, GAO-11-386 (May 2011), 34-35; *Car and Driver*, May 14, 2019, https://www.caranddriver.com/news/a27469407/us-postal-service-trucks-fire/.

17. "Size and Scope," U.S. Postal Service, January 4, 2021, https://facts.usps.com/size-and-scope/; CALSTART et al., letter to Megan J. Brennan, November 21, 2017; Historian of the U.S. Postal Service, *Electric Vehicles in the Postal Service* (Washington, D.C.: U.S.P.S., 2014).

18. *Buffalo News*, September 27, 2020, 3; *Trucks.com*, February 23, 2021, https://www.trucks.com/2021/02/23/oshkosh-defense-wins-giant-mail-truck-replacement-contract/; Sierra Club, press release, February 24, 2021; *Congressional Record*, 117th Congress, first session, 2021, 167, H1073; David Hemenway, "Government Procurement Leverage," *Journal of Public Health Policy* 10, no. 1 (1989): 123-24; Martin Albaum, *Safety Sells: Market Forces and Regulation in the Development of Airbags* (Arlington, Va.: IIHS, 2005), 114; Robert J. Cirincione, Jr., *Innovation and Stagnation in Automotive Safety and Fuel Efficiency* (Washington, D.C.: Center for Study of Responsive Law, 2006), 35; Michael R. Lemov, *Car Safety Wars: One Hundred Years of Technology, Politics, and Death* (Madison, N.J.: Fairleigh Dickinson University Press, 2015), 171-72

19. Monica Anderson, "About a Quarter of Rural Americans Say Access to High-Speed Internet Is a Major Problem," Pew Research Center, September 10, 2018, https://www.pewresearch.org/fact-tank/2018/09/10/about-a-quarter-of-rural-americans-say-access-to-high-speed-internet-is-a-major-problem/; D. Clayton Brown, *Electricity for Rural America: The Fight for REA* (Westport, Conn.: Greenwood Press, 1980), xv-xvi, xviii, 5, 16-17; H. Jerry Voorhis, *American Cooperatives: Where They Come From, What They Do, Where They Are Going* (New York: Harper & Brothers Publishers, 1961), 53-54; E. F. Chesnutt, "Rural Electrification in Arkansas, 1935-1940: The Formative Years," *Arkansas Historical Quarterly* 46, no. 3 (1987): 219; Ralph Nader, *Told You So: The Big Book of Weekly Columns* (New York: Seven Stories Press, 2013), 306; Audra J. Wolfe, "'How Not to Electrocute the Farmer': Assessing Attitudes Towards Electrification on American Farms, 1920-1940," *Agricultural History* 74, no. 2 (2000): 524.

20. Brown, *Electricity for Rural America*, 45, 73; Harry Slattery, *Rural America Lights Up* (Washington, D.C.: National Home Library Foundation, 1940), xiii, 105-31; Voorhis, *American Cooperatives*, 54, 58-59; Ronald R. Kline, "Agents of Modernity: Home Economists and Rural Electrification, 1925-1940," in *Rethinking Home Economics: Women and the History of a Profession*, ed. Sarah Stage and Virginia B. Vincenti (Ithaca, N.Y.: Cornell University Press, 1997), 240; Kline, *Consumers in*

the Country, 260; U.S. Department of Agriculture, *A Brief History of the Rural Electric and Telephone Programs* (Washington, D.C.: U.S.D.A., 1985), 6-7; Carl T. Kitchens and Price V. Fishback, "Flip the Switch: The Impact of the Rural Electrification Administration, 1935-1940," *Journal of Economic History* 75, no. 4 (2015): 1161-95; Lemont Kingsford Richardson, *Wisconsin REA: The Struggle to Extend Electricity to Rural Wisconsin, 1935-1955* (Madison: University of Wisconsin Experiment Station, 1961), 147-48; D. Jerome Tweton, *The New Deal at the Grass Roots: Programs for the People in Otter Tail County, Minnesota* (St. Paul: Minnesota Historical Society Press, 1988), 145-46.

21. Victor Pickard and David Elliot Berman, *After Net Neutrality: A New Deal for the Digital Age* (New Haven, Conn.: Yale University Press, 2019), 57-62, 112; Robert W. McChesney, "Be Realistic, Demand the Impossible: Three Radically Democratic Internet Policies," *Critical Studies in Media Communication* 31, no. 2 (2014): 94; *Los Angeles Times*, June 23, 2018, C1; *Forbes*, May 31, 2019, https://www.forbes.com/sites/ajdellinger/2019/05/31/heres-how-telecom-giants-spent-more-than-1-billion-lobbying-congress/; Katie McInnis and Justin Brookman, *State Broadband Privacy Legislation* (Yonkers, N.Y.: Consumer Reports Advocacy, 2019).

22. Sawicky, *U.S. Postal Service Is a National Asset*, 22; Bruce Schneier, *Data and Goliath: The Hidden Battles to Collect Your Data and Control Your World* (New York: W.W. Norton & Company, 2015); Shoshana Zuboff, "Big Other: Surveillance Capitalism and the Prospects of an Information Civilization," *Journal of Information Technology* 30, no. 1 (2015): 75-89; Richard M. Abrams, "The End of Privacy: 9/11 and the Ascendancy of the Surveillance State," *Asia Pacific Peace Studies* 2, no. 1 (2018): 17-19; Arthur S. Hayes, "The USPS as an OSP: A Remedy for Users' Online Privacy Concerns," *Communication Law and Policy* 19, no. 4 (2014): 473.

23. Cullinan, *Post Office Department*, 202-3; Government Accountability Office, *Overview of Initiatives to Increase Revenue and Introduce Nonpostal Services and Experimental Postal Products*, GAO-13-216 (January 2013); Selective Service System, *2020 Media Kit* (Washington, D.C.: S.S.S., 2020), 6; Department of Veteran Affairs, *Application for United States Flag for Burial Purposes*, VA 27-2008 (August 2020); Elliott Brack, "Deliver Us from this Latest Postal Efficiency," *Atlanta Journal-Constitution*, July 31, 1996, J2; *Washington Post*, September 23, 1996, A17; *Atlanta Journal-Constitution*, September 11, 1996, J2; *Bradenton (Fla.) Herald*, November 13, 1997, F11.

24. *San Francisco Chronicle*, July 1, 2020, CB1; "Tax Day—Forms and Special Hours," U.S. Postal Service, https://faq.usps.com/s/article/Tax-Day-Forms-and-Special-Hours; *Baltimore Sun*, July 26, 1984, 1B; Virginia Kase et al., letter to Louis DeJoy, September 1, 2020; *Houston Chronicle*, September 17, 2020, A1; *Houston Chronicle*, September 19, 2020, A3.

25. Margolis, *At the Crossroads*, 19; *Chicago Tribune*, September 22, 1985, 13/35.

26. *USA Today*, September 4, 2020, 1D; R. Jon Tester et al., letter to Louis DeJoy, August 13, 2020; Stacy Mitchell and Charlie Thaxton, "Ending Pharmacy Deserts," *The American Conservative* 18, no. 6 (2019): 28-31; Carol Miller (founder, Frontier Education Center, Ojo Sarco, N.M.), interview, July 19, 2005; LeNoir, interview, March 10, 2021; Special Panel on Postal Reform and Oversight of the House Committee on Government Reform, *Answering the Administration's Call for Postal Reform*, 240; USPS Office of Inspector General, *The Postal Service's Role in Delivering Wellness Services and Supplies*, Report No. RARC-IB-15-004 (July 2015), 15-17.

27. Heins, interview, February 5, 2021; Allen, *Guardian of the Wild*, 112-13; Anthony Licata, "Bucks for Ducks," *Field & Stream* 119, no. 1 (2014): 6; Doug Stang, "Federal Duck Stamps," *New York State Conservationist* 69, no. 3 (2014): 22-23; Government Publishing Office, *Keeping America Informed: The U.S. Government Publishing Office—A Legacy of Service to the Nation, 1861-2016*, rev. ed. (Washington, D.C.: Government Publishing Office, 2016), 110; National Academy of Public Administration, *Rebooting the Government Printing Office: Keeping America Informed in the Digital Age* (Washington, D.C.: National Academy of Public Administration, 2013), 37-38; *Baltimore Sun*, May 18, 2018, 2; Nancy Altman, "Social Security Closures Show 'Callous Disregard,'" *Baltimore Sun*, June 22, 2018, 13; SSA Office of Inspector General, *The Social Security Administration's Field Office Customer Service*, Report No. A-08-20-50898 (July 2020), 6.

28. LeNoir, interview, July 21, 2005; Steven Hutkins, "A New Agenda for Postal Reform," Save the Post Office, October 18, 2020, https://www.savethepostoffice.com/a-new-agenda-for-postal-reform/.

29. Scheele, *Short History of the Mail Service*, 92; Cullinan, *Post Office Department*, 81, 199; "Postal Money Orders Processed by the Federal Reserve—Quarterly Data," Board of Governors of the

Federal Reserve System, November 16, 2020, https://www.federalreserve.gov/paymentsystems/files/check_postalmosprocqtr.txt; U.S. Savings Bonds Division, *A History of the United States Savings Bond Program* (Washington, D.C.: Department of the Treasury, 1984), 5; Post Office Department, *A Wartime History of the Post Office Department: World War II, 1939-1945* (Washington, D.C.: Post Office Department, 1951), 52; John Morton Blum, *V Was for Victory: Politics and American Culture during World War II* (San Diego: Harvest Book, 1977), 16-21.

30. *USA Today*, September 8, 2003, 1B; *Buffalo News*, January 28, 2003, B4; Peter Tufano and Daniel J. Schneider, "Reinventing Savings Bonds," *Tax Notes* 109, no. 5 (2005): 2, 14; *St. Louis Post-Dispatch*, July 15, 2011, B1; Internal Revenue Service, *Allocation of Refund (Including Savings Bond Purchases)*, Form 8888 (2020); U.S. Savings Bonds Division, *History of the United States Savings Bond Program*, 27.

31. Federal Deposit Insurance Corporation, *2017 FDIC National Survey of Unbanked and Underbanked Households* (Washington, D.C.: F.D.I.C., 2018), 17, 19; Board of Governors of the Federal Reserve System, *Report on the Economic Well-Being of U.S. Households in 2019* (Washington, D.C.: Federal Reserve System, 2020), 27; John P. Caskey, *Fringe Banking: Check-Cashing Outlets, Pawnshops, and the Poor* (New York: Russell Sage Foundation, 1994), 84-106; Stephen J. Brobeck, *Do Big Banks Provide Affordable Access to Lower Income Savers?* (Washington, D.C.: Consumer Federation of America, 2020), 3-7; Constance R. Dunham, "The Role of Banks and Nonbanks in Serving Low- and Moderate-Income Communities," in *Changing Financial Markets and Community Development*, ed. Jackson L. Blanton et al. (Washington, D.C.: Board of Governors of the Federal Reserve System, 2001), 41; Michael Grinstein-Weiss et al., "Does Prior Banking Experience Matter? Differences of the Banked and Unbanked in Individual Development Accounts," *Journal of Family and Economic Issues* 31, no. 2 (2010): 212-27.

32. Federal Deposit Insurance Corporation, *2017 FDIC National Survey of Unbanked and Underbanked Households*, 23; Ken-Hou Lin and Megan Tobias Neely, *Divested: Inequality in the Age of Finance* (New York: Oxford University Press, 2020), 58; Bob Sullivan, *Gotcha Capitalism* (New York: Ballantine Books, 2007), 57-58, 60-61; David Cay Johnston, *The Fine Print: How Big Companies Use "Plain English" to Rob You Blind* (New York: Portfolio/Penguin, 2012), 11, 142-47; Gideon Weissman and Edmund Mierzwinski, *Big Banks, Big Overdraft Fees: The CFPB Defends Consumers Against Harmful and Deceptive Fees* (Washington, D.C.: U.S. PIRG Education Fund, 2016); *Consumer Reports* 84, no. 7 (2019): 34; Drew Dahl and Michelle Franke, "'Banking Deserts' Become a Concern as Branches Dry Up," *Regional Economist* 25, no. 2 (2017): 20-21.

33. *Philadelphia Inquirer*, August 6, 2018, C1; Lisa Servon, *The Unbanking of America: How the New Middle Class Survives* (Boston: Houghton Mifflin Harcourt, 2017), 7, 19; Karen Graham and Elaine Golden, *Financially Underserved Market Size Study, 2019* (Chicago: Financial Health Network, 2019), 9; "Payday Loan Facts and the CFPB's Impact," Pew Charitable Trusts, May 26, 2016, https://www.pewtrusts.org/en/research-and-analysis/fact-sheets/2016/01/payday-loan-facts-and-the-cfpbs-impact; Pew Charitable Trusts, *Payday Lending in America: Who Borrows, Where They Borrow, and Why* (Philadelphia: Pew Charitable Trusts, 2012), 8.

34. Christopher W. Shaw, "'Banks of the People': The Life and Death of the U.S. Postal Savings System," *Journal of Social History* 52, no. 1 (2018): 123; Gibbons, *John Wanamaker*, 1:284-87.

35. Christopher W. Shaw, *Money, Power, and the People: The American Struggle to Make Banking Democratic* (Chicago: University of Chicago Press, 2019), 15-72, 135-40, 166-68; Elmus R. Wicker, *The Banking Panics of the Great Depression* (New York: Cambridge University Press, 1996); Lester V. Chandler, *America's Greatest Depression, 1929-1941* (New York: Harper & Row, Publishers, 1970), 82.

36. Christopher W. Shaw, "When Pittsburghers Banked at the Post Office," *Pittsburgh Post-Gazette*, May 12, 2020, A11; Joint Committee on Printing, *Official Congressional Directory, 89th Congress, 1st Session* (Washington, D.C.: Government Printing Office, 1965), 45; Subcommittee on Postal Operations of the House Committee on Post Office and Civil Service, *Dissolution of the Postal Savings System*, 89th Congress, first session (Washington, D.C.: Government Printing Office, 1965), 4; Shaw, "'Banks of the People,'" 136-39; Shaw, *Money, Power, and the People*, 282-84; Shaw, *Preserving the People's Post Office*, 180-81.

37. Michael Lind, "Mailing Our Way to Solvency," *New York Times*, October 6, 2008, A29; Shaw, *Preserving the People's Post Office*, 171-86; Paul F. Jessup and Mary Bochnak, "A Case for a U.S. Postal

Savings System," *Challenge* 35, no. 6 (1992): 57-59; Richard D. Crawford and William W. Sihler, *The Troubled Money Business: The Death of an Old Order and the Rise of a New Order* (New York: Harper Business, 1991), 271-73.

38. USPS Office of Inspector General, *Providing Non-Bank Financial Services for the Underserved*, Report No. RARC-WP-14-007 (2014).

39. David Dayen, "The Post Office Should Just Become a Bank," *New Republic*, January 28, 2014, https://newrepublic.com/article/116374/postal-service-banking-how-usps-can-save-itself-and-help-poor; Elizabeth Warren, "Coming to a Post Office Near You: Loans You Can Trust?," *Huffington Post*, February 1, 2014, https://www.huffpost.com/entry/coming-to-a-post-office-n_b_4709485; Mehrsa Baradaran, "It's Time for Postal Banking," *Harvard Law Review Forum* 127, no. 4 (2014): 165-75; John Nichols "For a Post Office Bank," *Nation* 298, no. 4 (2014): 4-6.

40. Christopher W. Shaw, "Postal Banking Is Making a Comeback," *Washington Post*, July 21, 2020, https://www.washingtonpost.com/outlook/2020/07/21/postal-banking-is-making-comeback-heres-how-ensure-it-becomes-reality/; Office of Representative Marcy Kaptur, press release, April 15, 2021.

41. Federal Deposit Insurance Corporation, *2017 FDIC National Survey of Unbanked and Underbanked Households*, 23; Pew Research Center, *Public Holds Broadly Favorable Views of Many Federal Agencies* (Philadelphia: Pew Research Center, 2020), 5; USPS Office of Inspector General, *Providing Non-Bank Financial Services for the Underserved*, 6.

42. Shaw, *Preserving the People's Post Office*, 184-85; USPS Office of Inspector General, *The Road Ahead for Postal Financial Services*, Report No. RARC-WP-15-011 (2015), 16-17; USPS Office of Inspector General, *Providing Non-Bank Financial Services for the Underserved*, 16.

43. L. White Busbey, *Uncle Joe Cannon: The Story of a Pioneer American* (New York: Henry Holt and Company, 1927), 294; Bernard Sanders, letter to Steven T. Mnuchin, June 6, 2018; House Committee on Oversight and Reform, *Financial Condition of the Postal Service*, 11.

44. *Congressional Record*, 91st Congress, second session, 1970, 116, 20496.

45. David Bollier, *Public Assets, Private Profits: Reclaiming the American Commons in an Age of Market Enclosure* (Washington, D.C.: New America Foundation, 2001); Marvin T. Runyon, address to the National Press Club, Washington, D.C., April 14, 1998.

ACKNOWLEDGMENTS

Thanks to Douglas Carlson, Mark Dimondstein, Philip Dine, Tom Dlugolenski, Ed Fletcher, Ruth Goldway, Daniel Heins, Steve LeNoir, Bob Levi, Jim Sauber, Ronnie Stutts, Phil Tabbita, Gale Thames, and Chuck Zlatkin for generously offering their insights and knowledge. My work benefitted from the wonderful resource on postal affairs that Steve Hutkins established at www. SavethePostOffice.com over the past decade. I appreciate the contributions of Kate Marshall, Marlene Thorpe, and everyone at City Lights Books, especially Greg Ruggiero, Chris Carosi, Elaine Katzenberger, Stacey Lewis, Gerilyn Attebery, and Elizabeth Bell. Paulina Hartono provided vital support and assistance. Thank you, Ralph Nader and John Richard, for making this book possible.

INDEX

Federal Highway Administration, 166
Federal Trade Commission, 110-11, 146
FedEx Corp. *See also* Frederick W. Smith
 attacks Postal Service, 11, 101, 104, 107-10
 competitor to Postal Service, 93-94, 103
 contract with Postal Service, 109
 FedEx Office, 113
 fees assessed by, 111
 limited service of, 111
 lobbies for tax reduction, 105
 opposes ergonomics standard, 106-7
 opposes labor unions, 105-6
 political power of, 3, 104-6
 relationship with UPS, 107
 supports airline and trucking deregulation, 105
 support of foreign trade agreements, 105
Feingold, Russell D., 104
Feinstein, Dianne, 195n34. *See also* C. B.
   Richard Ellis Group Inc. (CBRE)
Ferrera, Peter J., 40
Feulner, Edwin, J., 11
financial crisis (2007-2008), 5, 80-81, 90-91,
   134
Financial Times, 33
Firestine, Theresa, 31
first-class mail, 12, 23, 92-94, 98, 103, 116, 136
 declining volume of, 80-81
Flexner, James Thomas, 44
Ford, Gerald R., 25, 65
Ford Motor Company, 168
foreign post offices, 31-37, 41
foreign trade, 105, 107, 123
Frank, Anthony M., 24, 103, 134, 159
Frank, Robert H., 139-40
Franklin, Benjamin, 14, 119, 144
Frederickson, David J., 67
Free City Delivery, 7, 15
free trade agreements. *See* foreign trade
Friedman, Milton, 42
fringe banks, 175-76
Fritschler, A. Lee, 112
Fuller, Wayne E., 14, 15, 38, 44, 46, 141, 144,
   166
Fuqua, Don, 153

Gabaldon, Eugene, 88
"gag" orders, 132-33
Galbraith, John Kenneth, 12, 21
Gallagher, Carolyn Lewis, 146
Gardner, John W., 53, 157
Gattuso, James L., 11
Geddes, R. Richard, 11, 21, 27, 40, 74-75, 131
General Accounting Office, 65, 79, 102. *See
   also* Government Accountability Office
general delivery, 60, 193n3
General Federation of Women's Clubs, 50
General Services Administration, 168
George Mason University, 146
Giuliano, Louis J., 146
Goldway, Ruth Y., 27, 96, 104
good roads movement, 166
Government Accountability Office, 95, 138.
   See also General Accounting Office
Government Publishing Office, 173
Great Britain. *See* United Kingdom
Great Depression, 77, 133, 177
Great Falls Tribune, 41
Great Postal Strike (1970), 134
Great Recession. *See* financial crisis (2007-
   2008)
Green, Alexander N., 171
Green, Mark J., 145
Greenlaw, David L., 70
Greenpeace, 53
Greyhound Corp., 29-31
Gross, H. R., 145
Grumman Long Life Vehicles, 166
Guardian (London), 35

Hamilton, Alexander, 43
Hanley, James M., 115, 150-51
Hauge, Gabriel, 134
Hayes, Arthur S., 170
Heins, Daniel M., 63
Henderson, William J., 68, 109, 113, 117
Henkin, David M., 15, 39, 44
Heritage Foundation, 11, 20, 53, 74, 131, 147
Hess, Lester C., Jr., 53
Hill, Rowland, 39
Hirschman, Albert O., 156
Historic Surplus Property Program, 77

ABOUT THE AUTHOR

CHRISTOPHER W. SHAW is a research fellow at the Center for Study of Responsive Law. He is the author of *Money, Power, and the People: The American Struggle to Make Banking Democratic* and *Preserving the People's Post Office*. Shaw received his Ph.D. from the University of California, Berkeley. His writing has appeared in the *Washington Post, Harper's, Foreign Affairs*, and several academic journals.

THE CENTER FOR STUDY OF RESPONSIVE LAW is a nonprofit Ralph Nader organization that supports and conducts a wide variety of research and educational projects to encourage the political, economic, and social institutions of this country to be more aware of the needs of the citizen-consumer. The Center publishes reports on a number of public interest issues. In 1983, the Center published *The Postal Precipice: Can the U.S. Postal Service Be Saved?* by Kathleen Conkey and in 2006 published *Preserving the People's Post Office* by Christopher W. Shaw. Center staff members have also participated in Postal Regulatory Commission proceedings and provided government officials and postal system stakeholders with policy recommendations designed to improve and preserve the U.S. Postal Service. www.csrl.org

ALSO AVAILABLE IN THE OPEN MEDIA SERIES

The Path to a Livable Future
A New Politics to Fight Climate Change, Racism, and the Next Pandemic
by STAN COX
foreword by Zenobia Jeffries Warfield

Build Bridges, Not Walls
A Journey to a World Without Borders
by TODD MILLER

A Short History of Presidential Election Crises
(And How to Prevent the Next One)
by ALAN HIRSCH

Loaded
A Disarming History of the Second Amendment
by ROXANNE DUNBAR-ORTIZ

American Nightmare
Facing the Challenge of Fascism
by HENRY A. GIROUX

The Meaning of Freedom
by ANGELA Y. DAVIS
Foreword by Robin D.G. Kelley

Breaking Though Power
by RALPH NADER

CITY LIGHTS BOOKS | OPEN MEDIA SERIES
Arm Yourself With Information